THE NEW
COMPLETE ENGLISH SETTER

A trio of Llewellin Setters, circa 1875–80. Artist, A. Pope, Jr.

THE LOOK OF AN ENGLISH SETTER

This beautiful head study of Ch. Stacia of Scyld typifies the gentle nobility and distinctive character of the breed—truly Gentlemen and Gentlewomen by nature!

THE NEW COMPLETE

English Setter

A COMPILATION OF INTERESTING FACTS, DATA, AND OBSERVATIONS ON BREEDING, RAISING, TRAIN-ING, SHOWING AND HUNTING ENGLISH SETTERS.

by DAVIS H. TUCK

Late President of The English Setter Association of America

revised by ELSWORTH S. HOWELL

Former President of The English Setter Association of America

and by JUDY GRAEF

Vice President of The English Setter Association of America

FOURTH EDITION—ILLUSTRATED

HOWELL
BOOK HOUSE
New York

Macmillan General Reference
A Simon & Schuster Macmillan Company
1633 Broadway
New York, NY 10019-6785

Library of Congress Cataloging in Publication Data

Tuck, Davis Henry, 1886-1953
  The new complete English setter.

  1. English setters.   I. Howell, Elsworth S.
II. Graef, Judy.   III. Title.
SF429.E5T8   1982   636.7'52   81-20267
ISBN 0-87605-116-6   AACR2

10   9   8

Printed in the United States of America

DEDICATED TO

my friends who have spent practically all of their otherwise leisure hours for many years of their lives in study and hard work, to the final goal of breeding, rearing, and training better pure-bred English Setters. Their tireless efforts and honest interest have always been an inspiration to me, and after a visit with them I am fired with enthusiasm and determination to do better with my own English Setters.

Redding Ridge, Conn., 1951   DAVIS H. TUCK

Davis Tuck

REVISERS' DEDICATION

This fourth edition is dedicated to all the officers—past and present—and members of the English Setter Association of America and local English Setter Clubs for their devoted service to this noble breed.

JUDY GRAEF
ELSWORTH HOWELL

Ch. Bogota Girl's Rowdy, first A. K. C. English Setter Field Trial Champion

Contents

Introduction

THE FIRST EDITION of this classic work was published thirty years ago. Its author, Davis Tuck, dedicated it to "my friends who have spent practically all of their otherwise leisure hours for many years of their lives in study and hard work to the final goal of breeding, rearing and training better pure-bred English Setters."

No one in English Setters has ever worked harder and contributed more to the benefit of the breed and its fanciers than did Dave Tuck. In his Silvermine Kennels he raised some of the finest examples of the breed to be seen in the show ring. He sparked the English Setter Club of New England and nurtured it to a high position of prominence among regional breed groups. Through his efforts, field trials for bench-bred stock were successfully initiated in New England. As its president in 1951 he revitalized the English Setter Association, revising its constitution to a more workable and democratic model and rebuilding its membership. For the many years of his devotion to English Setters, he extended a helping hand to newcomers and in fact encouraged scores of young people to take up the breed.

Hailed in its first edition as the ideal model for a breed book, the second and third editions — published respectively 12 and 21 years later — received the same high acceptance from the English Setter fancy. Now, with the fine efforts of Judy Graef, it is a great honor to present the fourth edition.

Like Davis Tuck, Judy Graef is a quintessential English Setter fancier. In 1957 as a youngster she fell in love with the breed when she attended the great Morris and Essex Kennel Club show where Ch. Rock Falls Colonel, winner of 101 Bests in Show including Morris and Essex, was being honored in his retirement. Judy then vowed that she would save her money for an English Setter. Before she had accumulated enough cash to buy it, she was offered a bitch by Joseph Rotella of the Manlove Kennels in Virginia. Judy's parents loaned her the difference between the dog's price and what Judy had saved toward it. That was the start of a fine collaboration between Judy and Mr. Rotella with Judy later establishing a Manlove "North" kennel in New Jersey.

Since then Judy Graef has made many superb contributions to English Setters and their supporters. She has bred and shown many dogs to championship and has always lent a helping hand to newcomers in the breed. She has served the English Setter Association of America as Vice President of the mid-Atlantic area for several terms, was Show Chairman of ESAA's New York Specialty and is one of the Directors of the Combined Setter Club for which she has also served as Coordinator with the American Kennel Club. With considerable competence she has judged five Sweepstakes coast to coast for the parent club and affiliated local English Setter Clubs.

In updating this Tuck masterpiece, Judy has retained Mr. Tuck's time-honored text on the breed's origin and history, its disposition and training for the field. She has revised parts of the chapters on the breed's "blueprint," care and management, buying a puppy, training for shows and breeding — but only in those areas where time has wrought changes.

Working in collaboration with George Alston, the accomplished professional handler, and Jerry Beal, an outstanding photographer, Judy presents an entirely new chapter on trimming and grooming. This is an absolutely essential revision because the techniques and tools used in trimming English Setters today have changed materially since Mr. Tuck's time.

The most painstaking and arduous task in updating this breed "bible" is the compilation, with pedigrees and lists of champion progeny, of the leading sires and dams in the decade since the third edition was published. Today's breeders will find this information of incalculable value in planning their own breeding programs.

The final chapter pays tribute to the breed's top winners from 1950 through 1980.

As the publisher of this book on my favorite breed, I am deeply grateful to Judy Graef for having made this fourth, new edition possible. I am sure that Davis Tuck would have shared in this gratitude for her splendid and *caring* effort to present the English Setter fancy with a new work that preserves the fine quality and usefulness of his original edition.

Darien, Conn.   Elsworth S. Howell

English Setter Pointing in Turnips.
By Philip Reinagle, R.A. (1749-1833)

This engraving by Scott was published in the "Sportsman's Cabinet" in 1803, illustrating an artist's conception of what a good English Setter was about 160 years ago. The Setter is on a close point with a black pheasant practically under his nose, yet he has a high head and is taking the scent from the air rather than from the bird's body. Note the characteristic wide head of the day which follows the idea that a large nose, deep flews, and wide head denote superior scenting powers.

Reproduction of a painting representing the ideal English Setter of the English Setter Club of Italy, 1949.

Reproduction of an etching by Leon Danchin showing a beautiful English Setter on point and another backing. It is interesting to note the slight dish face of these two dogs, as this dish face is still much to be desired in France and Italy. Compare these heads with the ideal of the breed shown in the yearbook for 1949 of the English Setter Club of Italy. Copyright Camilla Lucus, Art Publishers, New York.

13

CHAMPION STURDY MAX was considered by many to exemplify the closest approach to the standard of perfection of any modern English Setter. He was a big-boned dog with lovely dark eyes and typical English Setter expression. A good showman, with personality and gaiety. There is no doubt but that he set the style for the modern English Setter. This print can well be the breeders' ideal for which to strive—their star at which to aim. Data on Ch. Sturdy Max is shown in this book. Photograph by Tauskey.

1

Origin and History

FROM the best authorities on the subject, it appears that the English Setter was a trained bird dog in England approximately four hundred years ago. A perusal of some of the old writings leads us to believe that the English Setter had its origin in some of the older of the land spaniels that originated from Spain. We are indebted, however, to Hans Bols, who, in **Partridge Shooting and Partridge Hawking**, written in 1582, presents quite definite pictorial evidence that the setter and the spaniel breeds were quite different in appearance, and even at that time the tails of the spaniels appeared to have been docked, as they are today, and the tails of setters left as nature intended them. There is some evidence in the earliest writings of sportsmen that the old English Setter was originally produced from crosses of the Spanish pointer, the large water spaniel, and the Springer spaniel, and by careful cultivation attained a high degree of proficiency in finding and pointing game in open country. We can see from examination of the sketches in many of the old writings that

15

the setter-spaniel was an extremely handsome dog, many having a head much longer and with a more classical cut than that of the spaniel, while others had the short spaniel-like head, lacking the well-defined profile of the skull and foreface of the modern English Setters. Also most of these older setters had coats which were quite curly, particularly at the thighs. It can be seen from this brief review of the origin of the English Setter than even our oldest authorities were not entirely in accord as to the origin of this breed.

There is little doubt that the major credit for the development of the modern setter should go to Mr. Edward Laverack, who, about 1825, obtained from the Rev. A. Harrison "Ponto" and "Old Moll." The Rev. Harrison apparently had kept this breed pure for thirty-five years or more. From these two setters Mr. Laverack, through a remarkable process of inbreeding, produced "Prince," "Countess," "Nellie," and "Fairy," who were marvelous specimens of English Setters. Along about 1874 Mr. Laverack sold a pair of setters to Charles H. Raymond of Morris Plains, New Jersey. During the next ten years the English Setter became more and more popular, and it was about this time that many setters bred by Mr. Llewellin were imported into this country and Canada.

In considering the so-called Llewellin strain of English Setters, it is recorded in the writings of Dr. William A. Bruette that about the time the Laverack strain of English Setters was at its zenith in England, Mr. R. L. Purcell Llewellin purchased a number of Mr. Laverack's best show dogs of the pure Dash-Moll and Dash-Hill Laverack blood. These Laveracks he crossed with some entirely new blood which he obtained in the north of England, represented by Mr. Statter's and Sir Vincent Corbet's strain, since referred to as the Duke-Rhoebes, the latter being the two most prominent members of the blood. The result of these crosses was eminently successful, particularly at field trials, and swept everything before them. Their reputation spread to America and many were purchased by sportsmen in different sections of the United States and Canada, so that this line of breeding soon became firmly established in this country.

Probably the name that stands out most conspicuously in the foundation of the field-trial setter in America is Count Noble. This dog was purchased from Mr. Llewellin by Dave

Sanborn of Dowling, Michigan, who after trying him out on the prairies, was upon the point of returning him to England, but was persuaded not to do so by the late B. J. Wilson of Pittsburgh, Pennsylvania. On the death of Mr. Sanborn, Count Noble passed into the hands of Mr. Wilson, who gave him an opportunity to demonstrate his sterling qualities from coast to coast. The body of this famous dog was mounted at his death, and was in the Carnegie Museum at Pittsburgh, where it was visited by many sportsmen.

Dr. Walsh, in 1878, stated that Mr. Llewellin's dogs were Dan-Laveracks; according to him they were all either by Dan out of Laverack bitches or by a Laverack dog out of a sister of Dan. It is quite difficult to give a proper definition of a straight-bred Llewellin, but it is generally accepted that all setters may be called Llewellins which trace back in all lines to Duke-Rhoebe-Laverack. This, however, would shut out everything that had Dash II bloodlines, and this the Llewellin enthusiast does not wish to do, for under such definition it would eliminate a great number of the best known names that appear in the so-called Llewellin pedigrees. Mr. R. L. Purcell Llewellin is given credit for making the Duke-Rhoebe-Laverack cross, but, in justice to him, according to Mr. A. F. Hochwalt, one of our noted authorities on gun dogs, he is not responsible for the breed being named for him. The name was originated in America by breeders who imported dogs from Mr. Llewellin's kennels and, being great admirers of the man and the dogs he bred, they naturally gave his name to these dogs.

This somewhat orthodox or bland description of the history of the English Setter may be sufficient for most readers, but for the student or serious breeder it may be desirable to take the skeleton out of the closet and shake its bones, as thereby will be uncovered some information which has an important bearing on breeding and genetics.

The first book ever written on dogs was "Of Englishe Dogges," written by John Caius (1510-1573) and published in Latin in 1570 and translated into English in 1575. Caius was physician to the ailing King Edward VI and upon his death held the same office in the household of Queen Mary and upon her death was Royal Physician to Queen Elizabeth. He was the founder of Caius (Keys') College in Cambridge and a student

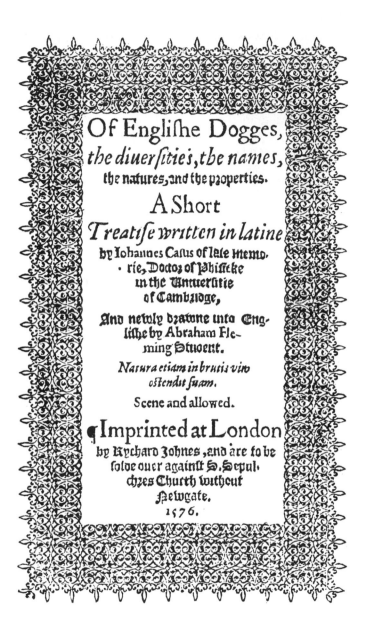

Of Englishe Dogges,
the diuersities, the names,
the natures, and the properties.

A Short

Treatise written in latine
by Iohannes Caius of late memo-
· rie, Doctor of Phisicke
in the Vniuersitie
of Cambridge,

And newly drawne into Englishe by Abraham Fle-
ming Student.

Natura etiam in brutis vim
ostendit suam.

Scene and allowed.

¶Imprinted at London
by Rychard Johnes, and are to be
solde ouer againſt S. Sepul-
chres Church without
Newgate.
1576.

Of gentle Dogges seruing the hauke, and first
of the Spaniell, called in Latine
Hispaniolus.

Vch Dogges as ſerue for fowling, I
thinke conuenient and requisite to place in this
seconde Section of this treatise. These are also
to bee reckoned and accounted in the number
of the dogges which come of a gentle kind, and
of those which serue for fowling.

There be two sortes {
The first findeth game on the land.
The other findeth game on the water.
}

Such as delight on the land, play their partes, eyther by swiftnesse of foote, or by often questing, to search out and to spying the byrde for further hope of aduauntage, or else by some secrete signe and priuy token bewray the place where they fall.

The first kinde of such serue { The Hauke,

The seconde, { The net, or, traine,

The first kinde haue no peculier names assigned vnto them, saue onely that they be denominated after the byrde which by naturall appointment he is alotted to take, for the which consideration.

Some be called Dogges, {
For the Falcon
The Phesant
The Partridge
} and such like,

The common sort of people call them by one generall word, namely Spaniells. As though these kinde of Dogges came originally and first of all out of Spaine, The most part of their skynnes are white, and if they be marcked with any spottes, they are commonly red, and somewhat great therewithall, the heares not growing in such thicknesse but that the mixture of them maye easely be perceaued. Othersome of them be reddishe and blackishe, but of that sorte there be but a very few. There is also at this day among vs a newe kinde of dogge brought out of Fraunce (for we Englishe men are maruailous greedy gaping gluttons after nouelties, and couetous coruorauntes of things that be seldom, rare, straunge, and hard to get.) And they bee speckled all ouer with white and black, which mingled colours incline to a marble blewe, which bewtifyeth their skinnes and affordeth a seemely show of comlynesse. These are called French dogges as is aboue declared already.

The Dogge called the Setter, in La-
tine *Index*.

ANother sort of Dogges be there, scruiceable for fowling, making no noise either with foote or with tounge, whiles they followe the game. These attend diligently vpon theyr Master and frame their conditions to such beckes, motions, and gestures, as it shall please him to exhibite and make, either going forward, drawing backeward, inclining to the right hand, or yealding toward the left, (In making mencion of fowles my meaning is of the Partridge and the Quaile) when he hath founde the byrde, he keepeth sure and fast silence, he stayeth his steppes and wil proceede no further, and with a close, couert, watching eye, layeth his belly to the grounde and so creepeth forward like a worme. When he approcheth neere to the place where the birde is, he layes him downe, and with a marcke of his pawes, betrayeth the place of the byrdes last abode, whereby it is supposed that this kinde of dogge is called *Index*, Setter, being in deede a name most consonant and agreable to his quality. The place being knowne by the meanes of the dogge, the fowler immediatly openeth and spreedeth his net, intending to take them, which being done the dogge at the accustomed becke or vsuall signe of his Master ryseth vp by and by, and draweth neerer to the fowle that by his presence they might be the authors of their owne insnaring, and be ready intangled in the prepared net, which conning and artificiall indeuour in a dogge (being a creature domesticall or householde seruaunt brought vp at home with offalls of the trencher and fragments of victualls) is not much to be maruailed at, seing that a Hare (being a wilde and skippishe beast) was seene in England to the astonishment of the beholders, in the yeare of our Lorde God, 1564 not onely dauncing in measure, but playing with his former feete vppon a tabbaret, and obseruing iust number of strokes (as a practicioner in that arte) besides that nipping & pinching a dogge with his teeth and clawes, & cruelly thumping him with y' force of his feete. This is no trumpery tale, nor trifling toye (as I imagine) and therefore not vnworthy to be reported, for I recken it a requitall of my trauaile, not to drowne in the seas of silence any speciall thing, wherein the prouidence and effectuall working of nature is to be pondered.

at Gonville Hall, Cambridge, and later became Master of this college. Caius very definitely places the setter in the spaniel class.

D. D. North, who wrote the chapter on English Setters in "The Book of the Dog" (edited by Brian Vesey-Fitzgerald, 1948), says, "At least it is certain that they were developed from spaniels." This book, 1039 pages, was published by Nicholson and Watson, London, 1948, and is an excellent one. Laverack in his book "The Setter" says, "In fact, the setter is but an improved spaniel." Stonehenge (1867) says, "There is no doubt that the setter is a spaniel brought by a variety of crosses — or rather, let us say, of careful selection — to the size and form in which we now find him." Hochwalt in his book "The Modern Setter" says, "The consensus of opinion among writers of canine literature, past and present, is that the setter is an improved spaniel."

One thing these early authorities are very explicit about is that the setting spaniel is an older breed than the pointer. They bring no proofs to substantiate these deductions, but the claim is made in order to convey the idea that no pointer blood was necessary to bring out the pointing instinct in the long haired bird dogs of the earliest days. Bernard Waters, in the "American Book of the Dog" (1891), says that the origin of the setter, like most other breeds, is obscure and all theories advanced are nothing more than guesswork and theoretical speculation. It is interesting to note that these authorities agree that the Setter was bred up from a spaniel but Setter includes all of them, the English, Irish, Gordon, and Russian, and it was not until later that the various classifications of Setters were made, and there is considerable proof that the four types were bred amongst themselves.

It is generally admitted that Laverack and Llewellin did more than any other two breeders to develop the English Setters of today, and this tendency to hero worship has possibly given more credit to them than they deserve. Edward Laverack was a native of a Westmorland village and in his youth was a shoemaker's apprentice. Early in life he came into possession of a legacy bequeathed to him by a distant relative. This legacy gave him an income sufficient for indulging his hobby of breeding English Setters and hunting them throughout

Edward Laverack, Esq. (1797-1877)
Broughall Cottage, Whitechurch, Shropshire, England

England, Scotland, Wales, and Ireland. In his book "The Setter" is shown the remarkable inbred pedigree of his Dash and he states that his Laverack setters are the result of nearly fifty years of breeding without ever resorting to an outcross from Ponto and Old Moll and that Ponto and Old Moll were the result of similar inbreeding by Rev. Harrison for thirty-five years prior to the time of his acquisition of Ponto and Old Moll. His contemporaries did not put much faith in the authenticity of his pedigrees. Laverack in "The Setter" says, "There are several secrets connected with my system of intercrossing that I do not think advisable to give to the public at present" (1872). Laverack admits that he tried several outcrosses but intimates that he promptly destroyed them and returned to his original strain, leaving the public to assume that he never used the get of these outcrosses in his breeding. In a letter to a friend about liver markings on one of his puppies he said, "He strains back to Prince's sire, viz; Pride of the Border, a liver and white. He strains back for 30 years to a change in blood I once introduced—the pure old Edward Castle breed—County Cumberland—liver and white, quite as pure and good as the blues." This letter was written in 1874, two years after the publication of his book and may be one of the "secrets" he did not think advisable to give to the public at the time. Stonehenge did not place much value on Laverack's pedigrees. Ponto was a dark blue belton and Old Moll was a light blue belton, and their breeding was supposed to be pure for thirty-five years. If Laverack did not bring in outside blood, as he claimed, where did the oranges and tri-colors come from?

The following interesting incident in Laverack's life is told by Rev. D. W. W. Horlock, who wrote the chapter on English Setters in "British Dogs," Third Edition, by W. D. Drury, Kennel Editor of "The Bazaar." "Some time ago Laverack, in the soothing atmosphere of a winter's eve-ning fire combined with the seductive effects of some good old port, disclosed a few faint shadows of his dark secrets. One of them is related here. Once upon a time there was a tract of country on the Borders called 'the Debatable Land,' nominally belonging to the Earl of Carlisle. Now, this country swarmed with gipsies, and that strange people had from time immemorial claimed the right to shoot over this tract at their own sweet will, so on August 12th in each year, they were accustomed to form a band of thirty or more, and with a large army of setters and pointers, made a regular raid on the said moors, and it is not surprising that the keepers gave them a wide berth. Well, on one Twelfth, Laverack accompanied this mob, and he had with him one of his best dogs. Among all the Setters which were ranging far and wide, Laverack's keen eyes noted one animal, liver and white, which was outstanding, and beat the whole lot in both nose and pace, though by no means a good looking one. 'Well, sir,' the old man said, 'I hunted up those gipsies. I found the dog, I bought him, and bred from him.' "

There is some reason to suspect that in later years (1870) a judicious cross was effected with the Pointer and there seems to be very little doubt at all that the Irish Setter also was called in to refresh the blood. Although there is little doubt that Laverack introduced outside blood from time to time, his setters were more closely inbred than any other strain of the time as evidenced by the similarity of his dogs, their susceptibility to disease and their usually poor nose, although there were some exceptions, as some of his dogs were good gentlemen's shooting dogs. Contrary to Laverack's claims to outstanding hunting ability and stamina, his contemporaries claimed that many of his dogs were worthless in the field. Mr. Laverack no doubt had complete faith in the superiority of his Laveracks, but other breeders were not satisfied with their hunting ability, so Statter, Field, Armstrong and others introduced the Duke-Rhoebe-Laverack cross.

Mr. Purcell Llewellin was a son of a noted Welsh sportsman of that name and began with Gordon Setters and some of the old fashioned English Setters. These he crossed and was badly beaten at the field trials. He then purchased some of the best Irish Setters in the country and crossed these with his other Gordon and English Setters. Not yet satisfied he crossed his Irish Setters with Laverack Setters and secured some outstandingly beautiful specimens which at the shows were practically invincible. Among them was a bitch named "Flame," a beautifully formed red and white of outstanding quality. This bitch is most noteworthy to modern English Setter breeders because a large number of the notable show winners of today carry her blood. For instance, the well known Mallwyd English Setters (Mr. Thomas Steadman, Merionitshire, Wales) contained

24

R. LL. Purcell Llewellin, Esq. (1840-1925)
Ashby-De-La-Zuche, Leicestershire, England.

25

a great preponderance of Mr. Llewellin's "Flame" and "Carrie." The Mallwyd importations to the United States and Canada were the very backbone of our present Bench Show type English Setters (Laverack). Mr. Kruger's Mallhawk Kennels of English Setters was founded on Mallwyd dogs, and we find the Mallwyd influence strongly in Rummey Stagboro's pedigree.

These Irish Setter-Laverack English Setter crosses, although outstanding at the bench shows, were almost entirely lacking in field performance. Llewellin was still dissatisfied. These years of hit or miss haphazard crossing of Gordon, Irish and English Setters had not given him what he was looking for—field trial winners, so when Statter and other were producing good field trial English Setters from the Duke-Rhoebe-Laverack cross he attended the field trial at Shrewsbury in 1871 and bought "Dan" and "Dick," both by Field's Duke out of Statter's Rhoebe, for the purpose of crossing with his Laverack bitches. This was Llewellin's beginning of the so-called Llewellin type of English Setter, and it should be stressed that Statter, Field, Armstrong, and others had really started the strain. Rhoebe was a cross of Gordon Setter and a black, white and tan English Setter of Lord Lovat's breeding. From this it will be seen that the so-called pure Llewellin blood is in reality a mixture of Gordon Setter and English Setter and what else nobody knows.

Thus we find by shaking the skeleton in the closet that our so-called Laverack bench show setters are a mixture of Irish Setter and Laverack English Setter with probably some "spice" thrown in on the side, and that our so-called Llewellin field trial type was not invented by Llewellin, and that they are a cross of Gordon Setter and Laverack English Setter with probably a little seasoning added when no one was looking. The Kennel Club in England was founded in 1873 and their stud book started 1874, so before that time pedigrees were not officially recorded and were therefore subject to considerable suspicion.

We occasionally hear reference to the Russian Setter. Laverack in his book "The Setter" (1872) refers to them as scarce in England at that time. They were white, lemon and white, liver and white, and black and white. They looked more like large spaniels than English Setters, and he did not consider them as good field dogs as his own Laverack Setters. He may have been somewhat prejudiced, because they were thought very

26

Mr. R. Ll. Purcell Llewellin with Kitty and Rosa Wind'em.

highly of by others, as many English Breeders of the time of about 1840 used the Russian Setter for the purpose of improving high head air scenting and stamina. In 1841 Mr. Lang wrote an article in the **Sporting Review** in which he highly praised the Russian Setter as a bird dog and especially a cross breed (English and Russian Setter) belonging to Mr. Joseph Manton which he bought for a hundred guineas. These Russian Setters are interesting because they are evidently in the blood of our present day Laverack and Llewellin Setters. They were also used as an English Cross again in our early native (American) English Setters.

The "Native Setter" is referred to occasionally and without doubt these setters have had a considerable effect on our present field trial Llewellin English Setters and our bench type Laverack Setters because they stemmed form the same origin as the Llewellins and Laveracks, i.e., a mixture of English, Irish, Gordon, and Russian Setters. When our forebears settled America they brought with them or later imported various types of setters to satisfy their sporting instincts, as the entire new country was heavily populated with game birds. The owners cared little for pedigrees and usually bred the best to the best in a given locality, mixing up the various setter breeds. Most of these Native Setters were orange and white and were of medium to large size. They did their share of winning both in the field and on the bench. A native of the Campbell strain, ."Joe Jr.," a mixture of Gordon and Irish and English defeated Gladstone on several occasions, and on December 15 and 16, 1879, he won by a very considerable margin against Gladstone, who at the time was considered the greatest exponent of the Llewellin Duke-Rhoebe-Laverack strain. Other well known strains of Native Setters were Gildersleeve of the Maryland section, Ethan Allen strain in Connecticut, and those bred by Mr. Theodore Morford of Newton, New Jersey.

Summary

Looking back at the history of the English Setter during the period between about 1819 and 1874 we find that from our

A typical Russian Setter slightly crossed
with English Setter blood. From Stonehenge.

modern breeding standpoint this was a most important period for English Setters. We had two outstanding breeders of some means who could indulge their fancy. Laverack was a sportsman who loved to hunt, especially in Scotland. He definitely wanted an English Setter of excellent appearance that would find birds for him. He and his keeper, Rattray, would break eight dogs in six days and a party of four would bag 3,000 grouse in a single day. In other words his ideal was a fine looking "meat dog."

Llewellin's idea was to breed a dog who could win field trials. The appearance of the animal was secondary to him. He foundered around for years trying all kinds of crosses, Gordons, Irish and English to each other but did not find what he was looking for until he copied Mr. Statter's cross of English to Gordon to Laverack's English.

Thus our English Setter accepted nomenclature of "Laverack" — the Bench Show English Setter — and "Llewellin" — the Field Trial English Setter — is not founded on fact, but was adopted from these men's **ideals** and not their accomplishments, because Llewellin crossed the English and Irish and accidentally got the show type (Mallwyd), and Laverack furnished Llewellin the missing link that produced Llewellin's field trial type.

During the last decade annual registrations of English Setters have ranged between 1200 and 1700 individual dogs ranking the breed in the low 50's in popularity among the 125 breeds currently recognized by the American Kennel Club. In 1970, 60 new bench champions were made. In 1978 that number increased to over 150 champions annually from over 10,000 dog show entries. Since many dogs are shown often, the number of individual dogs shown is much less than the number of entries. In addition, the American Field registers several thousand Llewellin type each year.

During the last eighty years a difference in type has appeared and constantly widened, so that in the United States and Canada there are now two distinct types of English Setters being bred, each having its own devotees. The Llewellin type is a comparatively small animal as compared with the Laverack type, although from a size standpoint the two types will overlap. The Llewellin type is the field-trial dog, and is

Photograph of Ch. Donora Prince, A.K.C. 94159. A typical Laverack type who was imported from the kennels of J. J. Holgate, Surbiton, England. He was a thoroughly broken field dog, and was at the height of his Bench Show career in 1906 and 1907. He was owned by Mr. William Rockefeller of Greenwich, Connecticut (Rock Ridge Kennels).

Donora Prince had seven Best of Show awards, including Westminster K.C. in 1907, over two thousand entries, and three Best of Show awards in England. He sired Donora Prince II, who was also a thoroughly trained field dog and was a consistent winner at the major Bench Shows in 1908–1913. Donora Prince II will be found as the great-great-grandfather of Kanandarque Chief. The boy in the photograph is Clarence Lewis, who judged N. W. Conn. Show in 1948 and Hartford in 1949.

This photograph is interesting, too, as a comparison of top flight English Setters of 1906 with our present day winners.

Typical Bench Type (Laverack) English Setter, CH. RIP OF BLUE BAR—C. N. Myers, Hanover, Pa., owner.

Typical Field Trial Type (Llewellin) English Setter, CH. SAM L'S SKYHIGH—Sam Light, Punxsutawney, Pa., owner.

usually distinguished from the Laverack type by the color—white, for the most part, with large black patches and, more often, white with large black patches and tan ticking on the head, muzzle and legs. Their heads are thicker through the skull; their muzzle, in comparison to their length of skull, is shorter than similar measurements for the Laverack type. The nose is inclined toward snipiness. They excel in speed and have a keen nose.

In color the Laverack type is usually blue belton, orange belton, or tricolor. Large black patches are usually undesirable. They are, on the average, larger than the Llewellin type—higher at the shoulder and generally heavier in build. Their heads are larger and narrower through the skull; the muzzle is longer and more square than in the Llewellin type.

There is a tendency for the devotee of either type to look down his nose at the other type, though actually each has its place. The field trial enthusiast's setter would usually make a sorry showing at a bench show as compared to a Laverack-type setter, while the bench show follower would generally have an "also ran" in a field trial of Llewellin-type setters. Both setters have one characteristic in common: both will do a good job at finding, pointing, and retrieving birds.

Intolerance is a defense mechanism to hide from oneself his own shortcomings. Intolerant people usually magnify the shortcomings of others, not admitting the good characteristics, and amplify their own points of excellence, suppressing their own faults. The intolerance exhibited between the followers of the field-trial English Setters (Llewellin) and the bench-show English Setters (Laverack) is a good example. The fair-minded will admit that the Llewellin English Setter from the field-trial standpoint is the last word in performance, but that it is not a very good looking dog, and that the Laverack English Setter is a beautiful specimen but lacks speed and bird-finding ability. The intolerant followers of the two sports, however, will not admit any good in the other type of English Setter.

The modern bench-type English Setter was developed in England from Laverack stock by Mr. Thomas Steadman of Mallwyd Kennels, his brother, Mr. D. K. Steadman of Maesydd Kennels, Dr. Price of Crombie Kennels, and by others. Many dogs from these kennels were imported from England to the

Reproduction of an oil painting by the incomparable dog artist G. Muss-Arnolt. The painting was owned by Anton Rost of New York and was sold to Mervin Rosenbaum of California.

This picture shows the Duke-Rhoebe-Laverack cross at its best from a conformation standpoint, and any English Setter breeder would love to produce a pair like these. Note again the slightly dished foreface. Col. Corn. Schilbred in his book *Pointer og Setter*, Oslo, 1927, remarked on the desirability both from the standpoint of keen nose and beauty, of this slightly dished foreface.

United States and Canada. This English breeding will be found in many of our modern bench-type English Setters at the 15th to 17th generations.

It is interesting to trace the background of one of America's outstanding English Setter kennels whose breeding we find in the majority of our present-day show specimens — the Mallhawk Kennels of Mr. Kruger. The Mallhawk Kennels is a combination of the Mallwyd and Mohawk kennel names. The Mallwyd strain traces back to Llewellin's cross of Irish Setter to Laverack Setter, and the Mohawk Llewellins trace back through Rodingo to Count Noble who was one of Llewellin's crosses from Gordon — Old English Setter to Laverack. Thus it will be seen that our top breeding of today is not too far away from a mixture of Gordon, Old English, Irish, and Laverack Setters.

Reviser's Note: Confirmation of parts of the foregoing history, and additional information, appeared in an article by the noted author on dogs, John T. Marvin, in the December 1968 issue of **Pure-bred Dogs—American Kennel Gazette**. Several years ago Mr. Marvin found in an old Memphis, Tenn., book shop a copy of Arnold Burges' **The American Sporting and Kennel Field** published in 1876 as the first formal stud record published in the U.S.A. Mr. Marvin writes:

> This particular copy was originally owned by a Dr. R. Liston of Albany, N.Y., who undoubtedly had a strong interest in the English Setter....he had used the book as a filing folder for a great and important accumulation of information on the breed.
>
> One of the most interesting items is an article from the February 1896 issue of *Outing*, written by L. H. Smith and titled 'The Llewellin Setter.' The article offers a brief but illuminating history of the development of the English Setter...and begins with the efforts of Edward Laverack in the 1820's. The strain, which carries his name, was begun with two animals, Ponto and Old Moll, and was brought forth through the breeding of brother and sister for some five generations whereby all of the strain traces back directly to these two progenitors. For those who decry inbreeding, this effort offers a strong counter-argument. In any event Laverack developed the strain which was absolutely tops for many decades. Circa 1870, Mr. Llewellin bought a couple of the Laverack bitches and in hopes of improving their hunting abilities decided to out-cross them with a dog named Dan, a consistent field trial winner. Great things came from these matings and a

new strain was begun. Many of the Llewellin Setters came to this country, but two of the best were Druid and Queen Mab brought over by the aforementioned Burges and campaigned on the bench by him.

Another startling insert is a pedigree of the dog 'Fly' which is a massive folded vellum sheet with no less than eight generations outlined thereon. Fly was a black and white dog bred by Ed. H. Lathrop of Springfield, Mass., circa 1876. He was by Duke ex Luna. Duke was a pure Laverack with pedigree traced back a full eight generations to Ponto and Old Moll. Luna had a less disciplined background and included at least one Gordon Setter among her ancestors. In any event, the pedigree traces back to the 1820's, a phenomenal task and an amazing revelation of the breeder's skill and records.

Many other added pedigrees are included. . . Last was a tipped in 'Catalogue of Thoroughbred English Setters' owned by Mr. Goodsell, 1883. E. I. Martin was listed as the manager of the kennel which was located in Wilmington, Del. This 31 page brochure offered five dogs at stud including Ch. Plantaganet at fees of fifty dollars each and another of lesser note for forty dollars. All were listed as 'Pure Laverack' strain. In each case a pedigree was provided together with a full listing of his winnings in England with a pen and ink sketch of the dog. Many of the kennel's bitches were also listed including the 'Pure Laverack Brood Bitch,' Ch. Petrel II.

Throughout the book, Dr. Liston has jotted down thoughts and opinions and some of these, with respect to his own dogs, indicated an honest and proper approach. For example, his dog 'Pinto' was described as 'long, low-dark brown, white ticked (good).' Actually, the information added by Dr. Liston, taken with the excellent exposition and records of English Setters that form an important segment of the Burges book, offers the student a rather complete history of the breed until about 1900.

Roderigo   Paul Gladstone

Reproduction of an etching by J. M. Tracy of Roderigo on point with Paul Gladstone backing. The gun is the Artist Tracy. Roderigo, whelped 1883, was a son of Count Noble, an importation from Llewellin, and was owned by W. B. Gates, Col. Arthur Merriman and J. M. Avent. As a producer he stood at the head of English Setters of the period. He sired twenty-seven winners. Paul Gladstone was a son of Gladstone, whose dam, Petrel (Laverack), in whelp to the Duke-Rhoebe dog Dan, was purchased from Llewellin by L. H. Smith of Ontario. Paul Gladstone was a field trial winner, a bench show winner, and the sire of seven field trial winners and one bench show winner.

The English Setter bitch "Countess" was purchased from Laverack by Llewellin. She was a sister to Laverack's "Dash," who was the culmination of Laverack's long line of inbreeding from "Ponto" and "Old Moll." The pedigree is reproduced here for its historical interest.

Countess was no doubt a beautiful specimen of what a good English Setter should be, with correct shoulders, wide, deep, well-angulated hind quarters, good back line, and well-carried flag. Her neck is long and well curved, and her head shows the well-defined stop with a suggestion of dish face which has been mentioned several times in this book as being very pleasing and much sought after in Europe today.

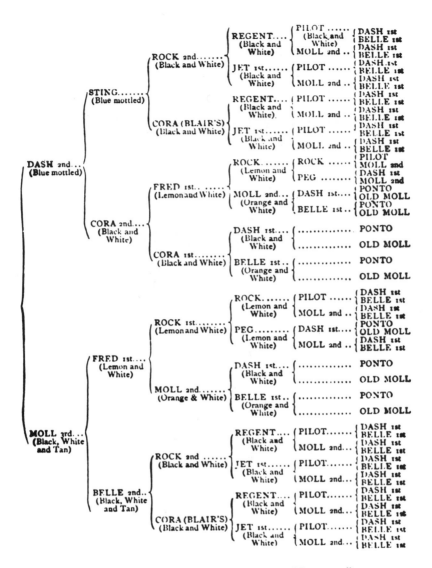

Pedigree of Laverack's English Setter "Countess."

Audubon and his English Setter. By Chappell.

John James Audubon (1770–1851), American naturalist. Father, French Naval Officer; mother, a Spanish Creole. Educated in Paris. Returning to America in 1798 he settled on a farm near Philadelphia where he made his bird drawings. In 1826 he went to England to secure subscribers for his book "Birds of America" (1838). In 1842 he purchased an estate on the Hudson River, now Audubon Park in New York City, where he, with John Bachman, published "The Quadrupeds of America" (1854). He died in New York City January 27, 1851.

That such a naturalist would choose an English Setter as his companion while in search of specimens, is additional proof of the unequalled disposition of the English Setter.

2

Temperament

THE English Setter has retained its popularity since its introduction into the United States primarily because of its usefulness, beauty, lovable disposition, loyalty and devotion. There is no doubt that its usefulness has been a prime factor in its popularity, and as a result of intelligent breeding it has been brought to a high state of perfection. There is always to be found a representative entry at bench shows and field trials. It is interesting to note, however, that at least half of the spectators at the ringside are not hunters or breeders of English Setters, nor even interested in showing them, but love them as pets. English Setters have a way of getting at your heart.

The mild, sweet disposition characteristic of the English Setter, together with its beauty, intelligence and aristocratic appearance in the field and in the home, has endeared it both to sportsmen and to all lovers of a beautiful, active, rugged dog, Their lovable disposition makes them ideal companions for children.

Contrary to the opinion expressed by some, the hunting ability of the English Setter is not spoiled but enhanced by making it a family pet. To this dog, love and affection are as necessary as food. Indeed food often will be left in the pan for a kindly word or a friendly pat. In fact, the pleasanter the association with people, from weaning through life, the smarter the English Setter will become; and its inherent good qualities will be more fully developed when there is more frequent chance of expression. Their natural instinct for bird-hunting cannot be developed unless given the opportunity to find birds in the field, nor will their outstanding characteristics of love and devotion be fully developed without close association with people.

The person who does not enjoy a close association with an animal should never purchase an English Setter. The breed demands large measures of love, affection and human companionship. For these reasons many never make good kennel dogs. Some become occasionally spiteful if left alone in the house without being crated. One six year old dog who had always been given the run of the house when his owners were out chewed the rung of a chair when denied a trip in the family car.

As in developing any effective relationship with man or dog the quality of time spent is often more important than the quantity of time spent. English Setters want to be noticed. They have a fondness for comfort and unless trained otherwise enjoy lounging on a chair or sofa. Even puppies enjoy being up if given the opportunity.

Although there are those who claim this breed can be stubborn and difficult to train, it is more likely that the dog has sized up a situation and has figured out a way to modify the owner's behavior. An example is the dog who rarely comes when he is called, but when offered a reward such as a liver snack, or when his dinner dish is rattled the response is immediate. It is imperative to train a setter with a gentle, yet firm hand and consistency. If allowed a transgression this dog will never forget that the owner has given in just that one time and he will continue to test for life.

Though gentle and devoted companions, English Setters also make good watch dogs. They sound an alarm to announce the arrival of any unknown visitor. Robbie thwarted a burglary by standing his ground at the sliding door frame. When his owners

English Setters are excellent with children. This photograph was taken at a Shooting Dog stake held by the English Setter Club of New England. The three-year-old child of one of the spectators was snapped by our photographer while playing with one of the English Setters who was entered in the stake. The child and dog had never seen each other before. This photograph is a good example of the incomparable disposition of an English Setter.

returned they found evidence of the attempt, slobbered windows, and the house intact.

Known as loving and mild mannered pets it seems inconsistent that English Setters can become ferocious fighters. Although they try to keep peace if attacked, they will stand their ground and usually be the winner if forced to fight.

English Setters have been known to perform acts of heroism. JoJo pestered his sleeping mistress by pushing his nose in her face and running in and out of the bedroom. Knowing he had been exercised his owner was hesitant to get out of bed. When he became frantic she followed reluctantly and he led her to the cellar door. When she opened it she discovered flames shooting from the defective gas heater. Without JoJo's persistence a tragedy would have resulted.

Its lovable disposition makes the English Setter a reliable companion for children. There seems to be a natural affinity between them. A year old bitch adopted from the local animal welfare league had been in her new home less than 24 hours when a visiting toddler fell across the sleeping dog. Toby raised her head in mild surprise, examined the child, and found a new spot for her nap. This action is typical for the breed.

When English Setter puppies are a week or so old their mothers love to have you and your friends come to see them, and never resent their being handled; in fact they seem quite proud of the attention and the opportunity to show off their children. There is no better way to teach your child the facts of life than to let him in on the entire procedure, from breeding to whelping. Two of my English Setter breeder friends have allowed their children to witness the entire breeding and whelping procedure since they were quite young and they point out that it is the best and most natural way for them to learn the truth about reproduction.

Dr. Gantt, in charge of the Pavlovian Laboratory at Johns Hopkins University, shows, in his studies of the behavior of dogs, that contrary to general belief dogs have a good memory. One of the dogs in his experiment remembered for nine years the type of food given him during his unpleasant experience at the laboratory, and remembered for eight years the man who handled him there. Dogs, like humans, Dr. Gantt reasons, may resent being uprooted from their home, and resent a routine that

This eleven year old male is taking time to become acquainted with his six week old grandson demonstrating the tractable nature of the English Setter.   *Sulzberger*

Ch. Hiddenlane's King George U.D. delights groups of children as he demonstrates his obedience skills. While George works the children are taught about pet care.

seems like punishment, and they may be frustrated by confinement in a place from which they cannot escape.

"English Setters are gentlemen by nature; they are of the best disposition, without fear or viciousness, mild-mannered, loving and devoted every moment of their lives, and a setter's eye is one of the jewels of the entire animal kingdom." (Capt. Will Judy)

English Setters react exceptionally well to obedience training which has become so popular in the last few years. This is only to be expected because they have been bred for training in the field and therefore take up obedience work willingly and naturally.

English Setters by nature are very sensitive to punishment. They are not so much afraid of the physical pain of the punishment as of the act. A sharp reprimand or a light slap with a piece of newspaper is an entirely sufficient punishment. A command should never be given unless you are in a position to enforce it. As with children, continual nagging invites disobedience. A system of reward consisting of an scrap of food or an affectionate pat as an acknowledgment of compliance is much better than punishment for disobedience.

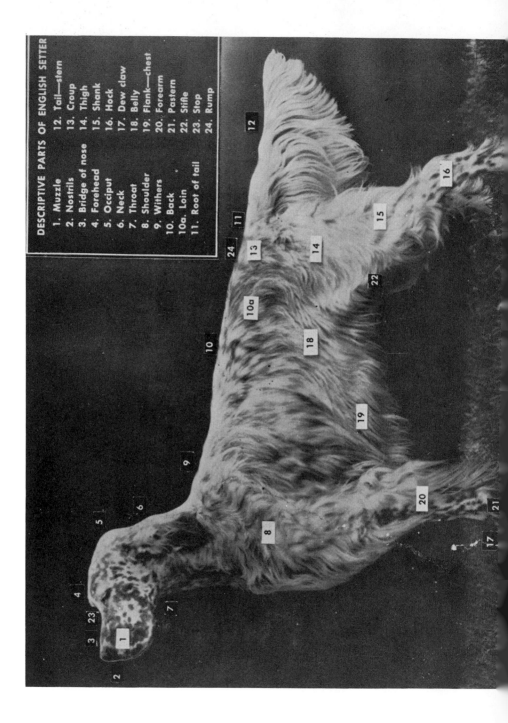

DESCRIPTIVE PARTS OF ENGLISH SETTER

1. Muzzle
2. Nostrils
3. Bridge of nose
4. Forehead
5. Occiput
6. Neck
7. Throat
8. Shoulder
9. Withers
10. Back
10a. Loin
11. Root of tail
12. Tail—stern
13. Croup
14. Thigh
15. Shank
16. Hock
17. Dew claw
18. Belly
19. Flank—chest
20. Forearm
21. Pastern
22. Stifle
23. Stop
24. Rump

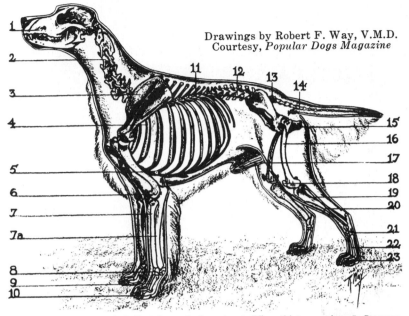

Drawings by Robert F. Way, V.M.D.
Courtesy, *Popular Dogs Magazine*

1 Skull, 2 Seven Cervical Vertebrae, 3 Scapula, 4 Ribs—thirteen pairs, 5 Sternum, 6 Humerus, 7 Radius, 7-A Ulna, 8 Carpal Bones, 9 Metacarpal Bones, 10 Phalangeal Bones, 11 Thoracic Vertebrae—thirteen, 12 Lumbar Vertebrae—seven, 13 Sacrum, 14 Coccygeal Vertebrae, 15 Os Coxae, 16 Femur, 17 Os Penis, 18 Patella, 19 Fibula, 20 Tibia, 21 Tarsal Bones, 22 Metatarsal Bones, 23 Phalangeal Bones.

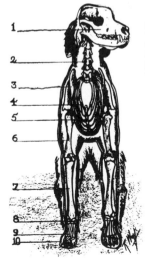

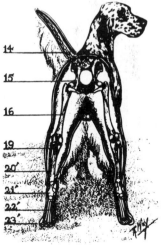

1 Skull, 2 Cervical Vertebrae, 3 Scapula, 4 Ribs, 5 Sternum, 6 Humerus, 7 Radius and Ulna, 8 Carpal Bones, 9 Metacarpal Bones, 10 Phalangeal Bones.

14 Coccygeal Vertebrae, 15 Os Coxae, 16 Femur, 19 Fibula, 20 Tibia, 21 Tarsal Bones, 22 Metatarsal Bones, 23 Phalangeal Bones.

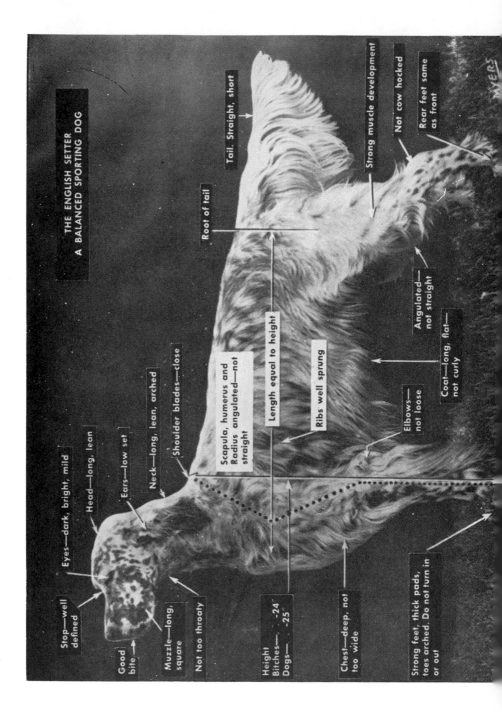

THE ENGLISH SETTER
A BALANCED SPORTING DOG

Tail. Straight, short

Root of tail

Strong muscle development

Not cow hocked

Rear feet same as front

Angulated—not straight

Coat—long, flat not curly

Elbows— not loose

Ribs well sprung

Length equal to height

Scapula, humerus and Radius angulated—not straight

Shoulder blades—close

Neck—long, lean, arched

Ears—low set

Head—long, lean

Eyes—dark, bright, mild

Stop—well defined

Good bite

Muzzle—long, square

Not too throaty

Height
Bitches— -24"
Dogs— -25"

Chest—deep, not too wide

Strong feet, thick pads, toes arched. Do not turn in or out

3

Description and
Standard of Points

(By courtesy of the English Setter Association of America)

Head. Long and lean, with a well-defined stop. The skull oval from ear to ear, of medium width, giving brain room but with no suggestion of coarseness, with but little difference between the width at base of skull and at brows and with a moderately defined occipital protuberance. Brows should be at a sharp angle from the muzzle. Muzzle should be long and square, of width in harmony with the skull, without any fullness under the eyes and straight from eyes to tip of the nose. A dish face or Roman nose objectionable. The lips square and fairly pendant. Nose should be black or dark liver in color, except in white, lemon and white, orange and white, or liver and white dogs, when it may be of lighter color. Nostrils should be wide apart and large in the openings. Jaws should be of equal length. Overshot or undershot jaw objectionable. Ears should be carried close to the head, well back and set low, of moderate length, slightly rounded at the ends, and covered with silky hair. Eyes should be bright, mild, intelligent and dark brown in color.

Neck. The neck should be long and lean, arched at the crest, and not too throaty.

Shoulders. Shoulders should be formed to permit perfect freedom of action to the forelegs. Shoulder blades should be long, wide, sloping moderately well back and standing fairly close together at the top.

Chest. Chest between shoulder blades should be of good depth but not of excessive width.

Ribs. Ribs, back of shoulders, should spring gradually to the middle of the body and then taper to the back ribs, which should be of good depth.

Back. Back should be strong at its junction with the loin and should be straight or sloping upward very slightly to the top of the shoulder, the whole forming a graceful outline of medium length, without sway or drop. Loins should be strong, moderate in length, slightly arched, but not to the extent of being roached or wheel backed. Hip bones should be wide apart without too sudden drop to the root of the tail.

Forelegs. The arms should be flat and muscular, with bone fully developed and muscles hard and devoid of flabbiness; of good length from the point of the shoulder to the elbow, and set at such an angle as will bring the legs fairly under the dog. Elbows should have no tendency to turn either in or out. The pastern should be short, strong and nearly round with the slope from the pastern joint to the foot deviating very slightly forward from the perpendicular.

Hindlegs. The hindlegs should have wide, muscular thighs with well developed lower thighs. Stifles should be well bent and strong. Hocks should be wide and flat. The pastern should be short, strong and nearly round, with the slope from the pastern joint to the foot deviating very slightly forward from the perpendicular.

52

Feet. Feet should be closely set and strong, pads well developed and tough, toes well arched and protected with short, thick hair.

Tail. Tail should be straight and taper to a fine point, with only sufficient length to reach the hocks, or less. The feather must be straight and silky, falling loosely in a fringe and tapering to the point when the tail is raised. There must be no bushiness. The tail should not curl sideways or above the level of the back.

Coat. Coat should be flat and of good length, without curl; not soft or woolly. The feather on the legs should be moderately thin and regular.

Height. Dogs, about 25 inches; bitches, about 24 inches.

Colors. Black, white and tan; black and white; blue belton, lemon and white; lemon belton, orange and white; orange belton; liver and white; liver belton; and solid white.

Markings. Dogs without heavy patches of color on the body, but flecked all over preferred.

Symmetry. The harmony of all parts to be considered. Symmetrical dogs will have level backs or be very slightly higher at the shoulders than at the hips. Balance, harmony of proportion, and an appearance of breeding and quality to be looked for, and coarseness avoided.

Movement and Carriage. An easy, free and graceful movement, suggesting rapidity and endurance. A lively tail and a high carriage of head. Stiltiness, clumsiness or a lumbering gait are objectionable.

RELATIVE WEIGHT OF VARIOUS POINTS

		Points	
Head			
Skull		5	
Ears		5	
Eyes		5	
Muzzle		5	20
Body			
Neck		5	
Chest and Shoulders		12	
Back, Loin and Ribs		10	27
Running Gear			
Forelegs		5	
Hips, Thighs and Hindlegs		12	
Feet		6	23
Coat			
Length and Texture		5	
Color and Marking		3.	8
Tail			
Length and Carriage		5	5
General Appearance and Action			
Symmetry, Style and Movement		12	
Weight and Size		5	17
Total		100	100

4

Blueprint of the English Setter

MANY English Setters are scattered about the country of whose merits their owners have no conception. Many of these dogs are of exhibition quality although, because of their owners' lack of awareness of that fact or indifference to it, they may never be entered in a dog show; while of others the owners know only that they have bought dogs with pedigrees and have them registered with the American Kennel Club. They assume that the pedigrees are an assurance of the excellence of the animals to which they are attached. It has often been said that there are more excellent show specimens tied up in someone's back yard than there are at the shows. There are also a great many poor well bred dogs.

A pedigree, even a good one, does not guarantee a good dog; otherwise a poor one would be an exception. A superior dog will almost certainly have a superior pedigree, but the converse to that statement is not necessarily true. A pedigree is only a record of an animal's ancestry for some three, four, eight or ten generations. It may be good or mediocre, but while it may indicate the attributes the dog to which it is attached is likely to possess, it is no assurance of the quality of the dog. It is merely a guide to be used in the employment of the animal for breeding purposes and in the choice of mates. If the animal is sterile or is not intended to be used for breeding, its pedigree is about as useful as a second tail.

A dog may win in one show under one judge and never be heard from in the prize lists again. On the other hand, a dog may fail to be within the ribbons at three or four shows at the beginning and finally attain recognition as one of the outstanding members of its breed. Such reversals have occurred with my own dogs several times. Some judges may demand in a prize winner certain attributes that other judges may ignore. Some judges appear not to know just what they are looking for. Many judges so take a dog to pieces and analyze his parts that they fail to see the dog as a whole functioning organism. Such a judge may become so engrossed in the minutia of type, the exact placement of an eye or the ears, or the length of the tail, that he may lose sight of the more important matters of shoulder placement or running gear. The old Army axiom applies here—"Quibbling over the minutiae is indicative of failure to grasp the spirit."

People who have an eye for dogs will be broadminded, having the capacity to appreciate various viewpoints. The true sportsman is a connoisseur, and the true connoisseur would rather revel in the perception of beauty and achievement than join the unhappy hunt for imperfections. Every expanded mind is first appreciative; every mean mind is first depreciating.

Thus the awards at a single show provide no absolute criterion of the merits of a dog. However, it is more to be wondered at that the opinions of judges are so much alike than that judges differ as much as they do. Excellence cannot be denied continually, and an outstandingly all over good dog will, in the long run, win. In this connection we must not lose sight of the fact that as a dog is exhibited several times he "catches on to the ropes" and so does his handler, so that after a few shows both he and his handler put their best foot forward.

As to the alleged dishonesty of dog show judges, it should be discounted heavily. This is not to say that the integrity of all judges is absolute or categorical, or that the possession of an American Kennel Club approval is a guarantee that a man or woman is more than human; but most judges are avid to make their awards as nearly in conformity with the merits of the respective exhibits as they possibly can. They take their judging assignments seriously, and their failures are to be charged more often to ignorance, nervousness, or inexperience than to undue influence brought to bear upon them or to outright dishonesty.

Then, possessing an English Setter, how is one to know whether it is good enough to warrant exhibiting it, even whether it is good enough to justify the owner's pride in it, whether it can be rightly claimed to be a representative specimen of the breed? The published Standard of the Breed as officially adopted by the English Setter Association and accepted by the American Kennel Club, is presumed to provide a guide to such an evaluation. However, the Standard of the Breed is compiled by men who are already familiar with canine anatomy and for other men and women who understand the more or less esoteric terms employed. Standards are of little use to the uninitiated, however valuable, even invaluable, they may be to persons familiar enough with the lore of the dog to understand or surmise their meaning and intent. Any breed of dogs requires to be officially defined, and the standard provides that official definition.

For the layman the specifications of the Standard of the Breed require to be taken apart, analyzed, interpreted and applied to the individual dog or bitch. That is what I shall try to do in this — **The Blueprint of the English Setter.** Nothing said here is intended to supersede or distort the specifications set forth in the Standard; that Standard, interpreted as best one can interpret it, must govern the breed. However, it is hoped that this **Blueprint** may enable the intelligent, serious minded amateur owner to apply the terms of the Standard to his individual dog and to reach some conclusions about the dog's merits and faults. It will help the owner to determine whether the dog is worthy of exhibition in a dog show, to be compared with other English Setters by a judge who may be depended upon to recognize its merits.

Perfection, it may be noted, is not to be sought; it can only be approximated. There are no perfect dogs of any breed. Since we

57

are not going to look for perfection, how much shall we penalize the faults we find? A well-balanced dog, one with a multitude of minor faults, a trace short of perfection here, there, and yonder, is to be preferred over a dog with a single outstanding fault which is so glaring as to be obvious at the first casual glance. And a fault that interferes with the usefulness of an animal for the purposes for which the breed was intended may be considered to be more grievous than a violation of some merely arbitrary specification of the Standard. For instance, it is more important that an English Setter shall have good feet than that the length of muzzle be as we should like to see it; correctly angled and powerful hindquarters are more important than a coat absolutely free from wave or curl.

The scale of points which is appended to the English Setter Standard of the Breed is not to be too seriously accepted, nor did the men who wrote the Standard intend it should be. It merely designates roughly the comparative importance that is to be attributed to the respective parts of the dog, with twelve points allotted to symmetry, style, and movement.

These twelve points can be added to any gross penalty for any fault that seriously mars an otherwise good dog, and they serve as justification for any judge to place a dog he considers to be a bad one under a good one in his awards, whatever their respective score might otherwise be. Symmetry, style, and movement cover a lot of territory.

For instance, let us take an extreme but by no means an unusual example. An otherwise excellent dog with miserable hindquarters, a veritable cripple, can be penalized only twelve points for his hindlegs. A better dog all over may be cut several points in each of the various departments so that his final score is less than that of the crippled dog. However, by adding the twelve points for symmetry, style, and movement to the twelve-point penalty already assessed for bad hind legs, a judge is able to justify his decision to put the cripple down to the dog with many well distributed but minor faults. To amplify this important consideration, I once made an additional breakdown of the point system so that I had 100 separate points to cover the various parts of a dog. Armed with this breakdown I went to see a dog that was for sale and bought him for a fair price based on his rating of 92%. I showed him consistently at the same shows for a year with another dog who rated only 80%. The 92% dog never went Winners Dog, but the 80% dog quickly finished his championship and afterwards proved his superiority by siring good dogs, whereas the 92% dog never sired anything outstanding.

Actually, the judges are called upon for no such official justifications. Their awards are final, and the American Kennel Club sustains them in whatever decisions they may make. They are under no obligations to explain or justify their decisions to disgruntled persons whose dogs have met defeat, nor to anybody else. However, most judges wish to be able to rationalize their decisions to themselves, and the twelve points in the scale for symmetry, style, and movement enable them to make decisions on the merits of the exhibits without being hampered by the exact terms of the scale of points.

The judge's task at a dog show is simply to evaluate a dog's merits in comparison with the merits of other exhibits and to declare by his awards whether the dog is, in his estimation, a better or a poorer specimen of the breed than his competitors. A judge's time is limited, and he is forced to make his decisions more rapidly than he sometimes would like to do. His knowledge of what to look for and his experience in comparing dogs together enable him to make decisions quickly and with comparative sureness. We, on the other hand, are not comparing our own dog with other dogs, but rather are comparing it with absolute perfection. We are trying to ascertain how good or how bad a specimen we have, not in comparison with some other dog or dogs, but in comparison with an ideal. We are not limited as to time, and we may ponder our decision indefinitely. We must not expect to make a cursory examination of our dog and determine for all time whether he is a sure champion or whether he is an arrant mutt. Dogs change from time to time, and opinions about them alter — sometimes because of changes in the dog and sometimes because of our own changed viewpoint. So let us survey our dog, digest our conclusions, and survey him again.

We are seeking now only to assess his worth as a show dog. It is not our purpose at this time to ascertain how smart he is, nor to assay his performance in the field. It is true that among sporting dogs the ideal show specimen is presumed to be the one best fitted for field work, but the show awards take no account of the heart, mind, disposition and instinct for hunting a dog may possess except as they may have a bearing on "CLASS."

It is assumed that the dog under evaluation has been bathed and groomed, that his nails have been shortened, and that his teeth have been scaled. It is further assumed that he is free from worms, is in good general health, well-nourished, neither a bag of bones nor hog fat. His flesh would be hard from plentiful exercise; his eyes should shine from health and from the enjoyment of living. No dog can endure neglect and appear at his best. That he is just a family pet, not destined for show dog competition, is no acceptable excuse for permitting a dog to go filthy and ungroomed any more than for letting his health stagnate through faulty nutrition or for an accumulation of parasites in his interior, or for that matter, on his exterior.

CLASS

Class as applied to animals and people means that they have an extra something that it takes to lift them from the mediocre to the top. Class is a well-known slang word and like so many slang words expresses in one word a meaning that would otherwise require paragraphs to explain, e.g., "The dame has **class**," or "She is in a **class** by herself." Class is an integration between zero and infinity of all the desirable attributes plus an extra something else. It is doubtful if class can be entirely cutivated, as it would appear that the individual must be born with it or without it. An old saying that you cannot make a silk purse from a sow's ear very aptly expresses this idea. It is also doubtful that class is an inherited characteristic.

Class is something that is easily and instantly recognized by the layman as quickly as by the initiated, and it is doubtful if any animal or person can to go the top pinnacle of endeavor unless he is gifted at birth with this quality. It does not follow, of course, that an individual endowed with class can attain top honors without hard study, discipline and training. An individual having class, however, and who is fortunate in having an understanding teacher, and given the opportunity of competition, has the best opportunity of becoming famous.

Class is the one outstanding desirable quality that is so seldom seen and which can go a long way toward putting over an otherwise mediocre individual. In English Setters it is well to recognize class at an early age and lavish your time in training, feeding, exercising, grooming and housing this individual. A kennel may breed a lifetime and produce only one or two specimens who are in a **class** by themselves.

COLOR

Although color is not the most important consideration in the Standard and counts only three points out of one hundred in relative weight of the various component parts, it is, from a practical standpoint, of more importance than one would assume from the three-point rating. The Standard of the Breed allows a wide latitude in color, but actually the only colors that will ordinarily receive consideration in the show ring are blue belton, lemon belton, orange belton and tri-color. All the beltons are marked alike. The ground color is white, and for the blue belton the black hairs fleck through the white to give a mottled or marbled appearance. In the case of the lemon and orange beltons the lemon or orange hairs take the place of the black ones in the blue belton. Sometimes the black, lemon, or orange hairs predominate so that practically no white appears, and such marking is called roan; that is, blue roan, lemon roan, and orange roan. The roans are not as desirable as the beltons.

Another color combination that is often seen is the tri-color. This is a blue belton with some tan markings on the muzzle, over the eyes, and on the front legs. This is often the color for Llewellin or field trial type English Setters. This tri-color marking is no doubt caused by the Gordon Setter blood introduced during Laverack's and Llewellin's time (1870).

We occasionally see the color mark of the Irish Setter also in our English Setters, especially in the blue beltons where the black hairs sometimes have a red or copper tinge, just as with the Irish Setter who sometimes has a tinge of black on his red hairs, due no doubt to the Gordon influence.

The orange beltons are particularly free from color abnormalities, which is one of the reasons for their popularity from a breeding standpoint.

Very dark blue beltons are an undesirable color as they do not show to advantage in the ring and are not attractive as compared with lighter colors.

Large black, lemon, or orange patches are also undesirable except in the case of the ears, which can be solid black, lemon or orange. A color spot at the root of the tail is not too undesirable and in fact often accentuates a good tail asset or a merry tail. Sturdy Max had this characteristic orange patch at the root of the tail. Large patches of color on the body are to be discouraged.

The blue beltons usually carry a more profuse coat than do the lemon and orange beltons, and this characteristic is also shared by the tri-colors. This more profuse coat, however, is more subject to curl, which is a penalty. The texture of the blue belton and tri-color coat is usually harder and more difficult to control and keep in order than is the case of the lemon and orange beltons.

The winning dogs at the shows today are mostly orange beltons, and the next in number are the blue beltons, with the tri-colors last in numerical popularity. There was a strong tendency years ago to breed blue beltons, but the available breeding stock was limited due to the overwhelming popularity of the orange belton. It would seem that the breeders' desires had not changed much since 1576 when Caius stated that Englishmen were "greedy gaping gluttons after things that are seldom, rare and hard to get."

There is another advantage of the lemon and orange belton color over the blue belton as regards trimming. Usually, though not always as regards individuals, the undercoat of the blue belton is darker than the outer coat, so that when any trimming is done on a blue belton it must be months in advance of the show, else we will have a two-toned job on our hands, which is most undesirable in the show ring. Many judges who have not bred and shown blue beltons assume that the trimming job was done on the tack crate before the judging and unconsciously penalize the two-tone effect as it gives a most amateurish appearance

There is no doubt that there is some complicated multiple gene factor between coat color, eye color, and vigor, because when orange beltons are bred together for too long a time the eye color is apt to become lighter and lighter, and vigor, vivaciousness, pep, and steam seem to lag. When the blue beltons and the orange beltons are bred together, approximately one third of the get are tri-colors. Tri-colors are more prevalent in England, though they are increasing in America.

COAT

Laverack in his book **The Setter** (1872) says, "A setter cannot have too much coat for me, as it is indicative of the spaniel blood. Quality of coat is a great desideratum, and denotes high breeding. The coat should be slightly wavy, long, and silky. The forelegs nearly down to the feet should be well feathered, as well as in the breeches; you cannot have too much of it as long as it is soft, bright, and silky."

The Standard of the Breed states that the coat should be flat and of good length, without curl; not soft or woolly. The feather in the legs should be moderately thin and regular. In the relative weights for various points the Standard allows 5 points for length and texture of the coat.

There is no doubt but that good coat is an hereditary factor and when we hear exhibitors say, "Summer is a poor time for showing English Setters because they are out of coat in hot weather," then this is an admission on their part that emphasis on coat has not been of prime importance in their breeding program. An English Setter with a really good coat, that is, thick and profuse, will always be in good coat provided of course that the basic elements of English Setter management are practiced.

Coat is best grown from the inside. There is no hair tonic that can substitute for a well balanced diet. With this grade "A" food should be added plenty of fresh water, fresh air and sunshine, exercise, and daily grooming.

The importance of grooming cannot be overestimated. For best results it must be done faithfully every day, and the longer the time the owner devotes to it, the greater his dog's chances of winning. This conditioning of the coat is closely tied up with "Class," and the very routine of standing your dog on a grooming table every day has a definite training value for the ultimate show ring. The dogs enjoy this daily grooming and quickly learn to jump up on the bench for this special devotion.

In grooming an English Setter the following routine is recommended. First, take him out for his exercise, which should be of about one half to one hour's duration. This exercise can be walking on a hard road on a lead or allowing him to run (attended) in a field. Each method has its advantages, as the hard road on a lead helps his feet and at the same time gives him lead experience, while on the other hand, running free in a field is greatly enjoyed by an English Setter and has the advantage that several dogs can be taken out at a time, which is a great time saver where several dogs must be exercised. When the dog is brought back to the kennel, put him up on the grooming bench and brush him over to get any dirt and weeds out of his coat. A large-tooth comb may be used if necessary to loosen up any mats or to get burrs or brambles out of the coat. He should then be brushed thoroughly, using a stiff, natural bristle brush with bristles at least one inch long, preferably one and one half inches. This operation will require about twenty or thirty minutes. Then should come the grooming with the bare hands, which is the one means of putting on a high polish. This hand grooming should include the front and hind legs, the length of the ear, head, body, and tail. Not only does this hand grooming take out the loose hair and make the coat lie properly, but it gives the owner the opportunity of looking over the dog carefully and feeling him over minutely so that any lumps, bumps, or skin trouble just starting can be caught before it becomes serious. It also gets the dog used to being man handled. It is recommended that the owner not wear rubber-soled shoes, as the static electricity developed causes disagreeable shocks to both the owner and the dog, and the dog's coat becomes so charged with static electricity that it is difficult to make it lie as desired. The next step is to sponge him off lightly with soft water. (Rain water or distilled water is preferable, especially in those cities where the tap water is heavily charged with chlorine, alum, and other chemicals.) He should then be dried off with a turkish towel, blanketed, and put in a crate for about two hours to finish drying.

When this coat conditioning routine is faithfully kept up day after day for several weeks, and proper diet and exercise are given in the meantime, and did the judge's decision rest solely on condition of coat, the dog to which this treatment has been faithfully administered would be a sure winner over all others that had been denied it.

Doubtless some English Setter owners will take the attitude that it is simply an impossibility for them to devote so much time to their dogs. Let him who takes this view be the last to complain when a good judge puts a poorer dog whose coat is in the pink of condition over his dog.

Of course a certain amount of trimming of the coat must also be done so that the entire dog will appear to best advantage. An entire chapter has been devoted to trimming an English Setter, and for the first time this important phase of putting down an English Setter in show form has been explained and illustrated in detail.

You may not have the best English Setter at the show, but you can have the cleanest and the best put down.

HEAD

A great deal of importance is placed on the head of an English Setter, as is indicated by the relative weights of the parts of the dog of 20 points out of a total of 100. Laverack describes his ideal head as one long and rather light, though not too much so. He did not like a heavy-headed or deep-flewed dog, as to him it indicated sluggishness. The Standard of the Breed subscribes to Laverack's ideal, as it also calls for a long and lean head. Some people object to a lean head on the basis that there is not enough "Brain room." Actually a dog has a comparatively small brain, and only a fraction of the total is ever used. The size of a dog's brain has no bearing on the dog's intelligence. So it is with human beings. Many men with extra large heads are morons. The Standard of the Breed mentions "Brain Room," but modifies it by saying, "But with no suggestion of coarseness."

Contrary to the Standard's conception of the ideal head, there has long been the feeling among sportsmen that superior noses were somehow tied in with broad heads. T. B. Johnson in his "The Sportsman's Cyclopedia," published in 1831 and reprinted in 1848 by Henry G. Bohn, discusses the sense of smell of various breeds and relates this sense to the broadness of the head.

The stop or abrupt change in direction at the junction of the foreface and the skull should be well defined. An English Setter whose head is so formed that a straightedge can be placed from the tip of the nose to the skull has a most undesirable wedge-shaped head and has little or no stop. A line drawn across the top of the head and one drawn along the top of the muzzle should be parallel to one another, but at different levels, the difference in level representing the stop.

The length of the skull from the stop to the occipital protuberance should be equal to the length of muzzle from the stop to the end of the nose. The muzzle should be deep enough so that a line drawn across the nose and foreface and one drawn across the lower part of the foreface should be parallel, but with sufficient depth to make the entire head in proportion and a pleasing picture. Compare the photograph of a poor head (Page 70) with the Standard of the Breed Illustrated (Page 50). The occipital protuberance is the bump at the back of the head and gives another almost right angle (the stop being close to 90°) between the end of the head and the beginning of the neck, which again makes a most pleasing picture. The occipital can be too well defined, and when this is the case it forms a bump on the back of the head that is not pleasing. This overdefined occipital is often seen in English Setter puppies about six months old and usually blends out properly later. A bone injury during puppyhood sometimes causes this overdefined occipital.

Fullness under the eyes and cheekiness spoil the chiseling of the face and are undesirable.

The nose should be black for blue beltons and tri-colors and dark liver in color for lemon and orange beltons. Sometimes during the winter the nose of lemon and orange beltons turns a lighter color.

A dish face is objectionable in the United States, although as already pointed out, a tendency in this direction is much to be desired in France and Italy. I am inclined to agree that a suggestion of dish face, as with a Pointer, is quite attractive, although I also agree with the Standard that a real dish face is most undesirable. A Roman nose is the opposite from dish face. For instance, the top of the muzzle instead of being a straight line is concave for a dish face and convex for a Roman nose. The Roman nose is undoubtedly hereditary. Not as many Roman-nosed English Setters are seen today as there were about forty years ago, at which time they were quite common, stemming for the most part from two kennels.

The nostrils should be wide apart and with large, as compared with small, openings. This nostril placement and size are supposed to have some bearing on the scenting ability, but at any rate, when the openings are close together and small they are not as attractive as when correctly formed. Spots on the nose that do not pigment in uniformly are objectionable and unsightly.

CH. SAMANTHA OF SCYLD
A Good Head

Although the standard calls for jaws of equal length and makes no mention of teeth there are two types of bites which are considered acceptable. The ideal bite is the scissors where the upper front teeth slightly overlap the front teeth of the lower jaw. In an even bite the front teeth meet and do not overlap, and the teeth eventually wear.

Overshot and undershot jaws are most objectionable for an English Setters, not only from the standpoint of conformation, but also from a utility standpoint. When the front teeth are too far out of line a bitch cannot properly deliver her puppies, because she cannot bite off the cord. The overshot jaw is where the upper jaw is longer than the lower and gives the face a chinless appearance. The undershot jaw is where the lower jaw is longer than the upper and gives a most unattractive appearance to the muzzle, both from the front and the side. A wry mouth is caused by one side of the jaw growing faster than the other giving the front of the mouth both an overshot and undershot appearance depending upon which side is viewed. Most poor bites are the result of heredity.

Puppies do not usually exhibit the tendency toward overshot or undershot mouths until they get their second teeth at about four and one half months of age, so in buying a puppy for show or breeding purposes it is wise to buy an older puppy and pay the extra price and be sure that it has a good mouth. In the show ring a poor mouth can spoil the chances to win of an otherwise good dog.

The ears are a very important part of the head of an English Setter, as their placement and texture frame the entire head. The ears should be set low on the head, at least level with the eye, and well back on the skull. Measuring from the occipital to the stop the distance from the ear set to occipital should be about one third, and the distance from the ear set to the stop should be about two thirds. The ears should lie close to the head and not stick out, especially where they are joined on to the skull. By trimming the hair out from between the ears and the skull they will lie closer to the head. The tendency of some dogs to carry the ears high is an objectionable trait.

The leather of the ear should be moderately thin and pliable and not of a thick cartilage type. This permanent thickness of the ear is often caused by a cankerous condition which in turn

68

CH. RUSTY OF HAON
A Good Head

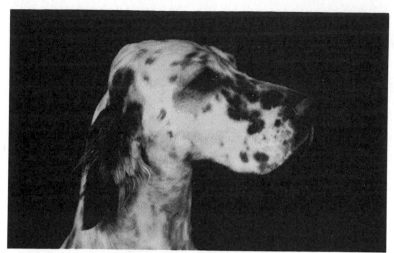

CH. MARY OF BLUE BAR
A Good Head

An example of an extremely poor head for a Laverack type English
Setter. Note the snipey foreface with lack of flews and the general
wedge-shaped appearance from skull to nose to neck.

70

causes a swelling of the leather. Trimming the top of the ear is discussed in the chapter on trimming and is also important in giving the ears their most pleasing appearance.

EYES

And last but not least by any means in making a good head are the eyes. The Standard of the Breed calls for eyes to be bright, mild, intelligent, and dark brown in color. While this is an excellent definition, it does not mention specifically their size, shape, and placement, or the pigmentation of the eyelids. Although the eyes have only five points in the relative weight classification, these five points may be called heavy points in the show ring, as the "Setter's eye is one of the jewels of the entire animal kingdom." He can ask the judge to put him up with his eyes just as well as if he could speak, and in a much more eloquent manner under the circumstances. I had this experience when I took a nine-months-old English Setter bitch to a match show for experience. She handled beautifully and when the judge went over her and then backed off to see her "all together," she slowly turned her head and looked him over also. The fineness and coyness were irresistible, and she finally ended up best of match. Her lovely dark eyes played no unimportant part in her win.

The eyes should be round rather than almond shaped (Oriental). They should be set neither too close (pig eyed) nor too far apart. They should be bright and clear and shining, suggesting health and energy. They should be dark, and the darker the better. The lame excuse, so frequently advanced, that the eyes, while not really dark, are dark enough for a lemon or orange belton is only wishful thinking. A liver belton is never born with dark eyes and the rims and nose do not pigment. The eye color remains the lightest yellow and gives a poor expression. The Standard does not indicate that an orange belton, or any other color, can have light eyes.

Prominent haws are unsightly and while not a specific disqualification in the Standard are nevertheless undesirable. The haw (membrina nictitans) is often termed the third eyelid or winking mechanism. It shows itself as a red and prominent

71

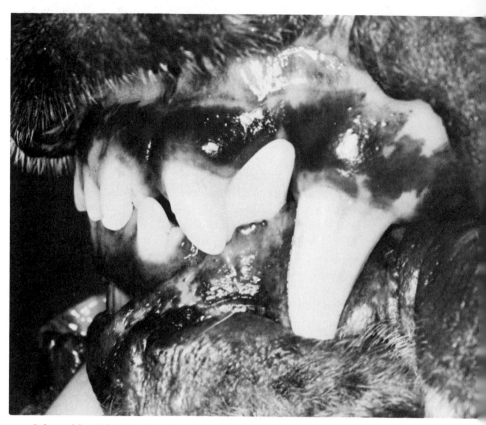

Scissors bite. The side view shows the tight overlapping of the upper teeth over the lower teeth. Ideal front teeth are uniform in size, pearly white and evenly set into the gum. *Beal*

covering over the eye, usually at the inside corner. The haw is prone to chronic inflammation and is most unsightly. Sometimes this inflammation can be temporarily helped by astringent washings of boracic acid, argyrol—5% solution, sulfathizol salve, etc. The only permanent cure is its removal by surgical means, which disqualifies the dog from being shown since no animal changed in appearance by artificial means is eligible to compete.

A not uncommon fault with English Setter eyes is incomplete pigmentation of the eyelids, so that the entire lid or parts of it are pink instead of black for a blue belton or tri-color, or dark liver for a lemon or orange belton. While this condition is not a disqualification by the Standard it cannot fail to be on the minus side when the competition is hot.

NECK

The Standard of the Breed gives the neck specification in a nutshell. However, there are some helpful hints that might be of value. A long neck gives a graceful appearance in the show ring and has its advantage in the field for winding birds. Its apparent length can be accentuated by careful trimming so that by comparison it shows to its best advantage. Trimming the neck is treated with thoroughness in the chapter on trimming. In posing an English Setter the neck should be almost perpendicular to the ground so that at one end the head will make almost a right angle and at the other end the shoulders will make almost another right angle. When an English Setter is set up with head and neck stretched out in front, it gives the dog an unbalanced appearance like a man with baggy-kneed trousers. The arch of the neck between the occipital and the shoulder is much admired and should be accentuated when trimming.

The Standard calls for the neck to be not too throaty. Of course a dog must have some throat, but in the show ring the less the better. We often see a handler, who thinks he is smart, gather the loose folds of skin which cause throatiness and pull them away from the judge or hide them in his hand. With all his efforts the dog is still throaty. The ringside sees it, the other exhibitors see it, and the judge sees it. A clean-throated dog will often become throaty with age, just as people get double chins with advancing years. There are some "fakes" whose only desire is to win and who care little or nothing about breeding who have the excess throat cut out of their dogs just as some people have their faces lifted. This practice is to be considered poor sportsmanship and against AKC rules.

Trimming the throat must be done carefully so that the coat will blend evenly from the throat to the chest. Otherwise the dog will have a goat-like appearance if there is an abrupt line between the throat and the chest.

SHOULDERS

From an examination of the rating of the relative weights of the various points one would gather that the shoulders are not too important, as the chest and shoulders together carry only twelve points out of the one hundred, and if we assume they are of equal importance, then the shoulders are worth only six points. However, when we consider that the shoulder takes into consideration only two bones, the scapula and the humerus, and that the remainder of the forequarters is taken into consideration under another classification, then the relative weight of six is not unreasonable. However, with some judges a good or poor shoulder may be a deciding factor in his placement, while other judges scarcely notice a poor shoulder. When it is considered that the rear legs of an English Setter are the real driving power and that the front legs are only to hold the dog up and guide him, then perhaps the shoulder is not too important. Yet an otherwise good English Setter can be spoiled by being loaded or too straight in shoulder.

It will be noted from the dotted line in the photograph illustrating the Standard of the Breed that two bones forming the shoulder, the scapula being the upper bone and the humerus being the lower bone, are placed at quite an angle and act with their connecting muscles as a shock absorber. Should this angle be too straight, the shock absorber action will be reduced in proportion.

A common fault in today's English Setter and many other sporting breeds is a poor front. Many dogs have good layback of the scapula but little layback of the humerus causing straight fronts and dogs which can never stand with the elbows posi-

74

Photograph of a throaty English Setter. Compare with photo below, showing a good clean neck.

This is an example of several good points. Note long arched clean neck, excellent top line, correct tail placement, fairly good angulation, good feet.

tioned directly below the point of shoulder. Such animals appear to have lack of brisket because of the elbow placement.

The scapulae should be curved in a lateral plane so that the two when they nearly meet at the top of the shoulder should be close together so that one or two fingers only can be placed between them when the dog is standing with his head up. A trick of some handlers is to lower the head and neck when the judge feels for the closeness of the scapulae, as this movement automatically brings them together. The shoulder should lie flat against the body so that the neck and shoulder flow together.

CHEST

The chest should be deep but not so wide as to interfere with the movement of the shoulders. When a dog is viewed from the front and the chest is too wide, then also the shoulders must be separated so that the space between the two scapulae will be wide, and the legs will then not be under the dog. When the chest is too wide the elbow will point outward and the toes will be turned inward. When this fault is present, it will be more noticeable when the judge pushes down on the withers, as the elbows then swing out and are called loose or out in elbow. When, on the other hand, the chest is too flat, the toes will point outward and the elbow inward, and the dog is said to be French or fiddle-fronted. Anyone can try this for himself by turning his two hands in or out and noticing what happens to his elbows. The chest must be roomy and deep, and extend far back so that the distance from the back rib to the upper rear leg, the flank or loin, will be short. This short loin is important because it is the weakest part of a dog, having no support except the backbone and the muscles. The ribs should be connected to the backbone at almost a right angle and then curve gracefully to the bottom of the chest. The depth of the chest should be such that the distance from the top of the shoulder to the bottom of the chest is one half the height at shoulder of the dog. (This does not include the feathering under the chest. You will notice judges pushing the chest feathers out of the way to establish this half way measurement.) The chest houses the heart and the lungs which are the dog's furnace, and without ample capacity of both, the English Setter cannot have endurance.

76

Example of a better than average front. The point of shoulder is directly over the point of elbow. The humerus and scapula could be of more equal length. *Fox Foto*

Some faulty chest conformations are called barrel-sided when the chest has insufficient depth, slab-sided when there is insufficient spring of rib, and razorbacked when the ribs do not spring out at the top.

BACK—LOIN—RIBS

The back line should be a gradual slope from the shoulder, being the highest point, to the root of the tail. The loin should be short. There should be no dip in the back line either just behind the shoulder or at the loin. A dip at the loin is a structural weakness, and an upward curve at the loin, although strong, is undesirable and is referred to as roached back. The loin should be supported by muscles and not fat. Some exhibitors try to make a dog appear short in loin by laying on fat, but this does not deceive an intelligent judge. A short loin is very important because the loin of a dog, like the small of our own back, is structurally weak. Bridges are arched in the center to give them strength, and if they were concave they would not carry the load for which they were intended. A slightly arched loin is therefore preferable to a dipped loin, although a well-muscled loin is preferable to either.

A not uncommon fault in English Setters is to be found where the back ends and the tail begins. The tail when stretched out should form a graceful continuation of the top line, for after all, the tail is only a continuation of the vertebrae of the back. Sometimes the back has a sudden drop or shelf between the hip bones and the tail which gives the dog a constipated appearance and interferes with his movement. You will usually find this faulty tail set connected with the tendency of a dog to sit down at every oppportunity.

The rib formation is very similar to that of a boat and it is for the same purpose, being a framework to protect the inner cavity which houses the vital organs—heart and lungs. The angle at which the ribs are joined to the backbone (the keel for a boat) will vary from the shoulder, being the sharpest there, to the center where the angle will be quite flat, and then gradually to a lesser angle. The spring or curve of the ribs should be minimum at the front, maximum about the center, and less again toward the loin. Just as with a boat, the lines, beauty, or symmetry of

78

the chest will be governed by the way the ribs are formed. Round barrel-like rib formation lacks the gradual spring from front to center to rear and is not only unsightly but interferes with the shoulder action.

FORELEGS

As already stated, the forelegs' function is to hold the dog up and is similar to the front wheel of a wheelbarrow, where the driving power is the pushers' two hind legs. The front legs absorb the shock of the dog when gaiting, the dog being continually in a state of falling on his face. The front legs are similar to knee action in an automobile, and the muscles which hold the bones together are the shock absorbers. Viewed from the front the front legs should drop absolutely straight and parallel to each other to the pasterns, and still viewed from the front the pasterns and feet should still be in the same straight line. Viewed from the side the frong legs should be angulated as illustrated by the dotted line in the illustration of the Standard of the Breed. It is from this side view that it will be noticed that the pasterns should be short and very slightly angulated forward to form another shock absorber. When this slight deviation from the perpendicular toward the front is too pronounced, it becomes a weakness, as the shock absorber leverage becomes so flat that it can no longer take the shock. This condition is called being down on the pasterns. It is a common fault in English Setters and is no doubt caused by incorrect management during puppyhood. Many judges will overlook a perfectly straight pastern (no shock absorber) because of their extreme dislike for the deformity of a dog that is down on his pastern so that the pastern looks like part of his feet. The pastern corresponds to a person's wrist.

Viewed from the side the forelegs should be well under the dog so that the radius (the bone in the front leg that is perpendicular to the ground) is in a vertical line with the top of the scapulae (shoulder blades). When the forelegs, shoulder, and elbow are not properly angulated the front legs are not well under the dog and are placed forward about under the neck. When viewing the dog from the front the front legs should not be too wide apart nor too close together. When the humerus and radius are in line the front will be correct. The length of the bones and the chest depth should be so proportioned that the lower part of the chest and the elbow should be in line.

HIND LEGS

The hind legs are naturally considered important in the relative weights of various points of the English Setters as they are his engine that give him the power to move. Twelve points out of one hundred are assigned to the hindquarters, being rated as of equal importance as chest and shoulders, or symmetry, style, and movement. The hindquarters or engine or propelling power must naturally be in harmony and in keeping with the remainder of the dog. A big car with a little engine or a little car with a big engine would be out of balance. The hind legs should be rugged with big bones and powerful muscles and should tie in generally with the overall animal. The hind legs are a series of levers and shock absorbers with muscles to coordinate these levers and shock absorbers. The bones which make up the leverage are the ilium, which is the hip bone and joins with the back bone or vertebrae. This hip junction is really the main bearing, as the entire effort of the hindquarters is transmitted through this joint to the vertebrae (the reason for a short muscular loin). The next bone is the femur or top thigh bone and sockets into the ilium. The next is the tibia or lower thigh bone and sockets into the femur so that the angle made by the two is about 120 degrees. This angle is called the stifle and is what is referred to as a well-angulated stifle when it is about 120 degrees, or a straight stifle when it is considerably more than 120 degrees, and overangulated when it is considerably less than 120 degrees. The reason for the 120-degree desideratum is that this particular angle gives the maximum driving power. The last bone of the rear leg is the metatarsus which is really an assembly of five bones and corresponds to the human instep. This is also called the rear pastern, and the junction of the metatarsus and the tibia with its protuberance, the oscalcis, is called the hock. The pastern should be short and round, and angulated very slightly forward. Looking from the rear the femur, tibia, and metatarsus form an angle so that if they are not in line the dog is called cow hocked. Associated with cow hocks,

Example of a good front. Notice the clean shoulder line, elbows that do not protrude and feet that do not turn in or out. The front legs are straight and the pasterns strong.   *Fox Foto*

A poor front. Legs bowed in, and too wide at chest.

naturally, the back feet are turned out. In looking for cow hocks, especially in a puppy, the animal should be at ease, as when frightened a hocked stance is often displayed, even when the bone formation is correct. When posing a dog at the show the pastern should be just about perpendicular to the floor when viewing the dog from the side and the rear, and when viewing from the rear the stifle should be in a vertical line dropped from the rear of the buttocks. For instance, looking at the illustration of the Standard of the Breed, the dog illustrated is pulled out too far so that the pastern is not perpendicular to the floor and this poor unbalanced position also reacts unfavorably on the undesirable sixty degree angulation at the stifle. The muscles around the femur and the tibia should be thick and hard as against thin and flabby.

FEET

As with man, the feet are a most important part of the body, although a dog is more fortunate in having four to support its weight. Man's hands correspond to a dog's forefeet and it is interesting to note that when a man falls, he instinctively makes an effort to break the fall by using his hands and arms as they were probably intended in the dim era of the past.

The feet on an English Setter should be strong with toes close together and arched, with the pads thick as against thin. A dog literally walks on his toes, although in some extreme cases of malformation they are inclined to use their pastern (our foot arch) and their hock (our heel). Poor feet are a serious fault in an English Setter and a common one. Poor feet are the result of a combination of inheritance, overfeeding when a puppy, lack of exercise, and poor footing. Puppies and adult dogs which are exercised on pea gravel develop better feet than those kept on cement or dirt. The combination of flat toes (not arched), splayed toes (not closely fit together), and thin pads is often coupled with poor pasterns (sloping too far forward). Attention should be called to the effect of long toenails as a contributing factor to poor feet, as when the nails become too long they interfere with the proper action of the toes and pads. Of course long toenails and lack of exercise, another contributing factor to poor feet, go hand in hand. It is doubtful that the toenails will ever be

Example of a good rear. The hocks are perpendicular to the floor. It is obvious this dog has well developed thighs and excellent bone. *Ashbey*

A poor rear. Note the cow hocks and the toe out which is a weak structure.

too long if a dog gets sufficient exercise, as he will keep them worn down to the point where the toes and pads function properly. While on the subject of toenails it is well to mention dew claws. English Setters have dew claws on the front legs only. They serve no useful purpose that we know of and mar the beauty of the front. They often become torn in the field and should be removed when the puppies are three or four days old.

TAIL

Next to the eyes, the English Setter's tail or flag is the most expressive part of his makeup and even when you cannot see the eyes, the tail tells you without doubt just how he feels about it — whatever it is. A tail carried down or between the legs indicates a disposition that is not characteristic of an English Setter. Although the Standard places considerable emphasis on the tail, it specifies its static requirements and does not mention specifically its dynamic action. The tail should be carried approximately level with the back so that a line from the base of the neck to the end of the tail should be a continuous pleasing slope. The Standard states that the tail should not curve sideways or above the level of the back. In fact, in the field trial (Llewellin) setters this is most desirable, as this high flag helps the handler locate the dog in heavy cover. English Setters are inclined to carry a high tail when they are in fine fettle or are looking for a fight. At any rate, a high tail carriage will usually not be penalized as much as a tail carried too low or between the legs. The tail should be animated and wag continually and in time with the dog's movement.

The tail is not merely an ornament and a means of expression, but has the useful purpose of serving as a rudder and a brake. The length of the tail should be not greater than to reach the hock. A shorter tail than this maximum is desirable. The tail should be covered with a silky fringe below, which should taper to a point at the end. A heavy bushy or fox tail is not desirable and much can be accomplished in this direction as well as length by careful trimming as explained in the chapter on trimming. In taking the superfluous hair off the tip of the tail, care should be exercised so that in our zeal to make the tail appear as short as possible it is not trimmed so closely as to cause a bleeding tail

Good feet and strong pasterns. Note the lovely bone, high arched
toes and beautifully manicured nails.   *Ashbey*

Example of poor pasterns, sometimes mistaken for poor feet. The feet are not good but the main fault is in the pasterns.

end when the dog is worked in the field. This word of caution is especially apt in the case of a dog with an exceptionally merry tail.

HEIGHT AND WEIGHT

The latest revision of the Standard of the Breed (1950) by the English Setter Association omits any reference to weight and defines the Standard for Dogs as height at shoulder about twenty-five inches and for Bitches about twenty-four inches. The intention of the committee on standard revision was twofold: (1) To raise the height standard of English Setters and (2) By the use of the word "about" to permit some variation in height above and below the suggested twenty-five inches for Dogs and twenty-four inches for Bitches. An examination of sixty-three English Setter Champion Dogs of earlier years showed that the average height at shoulder was 25.4 inches, so the change in the standard to 25 inches has a definite background. A similar study of twenty-two Champion Bitches showed an average height of 23.8 inches. While the word "about" is somewhat indefinite, as was the intention of the committee, its practical definition may be considered 24-26 inches for Dogs and 23-25 inches for Bitches with a preference for the 25 inches for Dogs and 24 inches for Bitches.

There is a marked tendency toward breeding English Setters higher than 25 inches for Dogs and 24 inches for Bitches (height being measured from top of shoulder). This is allowed under the standard by the word "about." It should be pointed out, however, that it is extremely difficult to produce a really good dog or bitch larger than the height suggested. Extreme care must therefore be exercised when breeding in this direction. In general, if the breeder will try to stay at about the height suggested, his chances of breeding acceptable specimens will be greater. Quality, not quantity, is desirable. In spite of the arguments against breeding for extra large size, it cannot be disputed that a larger dog has a better opportunity of receiving attention from the judge in the Sporting Group, assuming that it is otherwise good.

Photograph on an excellent tail set. Note how it continues the top line without a dip to tail set.

SYMMETRY

Some years ago a cartoon appeared in one of the dog magazines showing a store where they stocked and sold dog parts for all the various breeds. Heads, tails, feet, ears, fronts, and all other parts for each breed were orderly arranged in bins. If such a store really existed, it is extremely doubtful if anyone could go there and buy all excellent parts and from them assemble a dog that would have symmetry.

Symmetry is an integration of all the parts to form a whole which will be pleasing to the artistic eye or to the trained eye of the experienced dog judge. Amateur breed judges often become so engrossed in the "parts store" that they do not see the entire picture, good or bad. It is for this reason that a good experienced judge will usually pick out the symmetrical dog who is fairly good all over, while the breed judge may put up a specimen who excels in several parts but lacks symmetry. All too often a breed judge will forget to back away sufficiently to lose the details of the fine points and look for a picture of proportion or symmetry. Included in symmetry is "Class" which has already been discussed in detail.

We often hear the gallery and the ringside express disapproval of the judge's selection. They were too far away from the dogs to see the fine points but at their distance they recognize symmetry and express themselves accordingly. I well remember the judge of English Setters at the Morris and Essex show in 1938. He had a quick and trained eye for symmetry. He had very large classes and stood at about the center of the ring and watched the dogs as they came in the ring. He would motion the handlers as they came in to the right or left, and when the entire entry was in the ring he had the symmetrical dogs lined up on the right and those lacking in this quality on the left. To me it was a remarkable exhibition of an eye trained for an appreciating the beauty of symmetry.

From the foregoing one may assume that an artist, sculptor, or industrial designer, whose eye is trained in form and function, would make a good dog judge. This, unfortunately, is seldom the case, as to most of them a dog is just a dog, and they do not know enough about the different breeds to appreciate the fact that what may be symmetry for one breed may not be the

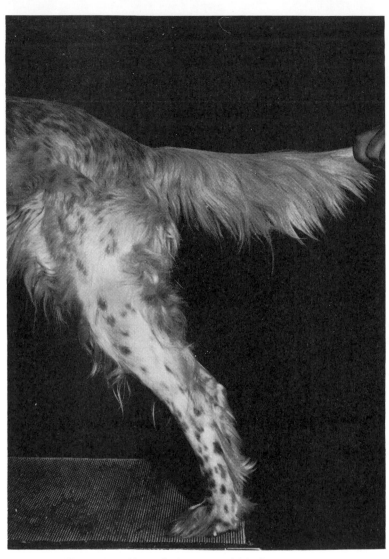

An illustration of low tail placement which gives a poor top line.

same for another breed. Quite often our Best of Show judges are people in the public eye, "name bands," and do not know much about the fine points of many, if any, of the breeds. They rely upon the breed and group judges to send them a representative specimen of the breed and therefore judge practically entirely on conformation, which is another word for symmetry.

MOVEMENT AND CARRIAGE

We have all seen dogs who when they move seem to get in their own way or who slink along like they were afraid of the unknown. This is very antithesis of what is correct in movement and carriage. We want an English Setter who functions and coordinates perfectly and who is bold and gay with it all.

The gait should be free and without apparent effort. We have often seen dogs who make a great show of moving by picking up their front legs high and making a big effort, but not going anywhere. This action reminds me of a Mississippi River steamboat. The paddle wheel goes around and around furiously, but the boat moves very slowly. This is sometimes caused by the handler using a tight lead so that the handler is holding up the front of the dog, and the front legs, whose function is to do this, are practically useless.

The first thing to look for is parallel hocks. A good handler can stand a cow-hocked dog so that it is fairly good, but when they are moved the truth will out. Also once in a while we will find hocks turned out, called "bandy legs," which is also a fault. Dogs with cow hocks will move with their rear feet turned out.

A narrow base with the rear feet moving so close together as to threaten interference, the one with the other, is poor movement and is a common fault with English Setters. There should be five or six inches between the hocks as they pass one another. However, a spraddling action of the rear legs is just as bad a fault as when the hocks are carried too close together.

As the dog returns toward him the examiner should look for the much desired perfect parallelism of the front legs, the elbows held close to the sides, but not bound or held too tightly. There should be no crossing of one foot over the other, known as weaving or trussing or paddling of the front.

While the dog in the walk or the trot (in fact in all gaits except the gallop) supports himself upon alternate front legs of necessity, the transition should not be apparent in the shoulders, which should be joined to the body so they do not slide up and down loosely as the dog changes from one foot to the other in the course of his locomotion. This is a common fault in English Setter movement. This movement is similar to the "tough strut" used to portray a bully in the movies, where the opposite shoulder goes up when the leg goes down.

The excessive lifting of the front feet and pasterns when moving on a level surface, called hackney action or steamboat action, is often applauded by the gallery and at best forgiven by some judges. It is a waste of energy and a definite faulty movement. This gait, although spectacular to the gallery, is a fault and should be penalized. It is frequently seen in the Pointer ring. This is not to say that an English Setter should drag his feet; he should lift them smartly so that from behind you can see his pads at every step, but he should not indulge in any goose-stepping calisthenics. Sometimes a similar high action of the rear legs is seen, especially on dogs with too wide a rear stance, and they are inclined to throw their feet outward as in a "Charleston" dance. Such dogs have, to the gallery, a spectacular but deceptive style, lots of action but little progress.

Having watched the dog move away and toward the observer, we should next watch him move from the side or profile. His top line should be good without rolling and without dips behind the shoulder or loin. His joints should move with rhythm, and his leg action should be long and free, simulating a glide forward with no ups or downs, as you would want in a good saddle horse. His head should be in the air, and his tail active. He should show liberty in his gait as well as soundness and power.

A smooth moving Setter with plenty of action forward and covering the space with minimum effort, head up and tail wagging in time to his movement with restrained enjoyment never fails to make an impression on the Group or Best in Show judge as well as the gallery. He is always a Best in Show contender.

FAULTS

The faults for English Setters are given in the following tabulation. Those preceded by an asterisk are not common

94

faults for English Setters as a breed; these points usually come good. Knowing which faults are not common is a help in breeding, as the drag of the breed will help to eradicate these faults; e.g., a short foreface is not a common fault for a Laverack type English Setter, so I would not hesitate to breed to an otherwise excellent dog who was slightly short in foreface, as I would not expect this fault to carry through to the puppies.

There are naturally various degrees of faults, such as a long tail. The maximum length of the tail should be such that it just reaches the hock; of course if it were one-quarter of an inch longer it would not be too bad, but if it were two inches longer it would be classed as too long. It is well, therefore, to qualify the fault by an adjective—eyes on the light side; slightly hocked, coat slightly curly, etc. Many of these faults are the result of the operation of the law of variation and are to be expected in your breeding operation. In the chapters on breeding, possible ways of minimizing them are suggested.

Several usual faults are illustrated in the group of photographs (pages 70-92), and a companion photograph of a good part is shown for comparison.

The head studies(pages 67-70) of several dogs and bitches will give the reader a good general idea of what is desirable in English Setter heads. Mr. Earl C. Kruger of "Mallhawk" fame and who judged the 1949 Morris and Essex Kennel Club Show, placing Ch. Mary of Blue Bar Best of Breed, described the ideal English Setter head for a dog weighing 60 pounds and 25 inches at the shoulder as measuring 10 inches overall, 4½ inches wide at ears, and 4¼ inches deep through the muzzle. A great deal of importance is attached to a pleasing head of an English Setter as evidenced by the relative weight assigned by the Standard of the Breed. One fifth of the total points going to make up a good English Setter are for a good head.

Admitting that a poor head may spoil the integrated picture of an otherwise good dog, the other eighty per cent of the dog is also important, so a word of caution is not remiss lest we unconsciously sacrifice the eighty per cent in favor of the twenty per cent.

I know English Setters who are admittedly weak in head but whose other eighty per cent is so superior that they have easily gone on to their championships over dogs that were much superior in head but weak by comparison in the other eighty per cent.

95

LIST OF UNDESIRABLE ENGLISH SETTER TRAITS

Light eyes
*Eyes too small
*Eyes not correctly placed
Eyelids not correctly pigmented
Progressive retinal atrophy (PRA)
*Curly coat
Woolly coat
Not enough coat
Poor spring of ribs — slab-sided
Straight stifle — structural
   fault
*Poor expression
Tail set too low
Tail carriage too high
Sickle tail
Slight bone
Lack of substance
Long loin
Snipey foreface
Short foreface
*High ear set
Cow hocked
Front toe in or out
Rear toe in or out
Angulation of front and rear
   not balanced
Too much throat
Too large
Too small

*Splayed feet
*Thin footpads
*Flat-footed
Short neck
Poor stop
Thick skull
*Undershot mouth
*Overshot mouth
Deafness
*Roman nose
*Cleft palate
*Shy
Roach back — structural fault
Sway back — structural fault
Out in elbow — structural
   fault
Front paddles when moved
Rear too close when moved
Front and rear not in line
   when moved
Hip dysplasia
High rump
*Undescended testicle
Navel hernia, inguinal hernia
Straight in shoulder — struc-
   tural fault
Lack of brisket depth
Body rolls when moved
Tail too long

* Traits which are not common with the breed.

5

Care and Management

THERE are some excellent books covering the feeding, housing, basic training and diseases of the dog in much greater detail than could be covered in an individual breed book. A must for any bookshelf is the *Dog Owner's Home Veterinary Handbook* by Delbert G. Carlson, DVM and James M. Giffin, M.D. (Howell Book House, 1980). This book offers sensible, easy to follow, up-to-date information on all aspects of dog care. Certain information on these subjects as it relates to English Setters is included below.

It is essential that the dog owner be aware that his behavior and methods of handling a young puppy help to model and create the personality and adjustment patterns of the grown dog. The desirable traits which are typical of the English Setter breed are there because of heredity and the animal's positive interaction with his environment. You are a critical ingredient

These two-month-old puppies exhibit good bone development. Notice the tight feet from feeding little and often, and unlimited exercise. They all weighed approximately fourteen pounds.

in promoting the positive behavioral adjustment of your pet. It is wise to become knowledgeable as to your role. A book such as, *The New Knowledge of Dog Behavior* by Clarence Pfaffenberger, (Howell Book House, 1963) provides the owner with important information on the topic.

Remember that there are critical periods in your puppy's development just as there are in the world of the human infant. The critical periods are:

1. Birth to 20 days
2. From 20 days to 49 days
3. From 49 days to 84 days
4. From 12 to 16 weeks.

It is obvious that almost three critical stages are already past by the time the puppy arrives in his new home which is why careful scrutiny of the breeder of the litter and his facilities should be a prerequisite to purchase. The physical and emotional health of a puppy are equally important in the development of an animal who has trust in and affection for people and a dependable temperament.

Attention should focus on preventing trauma and giving large amounts of affection. Children must not be allowed to abuse or to handle a young puppy roughly.

Respect a puppy's need for rest and individual space. Be sure a spot is provided where he will be undisturbed. A crate is ideal for this purpose and should be used for a life time. Until about 12 weeks puppies should be picked up, played with, and petted frequently. At about 12 weeks the training can become more serious and more directive. At this stage the puppy has progressed to the point where he is ready to learn. Basic obedience can be taught. Establish yourself as the boss through gentle yet firm correction. If the animal continues to have his way he will rule the household. Improper interaction now can create a setter with recalcitrant behavior patterns and give the owner a difficult to manage adult. It is said that parents often have the children they deserve. With few exceptions the same can be said of the family pet.

Feeding

Except in illness, English Setters require no specialized, esoteric or exotic diets. A healthy, parasite-free puppy or adult

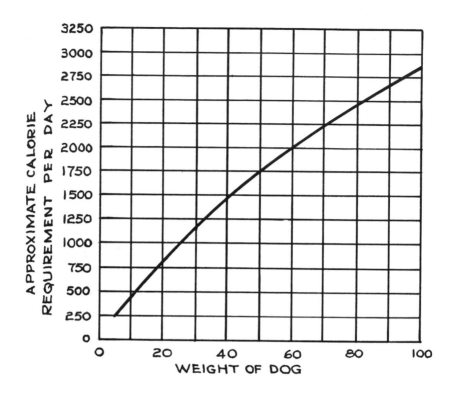

will thrive on a balanced diet containing the proper amounts and ratios of protein, carbohydrate and fat without fancy or expensive foods. Those interested in calories will want to know how many calories are required by a dog of given weight. A graph is reproduced in this chapter showing the relation of weight and caloric requirements. Though interesting, such charts should serve only as a general guide and not as an exact ideal. More useful to English Setter owners are the charts herein that show the age and weight relationships for dogs and bitches from birth to two years. Such age-weight curves are valuable to the breeder because they enable him to know at a puppy's early age if it will make the grade or not when mature.

Until recent years, breeders believed in stuffing young puppies until they become roly-poly butterballs. Today veterinarians are recommending that breeders keep puppies of the larger breeds somewhat on the lean side to avoid taxing muscular and bone development.

Adult dogs are usually fed once a day. Commercial dry foods supply a well-balanced nutritional formula for health and well being. Some people insist on feeding meat, cottage cheese or other types of protein mixed with the dry food. Although this is not a necessary practice, if you do add, never mix more than ¼ protein to ¾ dry food. Mixing the food with a little warm water aids in the digestion process.

When your pet reaches ideal weight with ribs and hip bones nicely covered, weigh him and use this weight as a guide. Feeding snacks between meals can put on pounds since many are prepared with large amounts of sugar. A hard baked biscuit type bone can be given as a reward when training, to exercise the jaws and keep teeth tartar free. Some dogs enjoy vegetables such as carrots, lettuce, and green beans which contribute natural vitamins and minerals to their diets. In spite of many commercial dog food ads which promote variety, a monotonous diet is the best diet. Adding table scraps can create digestive upsets and increases the probability of finicky eating habits.

A dog's appetite increases in cold weather or when exercise is stepped up and decreases in warm weather. Some dogs will eat and demand large quantities of food at all times and must be carefully monitored. Preventing obesity increases the life expectancy of your pet and decreases medical problems. The ideal weight is neither thin nor obese.

Age and Weight

In raising puppies, it is interesting to know what an English Setter puppy should weigh for any age. Such information is not only valuable for evaluating a puppy or grown dog for purchase, but it is well to watch the weight of developing puppies to see if they are gaining as they should. Available data of known accuracy on weight versus age of good English Setter puppies is somewhat meager. The following curves for dogs and bitches have been taken from two main sources and adjusted to fit the standard of the breed, and further adjusted between birth and maturity by several series of measurements made independently by Davis Tuck and Ward C. Green.

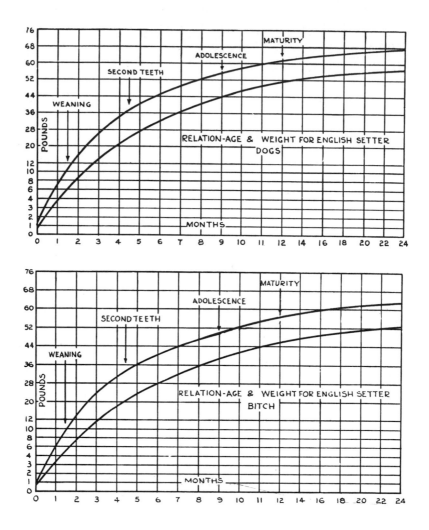

It is obvious that age-weight records for dogs and bitches who at maturity did not weigh the minimum required by the standard of the breed should not be included in the age-weight chart, so such animals have been omitted as we do not care to

102

to know the age-weight curve for substandard English Setters, but rather those who come within the limits of the Standard of the breed. Age-weight records are not complete, and the curve for dogs or bitches may have to be slightly revised when additional accurate data is available. It is believed by the author that sufficient data is available to establish within practical limits the age-weight curve up to six months of age. Additional data is needed for six to twenty-four months.

Such age-weight curves are very valuable to the breeder because they enable him to know at a relatively early age if a puppy is going to make the grade or not when mature.

These English Setter puppies are six seeks old which is the age for weaning, worming, immunization, training to ride in a car, crate breaking, lead breaking, house breaking, first trimming, teaching to stand, and generous feeding of the best food. They should weigh six to eleven pounds for dogs and five to ten pounds for bitches, and should gain weight according to the age-weight chart shown in this book.

From the charts showing the relation of weight and age for English Setter **Dog** and **Bitch** puppies who at maturity will meet the weight corresponding to the height requirement of the Standard of the Breed (revised 1950) it is obvious that a dog puppy at the age of five months weighing thirty-six pounds will, if kept increasing normally without severe setback from sickness, mature within reasonable limits of the Standard of twenty-four to twenty-six inches at the shoulder. On the other hand, should this five-months-old dog puppy weigh only twenty pounds, it is unlikely that he will reach the standard height at maturity. In using these curves some display of good judgment must be made, as evidently these curves do not apply to puppies who are hog fat or thin.

In compiling the data for the age and weight of English Setters similar data has been kept of age and height at shoulder, but such data is not sufficient for drawing any accurate conclusions. It was found, however, that there is a definite relation between the height at shoulder and the weight of good adult dogs and bitches. Using the data for the seventy-three good dogs and bitches it was found that the square of the height at shoulder in inches divided by the weight in pounds is 10.

$$\frac{ht^2}{wt} = 10$$

This formula is substantiated by many careful measurements of height and weight made by the author, and it has been found that when the height at shoulder of a good dog or bitch in show condition is carefully determined by using a scale and spirit level, the ratio of height squared divided by the weight is very nearly ten. This ratio is valuable in getting a dog in show condition, as show condition weight can be accurately forecast by measuring the height at shoulder.

Disease Control

Consult a veterinarian if your dog displays any of the following symptoms: loss of appetite for more than a day, fever, listlessness, diarrhea, lameness, cough, runny nose, watery eyes, evidence of pain, incontinent urination, vomiting, unusual thirst, skin eruptions, bad breath, persistent scratching of any area — or any other uncommon, unusual behavior.

The real costs of owning a dog vary according to the owner's interest in keeping the animal as a pet and companion or as a show dog, or field dog. Whatever your personal interests are there are some expenses which are constant and must be scheduled on a routine basis.

Keeping your dog parasite free is a must. Animals pick up internal and external parasites while outdoors and must be routinely checked for parasites. Have your veterinarian check a stool sample for the presence of hook, round, or whip worm. Tape worm infestation is caused by the ingestion of egg carrying fleas. After the worm matures it appears as small white segments on the stool and is best detected by the owner.

Heartworm is another parasite which has increased in incidence in various parts of the country. Unlike other types of worms dogs are infected through the bite of a mosquito. Yearly blood testing in the spring is the only positive way of checking for infestation. A preventive medication is given in liquid or tablet form during and until several months after the end of the mosquito season. The medication can only be administered to heartworm free animals. Heartworms cause damage to heart, kidneys and lungs and if they remain untreated will eventually cause death.

Fleas and ticks can cause a variety of mild to violent skin disorders. English Setters can be very sensitive to infestation. Flea bite dermatitis is caused by an allergic reaction to fleas and may continue even after the fleas have been killed. Treatment of the skin disorder by a veterinarian is necessary to control the reaction. In the warm months check your dog for the presence of fleas especially when biting and scratching persist. Fleas are sometimes difficult to locate. Dips, powders, sprays, and special flea and tick collars can be used.

105

Ticks attach themselves to the skin of the dog. A great many varieties are known to carry disease. Some dogs break out in a violent skin reaction with even the presence of one tick. In extreme cases ticks cause paralysis or other central nervous system disorders. Ticks can be killed by applying alcohol with a cotton ball. When the tick dies grasp it close to its head with a tweezer and pull gently to remove the head from under the skin. Leaving the head can cause infection. Avoid touching the tick with bare hands and flush or burn the remains.

Fleas and ticks which invade your kennel or home can be brought under control with insecticide sprays or by an exterminator.

Immunization

It is important to adhere to your veterinarian's vaccination schedule. When your dog is exposed to many other animals it is even more imperative to keep the shots up-to-date. The inoculations include Distemper, Hepatitis, Leptospirosis (DHL), Parainfluenza (CPI) commonly called kennel cough, Parvoviral Enteritis (Parvo), and Rabies.

There is a three year rabies vaccination given in many states. Some states require the yearly variety. Proof of a rabies shot is needed in many towns in order to obtain a current dog license.

Never vaccinate a bitch after she is bred. Be sure her boosters are current before-hand since live virus shots given to pregnant bitches can and often do cause severe problems with the normal development of the fetuses.

Poisonous Plants

All dog owners should be aware that many common house and garden plants are poisonous to dogs when eaten whole or in part. Some examples of toxic plants are ivy, azalea, boxwood, rhubarb, tomato, rhododendron, wisteria, and lily of the valley. Quick action by your veterinarian is essential if ingestion is suspected.

Training

English Setter puppies are fairly easy to house-train, given sufficient and frequent opportunity to perform outdoors when nature calls. A puppy from two to eight months of age should be taken outdoors the first thing in the morning, about every two hours during the day, after every meal and nap, and the latest possible hour before its owner retires at night. Fresh water should be available all day and removed at bed time. Giving inadequate supplies of fresh water causes severe kidney problems in later life.

Training to paper in the house is **not** desirable, since sooner or later the paper habit itself must be broken. If the puppy wets in the house, wipe up its urine with a rag or cloth which can be placed outdoors in the location best suited for the puppy's toilet habits. Always take the puppy to this location and it will soon get to know the place where it may perform without disciplinary action.

A normal, healthy dog will not foul its own nest or bed. For this reason, confining a puppy in a wire or wooden crate at night helps in the house-training process.

Crate-Breaking

Crate-breaking comes in very handy later for confining him and keeping him out of mischief when you are away for an afternoon or evening, or taking him to a match show, or along on your summer vacation. In later years many occasions will arise when you will bless the day that you crate-broke your dog. If you intend to show him at the dog shows or enter him in gun dog trials, crate-breaking is a great help, and the sooner he learns it the better.

In spite of the initial protests by a young puppy of being confined to a crate it usually becomes a haven for the grown dog and gives a sense of security wherever he is.

Begin training by keeping the crate door open. Leave an old towel or bath mat for bedding and supply the puppy with a tennis ball, natural hard baked bone or chewies. The first time the door is closed the puppy will probably howl. Do not give in. An English Setter has an elephant-like memory and will never forget when he has won and will continue to test you if you have weakened just once. You will find that if you leave the crate door open when it is not necessary to confine the puppy and place the crate in a convenient location that he will volunteer to use it for his nap.

Photograph of a five-months-old puppy who has been thoroughly crate-broken. He is outside all day but sleeps in his crate at night. At bedtime he runs most willingly into his crate. Wire crates are available and they can be folded for carrying. Purchase a crate that is 26 to 42 inches long, 21 to 24 inches wide and 26 to 30 inches high.

Puppies are easily lead-broken by coaxing them along with frequent petting and patience. They may balk a little for the first few days, but they will quickly learn to go along nicely. Do not be too severe with them; they do not know what you want them to do.

Exercise

It is also a very good idea to teach your dog to relieve himself while on a lead. This is very easy to do, especially if you catch him just at the time he really wants to go (first thing in the morning and immediately after eating). You will have to lead-break him anyway, so you will be killing two birds with one stone. In the city, on vacation, at the dog show or gun dog trial, you will be glad you trained your dog to relieve himself while on lead.

A responsible dog owner will never liberate his dog without supervision.

Allowed to roam at will, most dogs sooner or later connect with an automobile. Since they are hunting dogs, English Setters will roam. Assuming you love your dog, want to save him from injury and hope to avoid big veterinary bills, please fence him in! This need not be large nor expensive — a run 20 feet long, five or six feet wide and six feet high is sufficient. It can be made of wire called farm or turkey fencing, or of chain link if one can afford it. A fenced yard is ideal.

Chaining any dog to a post or pulley wire is to be avoided at all costs. Chained dogs bark a lot and often become vicious.

English Setter puppies up to four months of age will normally get enough exercise running about their yard and playing in the house. Older puppies and adult dogs (and their owners as well) will benefit from a brisk daily hike of one or two miles, or a run free from restraint in a field or woods far removed from traffic or other perils.

6

Buying a Puppy

YOU want to buy an English Setter puppy for a pet, a show dog, a shooting dog, or a combination of any two or all three uses. Where to go to look for a puppy, how much you should pay, what you should look for in a puppy, and at what age to buy it, are important questions to you.

Before you make a decision about where to buy a puppy it would be wise to contact two sources. Write to the American Kennel Club, 51 Madison Avenue, New York, N. Y. 10010 asking them to recommend reliable breeders in your vicinity. They can also supply you with the address of the current secretary of the English Setter Association of America. The Secretary will provide you with a list of breeders in your area and a booklet about the breed.

Be patient in your search. English Setters are often difficult to

An average litter for the breed is seven puppies.
This bitch proudly displays her ten day old babies.

English Setter puppies are usually born solid white with pink ears, feet, nose and eyerims. The pigmentation of the nose is beginning to appear on this three week old puppy.

At six to eight weeks the color begins to show through the body coat giving the puppy the characteristic belton appearance of the breed.

find and many litters are sold without any form of advertising. Avoid pet shops or other commercial establishments which sell a variety of dogs. No reputable breeder will sell puppies to them and the prices they command are usually substantially higher than those asked by a private breeder and for inferior quality.

Another place to look for a puppy is at your local dog show. When you attend watch the judging, paying particular attention to the winners in the various classes. Determine which dogs appeal to you. You can often locate the owners of the individual dogs at the show or write or call them using the addresses printed in the show catalog.

English Setter fanciers have a reputation for being among the most helpful people in the sport of dogs. Even when they have puppies of their own for sale which might not suit your requirements, they will often recommend other kennels. So do not hesitate to approach them and professional handlers who show English Setters, for their good and usually reliable advice.

You should let the breeder know what kind of a puppy you want: pet, show, or hunting prospect. The kind of a puppy you want will not only have a bearing on the price but also the breeder can recommend the proper puppy for your needs. If you want a pet, a loving affectionate disposition is of first importance to you. If you want a hunting dog then the nose and interest in birds will be the deciding factor. If you want a show prospect, the conformation, gait and markings will be important.

The price will probably range from $200 and up for a pet or hunting prospect, and $250 and up for a show prospect. A pet should be bought at about eight weeks of age; a hunting prospect from several months to a year old, and a show prospect from four months up. Although desirable, it is often difficult to locate an older puppy for sale since most breeders have immediate sales for young stock. One is often forced to gamble on a young puppy as a show prospect.

Buying from a small breeder often has its advantages since he can give each puppy in the litter his personal attention in feeding and sanitation. After the puppies are weaned he can also give them individual attention for exercise and training. It has been proven that this individual attention is very important in order to develop well adjusted adult dogs.

113

Puppies need to have intensive positive contact with human beings from at least the third week on. Frequent handling when the puppy is young can improve its physical and mental development and make it easier to train when it is sold. Simple grooming procedures such as cutting the nails should be introduced very early. Some breeders provide a radio stimulus as soon as the puppy is capable of hearing to provide human oriented sounds in order to enhance the socialization process.

For these reasons it is important for the buyer to determine what type of environment has been provided for the puppy's early development. In addition check the physical conditions and the cleanliness of the surroundings. A puppy can be easy to housebreak if it has lived in a spotlessly clean environment, is frequently taken out to relieve himself, or is provided with an in and out run.

Puppies are difficult to resist so determine in advance the conditions of the sale. Will you own the puppy outright or are there strings attached? Some sellers provide buyers with written agreements giving the terms of the sale. Is health guaranteed and if so for how long? Are heredity problems, such as Progressive Retinal Atrophy (PRA), which might develop as the puppy grows, covered? Is the guarantee in effect only if the dog is returned to the breeder? Will the animal be replaced or your money refunded partially or in full? If the puppy is sold as a show prospect and the mouth goes bad is there any recourse?

If there is a breeding agreement on the sale of bitch, who selects the stud, pays the stud fee, raises the puppies and pays their expenses, advertises and sells them? How many puppies must be returned to the seller and at what age will they be selected? Does the ownership in the bitch become unencumbered and revert solely to the new owner after the whelping and sale of the puppies? Whose name is recorded with the AKC as breeder of record?

If there is a breeding agreement on a male how many stud services are required? Who manages the breeding? Who selects and houses the bitch while she is being bred?

When showing is required who pays the entry fees, provides the transportation, grooms and conditions the dog? In other words, fully understand the terms of the sale if an agreement is to be negotiated. Also understand that most breeders will sell puppies outright with no strings attached.

While the price will be about the same for a pet or hunting prospect, regardless of age, the price for a show prospect will advance steadily with age. Buying a show prospect is a gamble, both for the breeder and the buyer. If you purchase a good show prospect for $300.00 at an age of four months, the breeder is taking a chance of selling you for $300.00 a puppy that might be worth $1,000.00 or more when it is two years old. On the other hand, you may be buying a puppy that may be worth only $150.00 when it is two years old. There is no positive way of telling at four months of age just how a show prospect will finish up when grown.

The basic structure of the animal is apparent at a young age but, where there is room for growth, there is always an opportunity for change to occur. For example, the head grows for 18 months and the jaw structure and bite can change for at least that length of time. What seems to be an excellent tail set can mature into a steep croup. Lovely rear angulation often straightens and noticeably heavy bone can become medium to light when the puppy grows to adulthood.

To judge the promise of a puppy is a guessing game based on knowledge of anatomy, the bloodlines which are combined, and previous experience with similar combinations. To keep your perspective, think of judging a future Miss America contest by peering into seven or eight baby carriages and making a selection. The potential for change is just as great with a puppy. English Setters mature slowly, and some faults do not show up in early puppyhood. When picking out your puppy, place a considerable amount of confidence in the recommendation of the breeder, but also make some examinations of your own.

There are few English Setter litters having uniformly good quality. An occasional litter may produce several champions, but this is unfortunately rare. Most puppies from most litters should be sold as pets.

If you are picking out a pet, look for a friendly happy disposition, and under no circumstances pick out a shy puppy. If you are looking for a hunting dog, pick one that is alert and watches anything that moves — a falling leaf, a butterfly, a sparrow, a grasshopper — and one that moves fast with a high head and tail carriage. Test this puppy with a bird wing tied to a cord or fishing line. The intensity of his interest will be apparent at an early age.

115

The experienced fancier and breeder prefers to acquire a show prospect over six months of age but the novice usually demands the youngest puppy available.

A show prospect should have a good mouth, not under- or over-shot, and a dark eye. Second teeth and permanent eye color come at four and a half to six months of age. Examine the belly for a possible navel hernia. Look for a dog that is bold and a good mover, with a long neck and high head carriage. The tail should not be set too low at its root. The muzzle should be square and not snipey. The length of the body should be about equal to the height at the shoulder. The puppy should not be cowhocked. It is best to watch for movement and hocks when the puppy is using his natural gait. When purchasing a male be sure both testicles are descended. Before going to look for a show prospect, review the chapter on the Standard of the Breed.

When going to a breeder to buy a puppy, make up your mind in advance the purpose for which you want the puppy and the maximum price you can afford to pay. Do not overlook the "priceless ingredient," the honor and integrity of the breeder. Inquire about this before you visit him. On the other hand, tell him the truth and do not ask for a pet because you think you can buy it cheaper and then select his best show prospect. Most breeders will give the buyer a good break in price on a show prospect if the breeder can be assured that the puppy will be shown consistently, but he does not want to sell one of his best show prospects only to have him lost in some back yard or neutered. On the other hand, a sincere breeder does not want to sell a poor show prospect as it will ultimately reflect unfavorably on his kennel.

The trait of bargain hunting with its attendant misstatement of facts and haggling over price is very apt to take possession of a buyer who has a dream of finding a "dumb" breeder who will sell him a top show prospect at a pet price. Such a buyer is usually not as smart as he may think and in almost every case gets at least no better than he pays for. My advice to a buyer wanting a puppy that has a good chance of turning out to be a show winner is for him to be perfectly honest with the breeder. Tell him the very top price that you can (and I do not mean afford to) pay and just what your intentions are from a show standpoint. Do you want a blue ribbon winner or one that can

116

win the Sporting Group? Are you going in for breeding or do you just want to have some fun at the shows? If you will take this honest attitude, you will get what you are after. If, on the other hand, you insist on bargain hunting, you will end up about third or fourth in your class with "just another dog."

When buying a puppy the purchaser has a responsibility as well as the seller. It is unfair for the purchaser to go from one kennel to another on the same day and handle puppies at each one as virus diseases can easily be carried on the hands, clothing and shoes and so by not thinking or being selfish one may easily be the cause of many litters of puppies becoming seriously ill or dying.

When you do select a puppy ask the breeder for a list of the shots that have been given and the date of the next recommended vaccinations. Also determine if the puppy has been treated for any worm infestations and what types were present. Continue checking stool samples with each routine veterinary visit as worms can cause severe physical problems in animals. When properly cared for, a worm free puppy provided a well balance diet develops to its optimum potential.

Continue the same diet as provided by the breeder. In puppies as in human babies a sudden change in diet or water can cause loose stools. Any change in food should be gradual. Mix the two types in varying degrees until the total change is accomplished over a number of days. A commercial puppy food is necessary for good development and is normally fed for one year. When provided with a well balanced diet a vitamin supplement is not necessary.

Never force a young puppy to exercise and do not allow him to become overweight. While in a rapid growth stage bone and joints are prone to injury. Keep puppies on secure, non-slippery surfaces so that they will not sprain muscles or ligaments or injure tendons.

Hold your puppy by supporting its full body weight with one arm under the chest and the other under the back legs. You can dislocate a shoulder or cause other permanent injury by picking a puppy up by the front legs.

Many physical and emotional problems are caused by owners with good intentions who handle the puppy improperly. Rely on the good advice of the breeder who obviously wants you to be satisfied with your puppy and is interested in your raising a healthy dog which is a credit to his breeding.

Best of Breed English Setters being judged by Dr. Dr. Thomas D. Buck of Rochester, N. Y., at the 1933 Morris and Essex Kennel Club Show. The Best of Breed dog on the right, was Ch. Gilroy's Chief Topic, owned and shown by Mr. W. F. Gilroy. The Best of Winners was Maesydd Modesty of Bromiley, owned by the late Mr. Irving Bromiley, being handled by Harry Hill. Modesty was an imported bitch from the Maesydd Kennels of Mr. D. K. Steadman of Merionitshire, Wales. Modesty was the most beautiful English Setter bitch that I have ever seen. The dog on the left is Ch. Hearthstone's Orkney Chief owned and handled by Mr. Richard Jennings of N. J.

7

Training for Shows

THERE is not much difference in training an English Setter for the show, training for a pet, or training for a shooting dog stake or for hunting birds. In all cases he must be trained to be obedient, to go on a lead at his owner's will, to ride in a car without getting sick, to be crate-broken, to stand as his owner wishes, and above all to be happy about the whole thing. We have already discussed training for car riding, training to go on a lead, and crate-breaking, all in the process of house-breaking and general training. It is advisable to start grooming your dog from an early age as well, for this will help the coat, making it lie well, and to teach him to stand still in the position you want him to stand, when and where you want him to stand. It also prevents him from becoming hand-shy, through the frequent handling of various parts of his body.

An English Setter should be groomed at least as well as his

owners. His hair should be washed, combed, brushed, and trimmed with the same care as you give yourself. His nails should be cut and filed. The hair on his head, ears, neck, shoulders, tail, hocks, and feet should be kept neatly trimmed to accent his beauty of form and to show off to the best advantage his good points. It is difficult for a veteran English Setter breeder to see the good points of a dog or bitch through a mass of unruly hair, let alone the dog show judge who has only a short time to look your dog over.

In grooming, trimming, lead-breaking, and other training you give your English Setter, do not forget the reward of a small piece of kibble or liver and some loving. Do this during the training process so he will associate this training with a good time and be merry about it. Remember you have more to learn than your dog, but the difference is that there is no one to reprimand you when you make a mistake, so take it easy and develop your patience. It is often said that the professional dog handler has an "in" with the judge and usually wins with his dog over an amateur handler. There are three important reasons for his many wins:

1. A top professional handler usually shows top dogs.
2. He knows how to handle a dog to get the most out of him.
3. His dogs are maintained in superior condition.

To keep your perspective know that the AKC expects a judge to examine and place 25 dogs an hour. Simply stated this means he has a little more thnan two minutes to evaluate the conformation and movement of each of the entries. A professional is competent and experienced and uses every minute to his advantage. The amateur is at a disadvantage when unsure of ring procedure and slow to position his dog for examination. Becoming a good handler takes time, practice, and application of skills gained through keen powers of observation. The professional dog handler has been doing for years what you are just starting to learn. Instead of finding fault, watch him closely, and you will learn to win over him when you have a better dog and should win.

Remember that you and your dog together present a picture in the ring and must work as a team. No manner of dress should detract from your dog. Your clothes must be neat, clean and well pressed. Wear low heeled, polished shoes that will give a firm footing on grass or any indoor ring surface. The color should silhouette your dog, not blend with him. For example, a white blouse and a light orange belton English Setter will blend together so that it will be difficult for the judge to see the dog's top line. Most all English Setters are orange and white (orange belton) or white with black ticks (blue belton), and your clothes should therefore be darker or lighter than the dog. Bright colors are acceptable, but very loud, vivid, or screaming colors are not suitable. A good rule to keep in mind is that you are showing your dog to the judge and the ringside, not yourself.

Most men wear slacks, sport jacket, shirt and tie. Women should not wear slacks and must remember to select an outfit which does not restrict movement. Have a pocket for a small comb and bait such as cooked or freeze dried liver.

A dog must be trained to respond properly to bait and not introduced to it in the ring for the first time. If you are using fresh liver boil it in water for about ten minutes, drain it thoroughly and then bake it in a moderate oven to dry it out turning the pieces several times. Cut the bait and freeze it in small containers so that it is available when you need it.

You must train yourself to gait with your dog, and this will require practice. Move with decision and precision and do not assume a pussyfoot, coaxing, or slinking movement.

A smooth clipped lawn or a carpeted strip on the floor, if indoors, should be used for moving your dog and in teaching him to move on a loose lead. It is best to use all types—grass, carpet, rubber mat strip, and grass mat strip—as your dog will later find all types for moving at shows, and may balk if he is not used to them. When attending a show with an unseasoned dog it is a good idea to get there early and move your dog to get him accustomed to the particular kind of floor. You will want the proper kind of slip show lead and not a collar and chain or too heavy a lead. A slip show lead measuring $3/8$" or $1/2$" wide will be correct for an English Setter. And by the way, never leave a collar on a show dog as it makes a ridge in the neck coat.

Posing for Shows

Some dogs are much easier to teach to pose for dog shows than others. In this connection I have often noticed that the ones who are well-balanced are the easiest to teach to pose in the desired show position, as when they are well-balanced, the pose position is a natural position which is easy to maintain for a considerable period of time without shifting. For example, when a dog naturally toes in or out in the front, it is an unnatural pose for them to stand with their feet placed as they should be, and you will find them taking their natural position at every opportunity.

Posing for the shows is best taught at an early age. Make it fun for the puppy by a reward of playing afterward so that it will associate fun and not punishment with the posing lesson.

Match shows provide good training for you and your dog. They give handlers an opportunity to gain ring experience in a relaxed atmosphere. Wins at match shows never carry the championship points associated with a win at an AKC licensed show.

It is the responsibility of every exhibitor to become familiar with the rules governing AKC point shows. The rules are updated each year and printed in booklet form. To obtain your free copy write or call the American Kennel Club.

Join your local English Setter club and the English Setter Association of America. Both will provide you with a monthly newsletter and other benefits of membership. Try to attend as many functions as possible. Your local club will give match shows, support the entry at selected local all breed shows, and perhaps run an independent Specialty. Take an active interest and ask what you can do to help the club. Willing workers are always welcome and they provide the backbone of any strong organization. If you really love English Setters, and you must if you ever hope to do anything with them, you will enjoy your new associations with dogs and doggy people.

To summarize, it is easy to train an English Setter for the shows if you begin basic training at a young age and have the time, patience, and determination to work with your dog. The most important ingredient in training is to make the sessions fun for the dog. The dog's lively ring attitude and happy tail weigh heavily in your favor. Tedious, frequent practice sessions and a heavy hand produce opposite than the desired results. Many English Setter have been ruined for show long before they have reached the ring for the first time. A dog who is a willing worker loves and respects the handler. Building that rapport is a necessary ingredient for success.

122

Powdering

English Setters should never be taken into the show or obedience ring without a bath. If you do not have time to bathe the dog do not show him. Unkempt, dirty animals discredit the breed, are disgusting to the judge, and reflect on the owner as well.

If you have entered a show circuit and are unable to wash your dog after a second day on the road you should know the correct method of powdering the coat to give a clean appearance. AKC rules prohibit the use of foreign substances left on the coat for breed judging. It is imperative that all the powder be removed.

Select the correct powder for the type of coat with which you are working. Use a coarse powder on silky feathering to add volume to the coat and a fine talc on harsh feathering to make it appear silkier. Experiment on your dog ahead of time to gain the best results.

Begin by spraying the feathering with water or a mixture of cream rinse and water. The proportions for the cream rinse spray are indicated under Grooming Techniques in Chapter 9. Lightly dry the feathering with a terry towel. Apply the powder working it through the feathering and towel the dog until it is dry. Thoroughly brush the dog parting the hair and working from the roots out. You can blow dry the dog and blow the powder out at the same time. You have done a good job if when the dog shakes there is no evidence of powder in the air.

The Lead

A well trained English Setter can be led by a length of thread. One who is continuously pulling indicates lack of training and control. Select a round leather collar or a nylon choke collar. A chain choke is used for obedience training but should not be left on the dog since it discolors and cuts the coat. In the show ring it is best to use a nylon martingale lead or a Resco show lead with a metal slip lock. Showing an English Setter on a metal choke collar and lead is considered in poor taste and communicates to the judge that the dog is difficult to control. A harness is inappropriate for the breed and is not used.

123

Junior Showmanship

Junior showmanship competition is offered at most AKC approved point shows. The child is judged on his handling ability not on the dog's conformation. Classes are divided into Novice Junior and Novice Senior, Open Junior and Open Senior. To be eligible for the junior class the child must be at least ten years old and under thirteen years. The open class is for children at least thirteen years old and under seventeen years. Novice competition is provided for those who have not won three first places in a novice class at a licensed or member show. To enter the open class in the appropriate age category the child must have won three first places in Novice. The book *The New Complete Junior Showmanship Handbook* by Brown and Mason (Howell Book House) is an excellent reference for those interested in more information on the subject.

English Setters are ideal companions for the junior handler. Their ideal temperament, willingness to please, and great patience when competing in large classes with a variety of dogs is evident. Through the years many have been used successfully by juniors. To be eligible for the Junior Showmanship class the dog must be owned solely or in part by the junior or a member of his immediate family.

Obedience

The versatility of the English Setter can be measured by his ability to perform in many arenas. It is up to the owner to train and bring out the dog's natural abilities for show, obedience, and field.

Obedience classes are divided into Novice A and Novice B which requires the dog to heel on leash, stand for examination, heel free, recall, long sit, and long down. By accumulating the required number of points the dog wins the Companion Dog (C.D.) title.

In Open A and Open B the dog performs drop on recall, heel free, retrieve on flat, retrieve over high jump, broad jump, long sit, and long down. Dogs qualifying for this degree are issued a certificate as a Companion Dog Excellent (C.D.X.).

The Utility Dog (U.D.) certificate requires a higher level of performance including the signal exercise, scent discrimination, directed retrieve, directed jumping, and group examination. In C.D., C.D.X. and U.D. work the dog and the owner are working toward their own best performance rather than against other dogs in competition.

The A.K.C. has recently granted the Obedience Trial Champion (O.T.Ch.) degree. To earn this title it is necessary to gain three first places as the highest scoring dog in trial in addition to earning one hundred points by placing first or second in the Open B or Utility class.

In addition, the A.K.C. issues the Tracking Dog (T.D.) certificate. The test is performed with dog in harness attached to a twenty to forty foot leash. The dog must scent a track 440 yards to 500 yards long locating an object placed at the end of the trail. There is no time limit provided the dog is working.

Locate one of the many local clubs which serve to train both dogs and owners in acceptable procedures for entering obedience trials. Obedience is an enjoyable sport for those who compete and creates a real challenge for both dog and trainer. If you are interested write to the American Kennel Club for your free copy of the *Obedience Regulations*.

Many English Setters have completed C.D. and C.D.X. degrees. Through careful training and devotion to their dogs several owners have been distinguished by having their dogs earn a combination of advanced titles. The first English Setter to obtain both a show Champion and Utility Dog title since obedience trials were introduced by the A.K.C. in 1936 is Ch. Hiddenlane's King George U.D. owned by Daniel and Jacquelyn Zerick.

Ch. Palomar's Artful Dodger T.D. owned by Brenda Parsons distinguished himself as the first of the breed to earn the show Champion and Tracking titles. Gunner's Lady Breca C.D.T.D. owned by Sharon Meng was the first English Setter to win a Tracking degree.

An eager worker and not surprisingly the first English Setter to complete the title of Obedience Trial Champion is O.T.Ch. Cornell's Queen Princess owned by Shahn Cornell.

English Setter owners have used their dogs as "working dogs" by giving of their time to visit schools as part of a program

designed to educate children on the responsibilities of pet ownership. The animal demonstrates obedience skills and thousands
learn how to care properly for their dogs.

English Setters have appeared in parades, mall demonstra-
tions, community programs of all kinds, in national T.V. com-
mercials and in plays. The versatility of the breed should not be
underestimated.

Given lots of affection and consistency in training the English
Setter will respond in direct proportion to the time spent on his
skill development.

This group of New England English Setter Club members enjoy team obedience work. Teams are composed of four dogs who perform most of the prescribed exercises simultaneously. The teams are scored on their ability to heel on leash, stand for examination, heel free, drop on recall, long sit and long down.

Ch. Rock Falls Colonel is pictured here at his retirement celebration at the famous Morris and Essex Dog Show in 1957. The Colonel and his owner Bill Holt are still considered the most successful amateur handler combination in the history of dogdom having won 101 Best in Show awards.

O.T.Ch. Cornell's Queen Princess is the first English Setter to win the title Obedience Trial Champion since its introduction by the AKC in 1977. Queen's exuberance makes her a crowd pleaser wherever she performs.

Ch. Leolair's Miss Constellation C.D.T.D. owned by Janice Leonard and Susan Fair is shown here in tracking harness working toward her Tracking Dog degree.

8

Trimming and Grooming

AN English Setter that is properly cared for is a handsome dog to own. Whether you keep your setter as a pet or show dog should make little difference in your devotion to its good care. Show dogs require more careful attention to trimming and brushing than a pet, but beyond these considerations, the conditioning which includes exercising, bathing and veterinary care is the same.

Any animal kept in optimum condition, and which is trimmed to conform to breed type provides visual pleasure. No matter what grooming products or practices are employed, the goal remains the same. The dog should look as natural as possible without a shaved appearance. The ultimate compliment is having someone remark, "Isn't it nice you don't have to trim that dog!"

Grooming your dog for show requires knowledge of the English

Setter standard and correct use of various pieces of equipment, shampoos and rinses. Many techniques are employed to get the best results. Each piece of equipment must be individually selected to perform a given task. No matter how superior the equipment is, it does no good if you don't know how to use it.

When the novice watches the practiced groomer he might walk away with the idea that using the equipment is an easy task. He must remember that the professional has years of practice; knows what tools to use on various parts of the dog and is experienced in working on a variety of coat textures and coat problems. Through evaluation the proper tools and techniques are used to get the job done.

A beginner often finds the equipment difficult to use and frequently either over grooms or under grooms his dog. Remember that any method employed to turn out a dog in final show trim is acceptable as long as the dog appears natural and neat in appearance when the job is done.

Some pieces of equipment work beautifully on one type of coat and are found to be completely useless on another type. Experimentation is the key to eventual success. The results are directly related to the time and effort put into the mastery of the grooming tools and the patience necessary to become proficient in their use.

There are advocates of various grooming styles and variations may be found from one area of the country to another. Judges, too, sometimes prefer certain styles. At one show it was known that the assigned judge liked setters with an "ungroomed" look. On that day handlers known for their polished grooming techniques showed dogs without much stripping or thinning. At the show the following day each of the dogs had been returned to routine trim.

The novice should be observant, ask and weigh the advice of others and use a good measure of common sense to evaluate what he has learned. A professionally groomed dog never looks freshly trimmed and is exhibited clean, well brushed, and with every hair in place. When the competition is close the best "turned out" dog has the obvious advantage. Good grooming can never turn an average specimen into an outstanding one but many an average dog in optimum condition can and does defeat a superior animal that is shown in poor condition.

130

One of the most difficult aspects of grooming is evaluating the various combinations of strengths and weaknesses in each animal. Trimming can be done which enhances these strengths and minimizes the weaknesses. Grooming cannot be expected to visually hide all faults but various techniques can camouflage them. A necessary first step is to honestly evaluate the dog's structure and movement before any grooming can begin. The owner-handler must develop an objective eye through reading the breed standard and through observation. Book knowledge is best coupled with experience to accurately assess the dog. Many professional handlers will evaluate for a fee if asked. Schedule a time which is convenient for both parties and agree on the fee in advance.

Grooming is a slow process which must be practiced in order to get the desired results. A last minute two hour session will never produce the finished results gained when trimming takes place in slow stages over a period of several weeks. Regular trimming at frequent intervals helps produce a dog which will exhibit the desired results.

No amount of proper grooming and bathing will pay off if your dog is not kept in good health; proper weight; and parasite free. Ninety per cent of coat growth problems are related to parasites, unbalanced diet and poor routine care.

EQUIPMENT

High quality tools are a must when engaging in any trade. Purchasing grooming equipment for your dog is no exception. Buy the most important pieces of equipment first. Then add a few pieces at a time until there is a wide selection of combs, thinners, brushes, and strippers available. See Photograph No. 1. It is not necessary to use all tools on any given dog and all cannot be used with the same effectiveness on any given coat since coats vary in texture and in thickness.

Many of the tools can be purchased in pet shops, from concessions at dog shows or at sizable discounts made available by mail order houses through catalogs for the dog fancy.

Clippers: Oster produces a professional small animal clipper model A2 or A5. It usually comes equipped with the standard number 10 blade although other blades are available. The A2

1. Tools used for trimming an English Setter: Oster Clipper with No. 10 blade, fine 48 tooth thinning scissors, straight edge scissors, regular 30 tooth thinning scissors, stone, variety of stripping knives, Resco nail clipper, grinding attachment for Oster A2 clipper, pin brush, flat natural bristle brush, furrier's comb, duplex dresser, steel comb, Weck Hair Shaper. All photos in this chapter were taken by Jerry Beal under the direction of George Alston, the noted professional handler.

model has a removable head. The A5 model has removable blades. The 10 blade is essential since it is used to trim ears, neck, face, and to remove the hair which grows between the pads of the feet. Some also use this blade to trim the hair from the top of the dog's head from brow to occiput. Others groom the top of the head without clippers by using thinning shears, stripping knife, and stone.

Clippers are cared for according to manufacturer's instructions. After each use blades are cleaned with a small brush and lubricated with oil or sprays to keep them sharp.

Scissors: Purchase high quality scissors recommended by someone who has grooming experience. A lot of money can be wasted finding an effective pair that cuts cleanly and maintains a sharp edge.

Straight Blade: Used for cutting whiskers, outlining the pad, and shaping the hair between the toes of the foot.

Blunt End: Adds safety for cutting whiskers at the brow or muzzle when a dog is most likely to move.

Thinning: These shears are available with both single and double blade thinning edges. The greater the number of teeth, the more hair can be removed in a single cut. Thinners are used for blending the neck, head, shoulders, hocks, feet, tail, and for removing excess coat over the hips and down the outer side of the back leg. These scissors cut most evenly when they are slightly dull.

Stripping Combs: Available in a wide variety of types and price range. This tool varies in its effectiveness on individual dogs. It is best used where there is a dense undercoat without a lot of protective, heavier top coat or guard hair. Used for removing dead coat and undercoat from the head, body, and flank, and for blending the hair on the neck. The groomer must experiment with the use of the tool on his dog to find which does the best job. Effectiveness can also vary during the seasons as dogs go through the shedding process or are growing new hair. When new, stripping combs can leave sharp cut marks across the dog's coat giving a scissored appearance. The goal is to dull the blade and then to drag it through the coat to pull out the dead hair.

Magnetized Stripping Comb: Similar to a stripping comb but with finer teeth. This tool is best used for removal of dead coat from the body, neck, and top of the head.

133

Duplex Dresser and Weck Hair Shaper: These two tools are equipped with removable blades. They are used for removal of hair on the top of the head, and blending the neck and shoulder area. Since this tool is meant to cut hair the blade must be kept sharp and therefore frequently changed.

Stone: Has rough edges and is shaped like a brick cut in half lengthwise. Drag over the top coat, top of head and neck. Can also be broken into smaller pieces and used with tension between the stone, hair, and thumb for removal of hair.

Brushes: It is best to select a natural bristle brush because it will not tear the coat like synthetic materials. Keep the brush clean. The wooden handled brush helps absorb the natural oil which is deposited on the bristles. Select one that has a broad enough face to smooth the top coat as illustrated in Photograph No. 1.

Pin Brush: Named for the one inch wire pins inserted in the wood backed rubber cushion. This brush is best used to separate hairs in the long furnishings. Never pull this or any other brush through the feathers when you meet resistance since you will tear coat which takes a long time to grow. Section the hair and work in small areas. Brush from the roots to the end of the hair shaft. The long furnishings will then hang free. If the pins get bent remove them with pliers so they will not snag and damage the coat. Never leave the pin side up on the grooming table.

Wire Slicker Brush: Also separates the coat and can cause damage by tearing if not used carefully. The wires on this brush are much finer and more dense than on the pin brush. Slide this brush lightly over the top coat and long feathering to align the hair before toweling.

Hound Glove: Removes loose hair and gives a gloss to the top coat. Used shortly before the dog appears in the ring to give a smooth well groomed look.

Steel Comb: Select one with graduated teeth. A wide tooth comb separates the hair. After fully combing the feathering repeat with the narrow tooth comb. A furrier's comb has the shortest and finest set of teeth and can be used to align the hair in the top coat. Avoid continuous use of the steel comb on the feathering since it breaks the coat. Many handlers use a comb in the ring when it would be difficult to carry a pin brush. The pin brush is the best piece of equipment to use on the feathering.

134

Nail Cutters: The guillotine type is a favorite of many. This cutter has an oval opening for insertion of the nail. The blade that slices across the opening for cutting may be replaced when it becomes dull. Any amount of nail can be removed so care must be taken to avoid cutting through the quick. The plier type has a guard which can be set to avoid cutting too deeply into the nail. This one squeezes the nail from both sides as it cuts.

Grinding: The Oster A-2 clipper is made with a removable head which exposes a drive shaft to which a plastic grinder can be attached. Sandpaper discs are inserted in the grinder head for polishing the nail after it has been cut. You must be careful to avoid catching the leg feathering in the drive shaft when grinding. Do not grind a dirty nail. The grinder will force the dirt into the nail bed which can cause infection.

A high power hand tool with a stone attachment is used by some. It is dangerous because of its high speed and quick action. Goggles must be worn to protect your eyes from flying pieces of nail. Many professionals will not allow this particular tool in their kennels. They prefer the Oster A-2 clipper attachment since it is slower acting and gives better control.

Filing is a slow process achieved with a variety of metal hand files. You can smooth rough nail edges after cutting without the danger of suddenly producing a bleeding quick.

Kwick-Stop: This commercial product is sold in powdered form for stopping bleeding of nails when they are cut, ground or filed too short. Use according to manufacturer's instructions.

Tooth Scaler: There are many types of scalers available for the removal of tartar build up. The type with a flat quarter inch blade seems adequate and does the job. The amateur must be careful not to damage the flesh of the gum. Dogs generally do not enjoy having their teeth scaled so most owners are working on a moving target. Begin slightly under the gumline and pull with pressure against the tooth to the end. Tartar left under the gumline can cause irritation and infection. Brushing with a toothbrush and paste of baking soda and water will help keep the teeth clean. Feeding hard baked dog bones deters tartar build-up. For chronic cases a veterinarian puts the dog under anesthesia and removes the tartar with an ultrasonic device. Tartar accumulation causes bad breath.

Grooming Table: Excellent for training the dog for show and

2A. Before trimming.

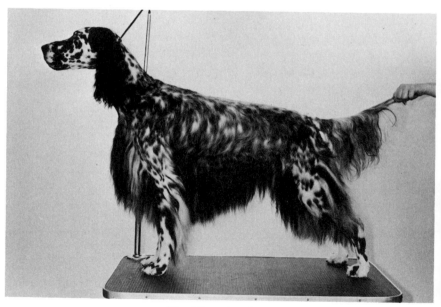

2B. After trimming.

to gain the necessary control while grooming. The rubber mat prevents the dog from slipping and the arm and loop hold the dog in position for trimming. It is much easier to work on a dog which is elevated above the ground. The table is worth the investment as a back saving device for the owner as well.

GROOMING TECHNIQUES

Brushing and Combing: Keep your dog free of knots and tangles. This is best accomplished using proper brushing and combing techniques. Dogs which are consistently shown are bathed once a week and thoroughly brushed out twice a week. Correct brushing never tears out the coat. Never brush a dog when the coat is thoroughly dry. Use either plain water or a mixture of one quarter balsam or creme rinse to three quarter parts of warm water in a plastic spray bottle. Shake it to mix the rinse with water then mist the dog with the spray.

Brush the back of the dog with a natural bristle brush in the direction the hair grows. The longer feathering on the ears, ruff, legs, belly and tail is combed first with the wide tooth comb to free the hair of tangles; then followed by one with finer teeth. The pin brush is used next to separate the hair so that it hangs freely.

A good brushing is worth a good feed. Yanking and pulling tears the coat and destroys the growth that you are trying to promote. If the comb or pin brush meets resistance as you work stop and untangle the coat by hand.

Be sure to lift and part the heavy feathering as you work. Brush the dog in sections. Notice places where the dog mats because of friction between the body parts. One example is behind the elbows.

TRIMMING

Anyone who doubts the necessity for trimming a setter need only look at the before and after photographs to see how trimming has enhanced the dog's natural beauty.

The best time to trim is three to four days after the dog's bath when the hair has regained some of its natural oil and is still

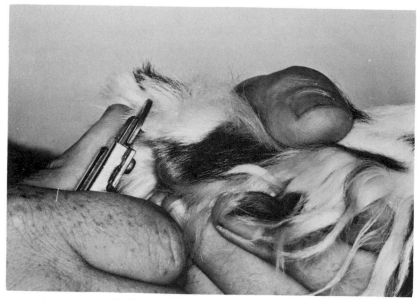

3. Proper use of the Resco nail clipper.

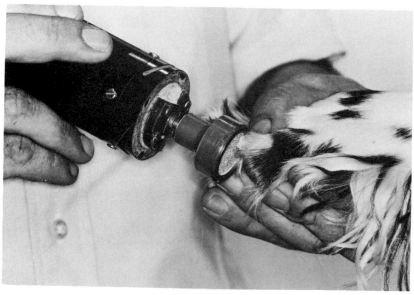

4. Proper use of the grinding attachment.

138

clean enough not to dull clipper blades, scissors, and a sharp razor edge. The hair seems to stay against the body naturally without the fluff associated with a new bath. Plan to begin to trim about three weeks before the show.

Begin by cutting the nails with the Resco nail trimmer. Since the nails and foot are extremely sensitive it is important to separate the time spent on nail cutting and trimming the foot. Cut the nail back at an angle to remove as much of the top of the nail as possible. See Photograph No. 3. With light colored nails the quick is easily seen but with black nails it is not as easy to determine where to stop. Cut close to but not through the quick of the nail. Cutting through the quick is not only painful to the dog but can make him foot-shy.

If the nail does begin to bleed use Kwik-Stop to halt the flow of blood. Nails must be cut at least once a week to keep the dog walking on the pads of the foot. Nails allowed to grow too long click on the kitchen floor and also can be heard as the dog gaits in an indoor ring. Nails cut to their proper length do not touch the floor as the dog stands. A file or grinder can be used afterwards to shape the cut nails. If the quick is left slightly exposed it will recede by itself as the process is repeated often enough. See Photograph No. 4.

As you work keep the dog in a standing position. Begin by trimming under the neck. Hold the electric clippers like a pencil. The free hand positions the dog's muzzle up to expose the neck to the clipper blades. Start at the chin and cut down the middle of the underside of the neck to about two fingers width above the breast bone. Give time for the clippers to do the job. Do not rush. See Photograph No. 5.

Trim with the hair to an imaginary line drawn parallel to the lower edge of the jaw, under the ear to the side of the neck. Hold the ear away from the neck and continue trimming. Stop where the hair changes direction under the ear to where the neck joins the shoulder. The long hair that remains will be removed with thinners, stripping combs and the stone. It is important to view the neck from the front and side while trimming to gain the best possible effect. See Photograph No. 6.

If the dog has been trained to the grooming table and is not frightened by the clipper it is possible to slip the grooming loop over the muzzle and to tighten it. This allows the groomer access

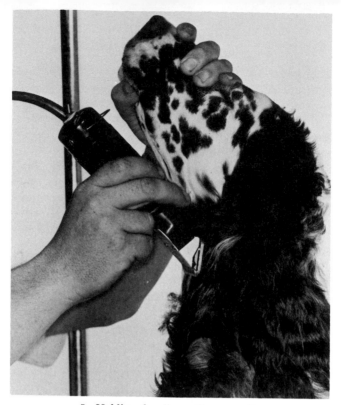

5. Holding the clipper like a pencil.

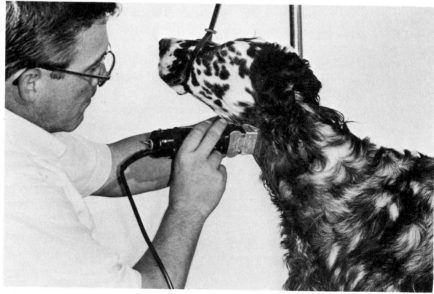

6. Trimming the side neck.

to the entire neck. When the neck is more carefully groomed tighten the loop on the neck once again. Most dogs will not be terribly cooperative during any phase of the grooming process if they are not exposed to the equipment in easy stages.

Ear: Begin where the ear cartilage meets the skull and trim about one third the length of the ear. It is best to hold the ear leather near the bottom and trim with the hair. Never trim the hair that covers the fold at the front of the ear. Leaving the hair along the fold softens the ear and helps enhance the much desired mild expression which is characteristic of the English Setter. Trimming gives the appearance of lowering the ears which act as a frame for the eyes. See Photograph No. 7.

Turn the ear over and clean out the hair from the inner surface and close to the ear canal. This allows air to circulate in the canal and helps keep the ear free of infection. Next, raise the ear and trim the ear burr. Be careful not to nick the sensitive, small split part on the underside. The ear hangs closer to the face once the hair is removed. You may trim against the grain of the hair under the ear and on the ear burr. Make sure that when the ear hangs naturally that the long hair under the ear is cut down as far as the hair that has been trimmed on top of the ear. See Photograph No. 8.

Face and Head: Shape the hair on the dog's muzzle by holding the clipper on the flattest part of the face sideways to the grain. As you work remove the whiskers. Check the muzzle from several angles as whiskers are often missed with even the most careful attempt to remove them. See Photograph No. 9.

Touch-up the cheek using the Duplex Dresser or Weck Hair Shaper. Remember that each contains a razor blade and will cut the hair. Heavy growth left here will add apparent width to the cheek of the dog and coarsen the head. As you work with the razor comb it with the growth of the hair. The Weck Hair Shaper can also be used to remove the whisker nubs by pulling it sideways to the whisker grain. See Photograph No. 10.

Blend the ear to the head with thinning scissors held against but not across the grain of the coat. As you cut brush the coat to remove the results of each scissoring. Do not cut several times in one spot without brushing and inspecting the results or you will make a hole in the coat or the hair will appear as if it were cut in steps.

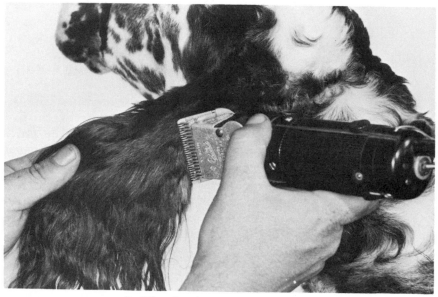

7. Trimming the top of the ear.

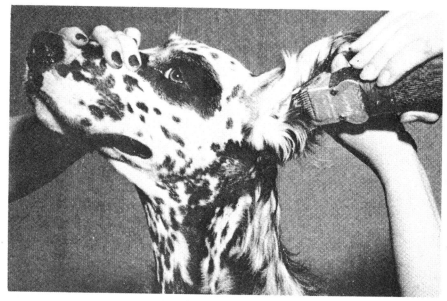

8. Trimming the ear burr.

142

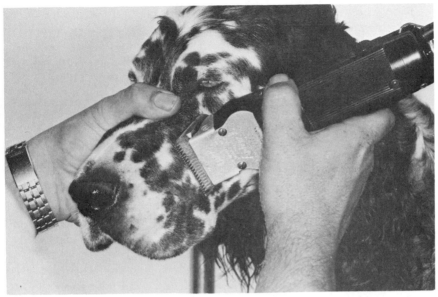

9. Use of clipper sideways to the grain.

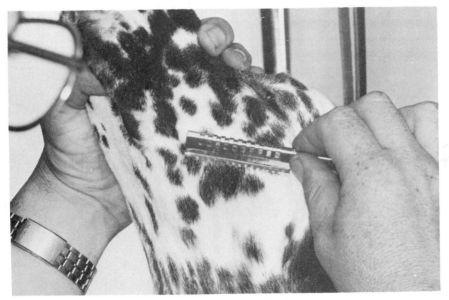

10. Weck Hair Shaper on cheek.

143

Next, use the stone on top of the head to take off the fuzzies. Drag it. Do not pull against the hair. Keep the stone clean as you work. See Photograph No. 11. When you have made the head appear as smooth as possible take the thinning scissors and begin to blend the short clippered hair at the mid point under the ear into the long hair on the side and back of the neck. Once again, cut against the grain into the coat and brush after each cut. Do not leave steps by cutting across the grain as illustrated. See Photograph No. 12.

To establish a clean neck line between the clippered hair and the longer neck hair use the thinner straight along the neck edge to form a line between ear and shoulder. Then, take the thinning shears and begin to blend the short clippered hair at the mid point under the ear into the long hair on the side and back of neck. See Photograph No. 13.

Never use thinners by cutting across the grain of the coat. Blend against the grain into the hair. After each cut brush the hair away. Try to layer the hair evenly and gradually so that there is a smooth transition from the longer two inch hair on the back of the neck to the short clippered hair on the front of the neck. See Photograph No. 14. The change in hair length from longest to shortest is gradual and when properly done is almost imperceptible.

A stripping knife will remove the dead undercoat and help smooth the neckline. Drag the stripper against the coat and with the grain of the hair. See Photograph No. 15.

The photographs show a dramatic difference in the before and after head and back of neck of the dog and clearly show how necessary a good grooming is to enhance the natural good looks of your dog. The outstanding qualities of this animal would be difficult to discern if left ungroomed. See Photographs No. 16 and 17.

The careful trimming of the blend from neck to shoulder is very important. The hair on the shoulder has a tendency to curl and add bulk where there should be refinement. It is difficult enough to breed an English Setter with good clean shoulders without allowing a heavy coat to accentuate one that is already loaded. Since there are so many English Setters with wide set shoulder blades and straight fronts it is best to concentrate on de-emphasizing heaviness through proper grooming. Stress a

144

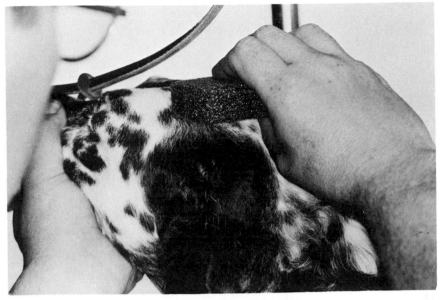

11. Dragging the stone to remove fluffy coat.

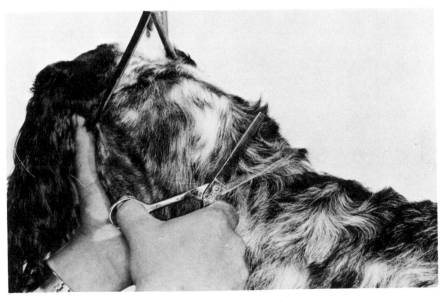

12. Improper use of thinning scissors.

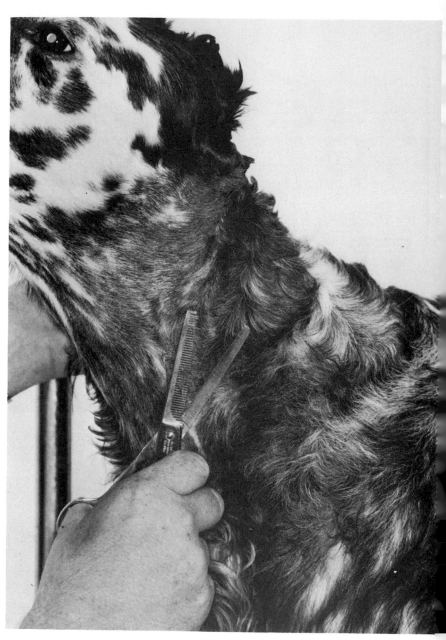

13. Blending the neck.

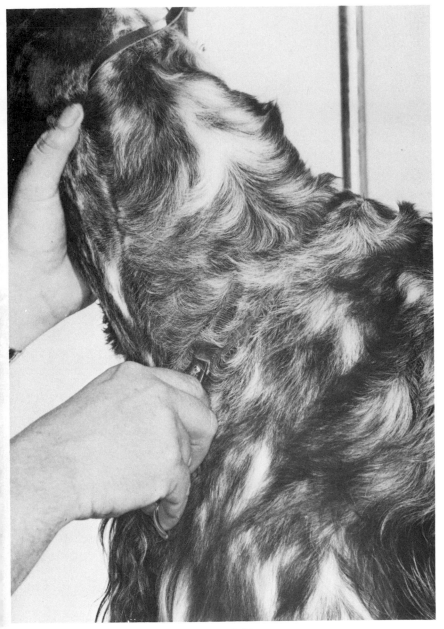

14. Proper use of thinners.

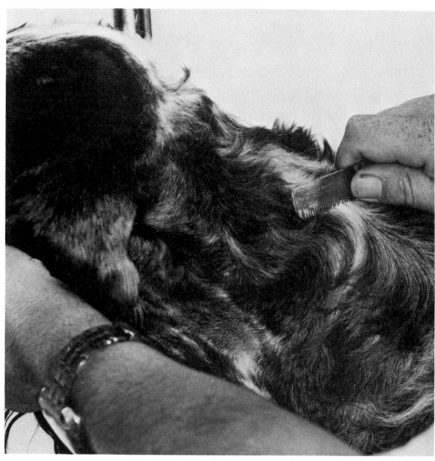

15. Stripping knife on the neck.

16. Trimmed and untrimmed head front view.

17. Trimmed and untrimmed head rear view.

18. Front view neck and shoulders.

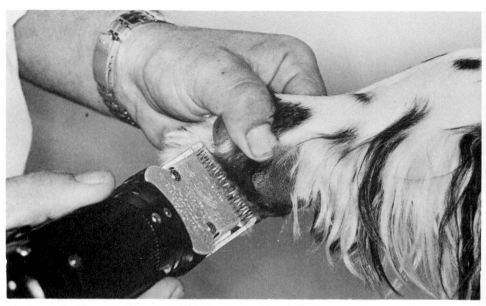

19. Trimming the bottom of the foot.

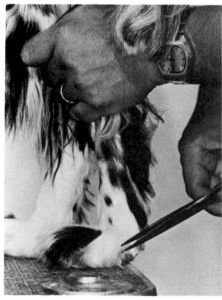

20. Edging the foot.

21. Scissoring the foot.

clean shoulder. This particular part, the blending of the neck to the shoulder can be one of beauty or can look unkempt. The overall picture of head, neck, and shoulders should be balanced and pleasing to the eye. See Photograph No. 18.

Feet: Trimming feet is a time consuming job. It is best to undertrim them at first. You can always take some more hair off but you cannot put it back in time for the show. The most common error here is making holes in the hair between the toes. The goal is to shape the foot to give a clean, compact look.

Cut off the extra hair from the bottom of the pads using the Oster Clippers with a number ten blade. The foot must be clean or you will dull expensive blades as you work. Avoid cutting hair from between the bottom of the pads. Keeping the hair short allows the pads instead of the wads of hair to touch the ground and makes the dog use his toes in walking as he should. It also prevents the dog from bringing extra dirt into the house and minimizes the chances of fungus infection. Be careful not to cut the pads or the toes. See Photograph No. 19.

Next, edge around the toes with a sharp pair of straight scissors exposing the pads. You will use both the points and the blades to achieve a clean, neat appearance. See Photographs No. 20 and No. 21.

Shape the long feathering which grows between the toes. From the top, angle the straight scissors from the arch of the toe to the nail. Continue to blend by using the thinners with the tips pointed toward the toes. See Photograph No. 22.

If you discover mats between the toes separate them with your fingers or comb them out with a fine tooth comb. If the mats are allowed to develop the hair retains moisture which helps promote undesirable infections.

Shape the fetlock with a straight scissor cutting at an angle. The hair here must not drag on the ground and should be cut short enough to show off the foot. Never shave the fetlock with the clippers. See Photograph No. 23.

The feathering which grows on the hock is also shaped. First brush the hair up. Do not clipper the hair here or the dog's bone will appear slight and the total look unbalanced. Angle the shears toward the dog's heel and thin at a slight distance from the bone. How much hair you leave will depend on the amount

22. Proper angling of scissors.

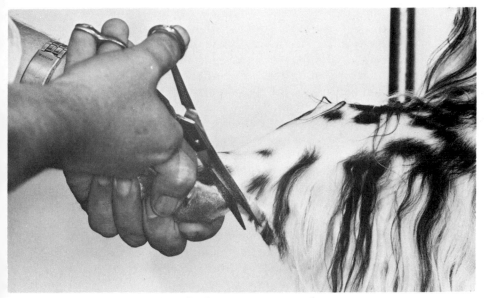

23. Shaping the fetlock.

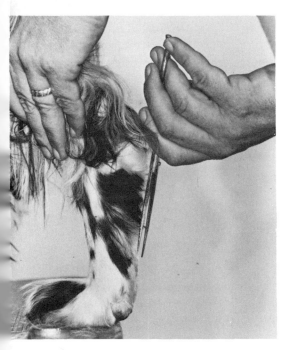

24. Trimming the hock.

155

of bone the dog has. Brush the hair up again. Trim the ragged ends with the straight scissor. See Photograph No. 24.

Notice the difference in the Before and After appearance of the front foot. One foot seems to be compact and neatly manicured and strong in pastern. The untrimmed foot looks flat in comparison because of the illusion created by the length of the hair. The benefit of grooming is obvious. See Photograph No. 25.

Rump and Tail: Most English Setters when left untrimmed will develop a profusion of coat over the rump, base of tail and rear legs. This mass of curls is made manageable with thinning scissors. Always make the cutting strokes against the lay of the hair. Patience is necessary. Take one scissor bite at a time and brush out the hair. Always keep in mind that trimming is creative work and your artistic point of view plays an important role in the look of the finished dog.

Trim along the outer thighs exposing the clean lines of the leg. If too much hair is left it gives the effect that the dog is wearing pants. See Photographs No. 26 and No. 27.

Raise the tail and trim away the long hair that grows at the root of the tail. Use the straight scissors here. The blunt ended type are the safest. Remove the hair for one to one and one half inches. Do not use clippers here. The hair removal not only promotes cleanliness, but also gives the tail an attractive carriage and defines the body line. See Photograph No. 28.

In a well coated dog the hair usually grows too thick along the top of the tail. Proceed with the thinning scissors and brush until the tail gracefully tapers from root to tip. Pull all the tail feathering over the last vertebra and cover the tip with your thumb and forefinger. Leave about one half to three quarters of an inch of hair to protect the end of the tail. All the remaining hair is thinned across the end. See Photograph No. 29.

Next, use the stripping knife to taper the end and eliminate a clean cut appearance. See Photograph No. 30.

The finished tail has roughly the shape of a triangle. See Photograph No. 31.

As you trim, inspect how the dog looks from a distance. Have someone hold the dog in show position to see the results of your effort. Judges often "buy" a standing picture of the dog. This means that the profile of the animal at rest can become more important than the moving picture. Be sure to know how your

156

25. Trimmed and untrimmed foot.

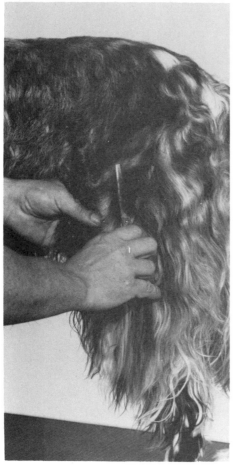

26. Thinning the leg.

27. Finished rear view.

28. Trimming the line of demarkation.

29. Thinning the end of the tail.

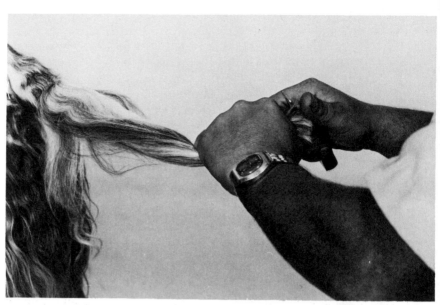

30. Stripping the end of the tail.

31. Finished tail.

160

dog looks in motion too. Hair may begin to fly in areas where it should remain flat. Touch-up grooming is almost always necessary. Also view your dog at a distance. How will he compare in profile with other dogs as he stands in line. Trim a dog for what he will look like at twenty feet.

The stone is used to remove hair and smooth the top coat. If you need to remove more hair than dragging the stone through the coat will accomplish, grip the hair between the stone and finger. Then, do not yank but pull gently. See Photograph No. 32.

Complete shaping the long feathering which grows over the rib cage by blending the coat so it will remain flat against the body of the dog over the greatest rib spring. A stripping knife will do a good job here. See Photograph No. 33.

A good time to clean the ears and check them for infection is prior to the dog's bath. Put your nose close to the dog's ear canal. Any unusual odor is a sign of wax accumulation or infection. Another sign is a dog that holds his head to the side or frequently shakes his head or scratches his ears and groans. Routinely clean the ears with a cotton ball dipped in mineral oil or hydrogen peroxide. A veterinarian will recommend an antibiotic ointment in case of infection.

BATHING

A necessary first step is to purchase a quality shampoo and rinse. Since different types of coats require different combinations of shampoo and creme rinse it is important to experiment to find the best combination for your dog. Be sure to ask what others use. You might find that as the seasons change so does the quantity and quality of your dog's coat. What works beautifully at one time of the year might have to be changed to gain the desired results at another time. Certain high suds shampoos can cause matting of the furnishings and produce hot spots on the skin in warm weather.

Try buying small bottles of any shampoo until its contents prove their usefulness on your dog. Small bottles are expensive for continuous care since the shampoo has already been diluted. The gallon size is more economical since the shampoo is full

161

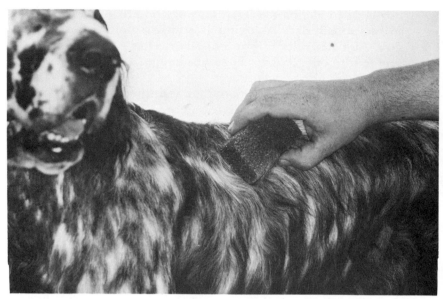

32. Use of stone on top coat.

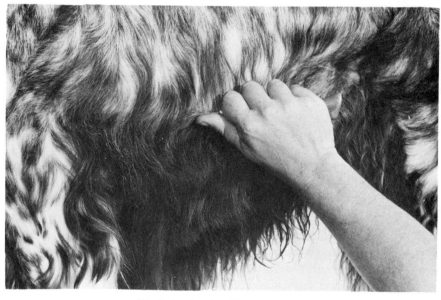

33. Stripping the side coat.

162

strength. Save the empty small plastic bottles to mix the shampoo for the bath. Squeeze bottles are both easy to use and safe to handle with your dog in the tub.

It is usually necessary only to suds and rinse your dog once. When the hair becomes brittle or appears lifeless conditioning involves putting the dog down in oil. Dogs are sprayed with a mixture of oil and water. Ch. WuPi is a brand name oil preferred by many professionals. It is diluted according to manufacturer's directions in a plastic spray bottle and misted onto the coat. The coat becomes mildly greasy and picks up dirt. The dog is bathed to remove the oil once a week. When the dog is put down in oil it is necessary to shampoo twice and rinse with warm water. When the dog is dry, brush thoroughly and respray with the oil conditioner. Never show a dog that is put down in conditioning oil without bathing first.

Begin the bath by thoroughly wetting the dog's coat. A hose fitted with a shower head makes bathing an easy task. Protect the dog's eyes by putting a drop of mineral oil in each. Apply the shampoo on the head and then generously apply more to the body, legs, and feathering. Work it into a lather. Be sure to pick up each foot and work the lather in between the pads.

Care must be taken to rinse all the soap out of the coat. When you are finished, the rinse water must be totally clear. Check for soap under the elbows and other difficult to reach spots. When you are finished squeeze out the excess water. Mix a half dollar size glob of creme rinse at the bottom of a bowl with a quart of warm water. Pour the rinse over the dog just on the top coat. Do not rub the rinse into the undercoat because it causes lifting of the coat when dry. Balsam rinses can cause flaking of the skin in the dry winter months.

While the dog is wet, brush lightly with the slicker brush. See Photograph No. 34. Select a bath towel that is large enough to cover the dog from high on the neck to half way down the tail. It must be wide enough to reach around the dog. Pin the towel under the neck with horse blanket pins. Without disturbing the coat on the dog's back, snap the towel back pulling tightly. Without easing up on the towel pin it in place under the tail. Smooth the sides and pin again between the chest and loin. See Photograph No. 35. Toweling keeps the coat flat and is left on the dog until shortly before show time. Another purpose is to

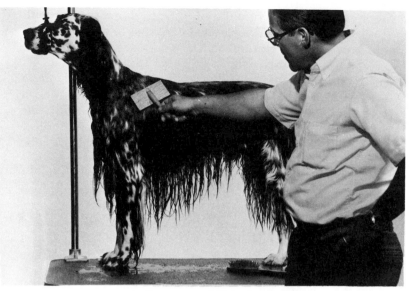

34. Proper use of slicker brush.

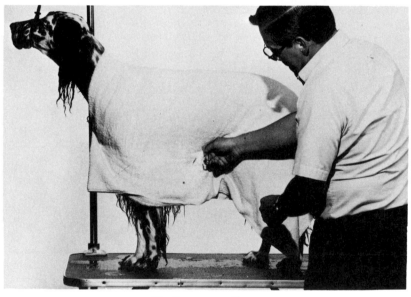

35. Proper toweling.

164

keep dust and dirt away from the coat. If the dog is to be shown again the next day, towel it again. Remember that the bathing, toweling routine is as important to the final appearance of the dog as proper trimming.

Some people prefer to brush their dogs until dry. Others use a hand held dryer while brushing. Although it is convenient, avoid continuous blow drying since it tends to break the coat and causes split ends.

Grooming is never completed. After the initial roughing out frequent touch-ups will prevent continuous hours of work which are tedious for both the owner and the dog. Also keep in mind that each dog is different in conformation and coat quality. Continue to experiment until you find the right combination of grooming techniques to produce the best possible finished look for your dog. Learning is a continuous process and grooming your dog is no exception.

SPIRON JAGERSBO pointing quail.

This great blue belton dog was the father of Rummey Stagboro
and was owned by Erik Bergishagen of Birmingham, Michigan.

My Setter ranges in the new-shorn field,
His nose in air erect; from ridge to ridge,
Panting, he bounds, his quartered ground divides
In equal intervals, nor careless leaves
One inch untried. At length the tainted gale
His nostrils wide inhale; quick joy elates
His beating heart, which, awed by discipline
Severe, he dares not own, but cautious creeps,
Low-cowering, step by step; at last attains
His proper distance; there he stops at once,
And points with his instructive nose upon
The trembling prey.

—Somerville

9

Training for the Field

THIS book has been written about the show type
(Laverack) English Setter. They make excellent shooting dogs
for a day's sport on grouse, woodcock, quail and pheasant, but it
is doubtful if one will ever be able to compete successfully with a
field trial type (Llewellin) English Setter in the big time field
trials when race-horse speed over long heats is required. Edward
Laverack in his book **"The Setter"** (1872) has a chapter on
breaking, and it is so interesting, meaty and to the point that I
am sure you too will enjoy the parts that I quote.

"Young dogs vary much in their tempers, and their early
disposition to hunt and find game. I have frequently shot over
my setters at nine and eleven months old, as steady as need be,
and continued to shoot over them daily the whole season; some
come sooner into work than others, get their strength, and
furnish quicker.

"Like children, many are more precocious than others. My breed (strain*) hunt, range, point, and back intuitively at six months, and require comparatively little or no breaking.

"The system of tuition I adopt is to take the dogs to my shootings in Scotland, uncouple, and let them chase everything (game) until they are tired, having previously accustomed them to lie down at the word 'Drop.'

"After having run themselves down, they naturally point and back. When pointing, walk quietly up, slip a thin cord through the collar, and stand behind, making no noise, holding the cord rather slack in your hand. After the dog has stood some little time, he naturally, to ascertain by his nose where the game is secreted, will prick up his ears prior to making a spring at feather or fur, whichever it may happen to be. In attempting to do so, jerk him sharply back with the cord, calling 'Drop!' Keep him down until the birds are out of sight, to teach him patience; then withdraw the cord, and let him range.

"By repeating this, the dog will very soon be broken. When I rented the shootings of Cabrach, in Banffshire, belonging to the Duke of Richmond, I and my keeper, Alexander Rattray (now keeper to the Duke of Richmond Glentiddich), by this system once broke eight dogs in six days; and all at the week's end were as steady as could be—pointing, backing, footing and free from 'chase.'

"When you get the dog to drop well to the word, it is easy to teach him to do so at 'wing' or 'fur'; to 'down charge,' to come close to heel, and to ware fence is nothing to teach.

"My dogs are invariably broken on the open moors, and not in small enclosures, which always cramps their range and checks their spirits; it is distressing to hear a breaker crying out every instant 'ware fence,' whistling and shouting: you cannot be too quiet on all occasions.

"I seldom use whip or whistle, but allow my dogs to use their own natural sagacity in making their casts and finding game.

"I have ever found those dogs who range wide turn out the best. It does not follow because a dog ranges wide he will not

* Strain has been inserted by the author as in the past the word breed was used to designate that which we now call strain. For instance, we would now say the Laverack and Llewellin strain, whereas at that time they were referred to as the Laverack or Llewellin breed.

168

range close. Where game is plentiful a wide ranging dog must necessarily become a close ranger because the game stops him; he cannot get far without finding, his natural sagacity tells him to hunt close; it is his high courage and anxiety to find game that causes him to range wide.

"A wide-ranging dog too saves you a great deal of walking. Every shooting man knows that he may occasionally tramp over two or three miles without coming across anything; here it is a wide-ranging dog is of greater ability than a close ranger.

"I will give an instance of the advantage of selecting good and lasting dogs. I was one of a party of four that on September 11th had bagged 3,066 head of grouse — one gentlemen killed within seven head, to his own gun, as much as the whole party, solely by having superior dogs, and in addition he lent a brace of dogs several times to his friends. I was one of another party of four on a Scotch moor. In four days the four guns had killed 1,654 head, and one of them bagged 127 brace in one day, over a brace of setters. None of us ever used relays of dogs, or did any of us possess more than two brace each.

"Many years have passed over my head, bleached my locks, and withered the sap of youthful vigour since I took my gun and dogs and made bonnie Scotland my home. I loved it then, I love it still, and ever shall I yet go there annually, and feel ten years younger when I catch sight of those wild, glorious, healthy, purple clad mountains, far away from the busy hum of the world, and ever-crowded and ill-drained cities. It is in Scotland I find repose, contentment, amusement, and health.

"I cannot understand **Pater Familias** taking his wife and family away to the Continent, or to some expensive watering place for the autumnal months, when we have such lovely and magnificent scenery within twelve hours of us. I may be an enthusiast on this point. The used-up **blase**, worn out with dissipation and late hours, broken in health, constitution, and spirits, is often now recommended by his doctor to take a Highland shooting. What for? Not with the idea that he may kill much game. He is too prostrated, too feeble for a long tramp over the hills. It is not for the sake of shooting, but to wean him in some measure from dissolute habits, which if persisted in, must eventually carry him to a premature grave. It is in the hope of saving him, invigorating him, and restoring his shattered constitution.

169

"I remember the remark of an old Highlander to a cockney sportsman who was grumbling at the country and asking 'What was to be found in it' Sandy replied, 'Hoot mon, there's health behind every rock and stane.'

"Burns' beautiful lines are now recalled to my memory:

> 'Now wrestlin winds, and slaught'ring guns,
> Bring autumn's pleasant weather;
> The moorcock springs, on whirring wings,
> Among the blooming heather.'

"These lines again bring to mind many stories I heard; scenes I have seen, in years long gone by, never to return. Relentless old Father Time serves us all alike; shows no favour to rich or poor, and with that terrible scythe of his cuts all down in turn."

I think Edward Laverack probably had the correct psychology of hunting in the field with his English Setters. He did not care to have his dogs trained to all the niceties and etiquette of the field trial. He wanted a dog that could find and point birds day after day. He loved the sport and the comradeship of his good friends in the unspoiled open country. I suspect, however, that his keeper, Alexander Rattray, spent many hours on his dogs before he and Mr. Laverack trained eight dogs in six days. Nevertheless, his basic methods were sound. Years ago I followed his methods with a bitch named "Brenda" (a daughter of Ch. Sturdy Max). Five hours at a game farm made her a shooting bitch. She placed in several field trials and never lost a wounded bird. Of course, as Laverack pointed out, "Brenda" was a precocious child.

Stonehenge, in Dogs of the British Isles—4th Edition (1882), points out that in his opinion a quiet tail is usually accompanied by a nose of equal dullness. I am fully in accord with Stonehenge's observation as it has been my own experience also that merry English Setters make the best hunters and there is no doubt that they show to great advantage in the show ring.

Mr. Ralph E. Yeatter is the author of a booklet, **Bird Dogs in Sport and Conservation**, which contains a section on amateur training for hunting that is so practical and simply expressed that I have secured permission to use parts of Mr. Yeatter's material here. The parts that do not apply to English Setters

170

Ch. Chearta Manlove Cantique pictured scenting quail proves a bench Setter has ability in the field.   *B. Kline*

have been omitted. The methods outlined by Mr. Yeatter are proven, practical methods used for many years by trainers, and can be relied upon to produce results.

There are two "musts" that should be stated here at the very beginning of this chapter on training, for lack of them will result in failure in whole or in part:

1. You must have patience.

2. Your dog must be birdy and normal, both physically and mentally.

The Amateur Trainer

Sportsmen who buy trained dogs or have young dogs fully trained by professionals are relatively few compared with those who buy young dogs and train them during spare time. That numerous capable hunting dogs have been trained by their owners speaks well, on the whole, for amateur trainers. Nevertheless, many dogs develop bad hunting habits that might been avoided or minimized if the owners had been better informed on training.

There are several books on the subject of training hunting dogs. Unfortunately for the average reader, authors sometimes fail to bridge the wide gap between the professional trainer and the amateur and they outline rough training methods which, in the hands of the beginner, may ruin the dog as a hunter.

Most dogs are by nature anxious to please their masters, but they cannot do things they do not understand: Lessons need to be repeated until they are thoroughly mastered. Patience on the part of the trainer, whether natural or acquired, is the first requisite in successful training.

Obedience training is an essential part of the education of any dog. In hunting dogs, this is especially important, since the disobedient dog hunts mostly for himself and takes most of the owner's time in trying to keep up with him or to find him. The obedient dog, which responds to directions and hunts for his owner, stands a good chance to find as many birds within gun range as the wild, disobedient dog will find for himself a mile away.

The successful amateur trainer develops a knack of teaching obedience without cowing or alienating his hunting companion. The following quotation from a widely known English authority (Carlton 1945) can well serve as a guide when the puppy's obedience training is begun:

"You should no doubt teach the puppy his name, which may be done by calling his name and patting him or giving him a piece of biscuit. You should also, no doubt, make the puppy gallop up to you on his name being called — which may be done in much the same way. And you should make him go to his kennel when desired. This presents more difficulty. Personally, if a puppy is recalcitrant in this respect, I generally get him to me, and either pick him up and carry him in or put on him a collar with a short, light cord attached and make him comply by an admixture of cajolery and gentle force, and end up with a reward.

"In these early lessons, as•with all other lessons during early puppyhood, the four cardinal principles are:

"(1) Never given an order without seeing that the puppy complies with it; he has got to learn to obey you always, not sometimes.

"(2) Always be absolutely gentle, both in voice and action — when you come to work in the field, you want a bold, keen dog, not a cowed and listless wreck.

"(3) Never give an order with which you cannot secure compliance without a display of harshness.

"(4) Never persist in any lesson which is becoming a bore to the puppy.

"The nearer these early lessons can be approximated to a game, in the puppy's eyes, the better."

As the puppy develops and learns to take directions, you should become accustomed to giving them in a firm, distinct voice, making sure that each command is understood and carried out. The commands should be short, and the same words should always be used for each response expected. Be sure each command is audible, but do not get into the habit of raising your voice, or the pupil will probably think he does not need to mind unless you shout.

Teach a few basic things well rather than attempt a large number, which may be only half learned.

At each step of training, make every effort to see that the dog understands what you want, and, whenever possible, why you want it. When the lesson is learned, it should be practiced until response becomes habitual. This is the background of obedience training. Such training calls for ingenuity, common sense, and much patience in getting the lessons over to the dog. Harsh treatment and punishment not understood have permanently intimidated many promising hunting dogs. The dog's span of attention is short. Lessons should be only four or five minutes long for the young dog. They should not be prolonged until the dog becomes bored or sour, and the trainer loses patience.

Dogs vary in intelligence and temperament just as do humans. This variation calls for study of the individual characteristics of the pupil and adaptation as far as possible of the training program to his needs. Some dogs need more rehearsals of each step than others. Some must be praised and encouraged more than others.

Although considerable emphasis has been laid on the preparation of the trainer, there is no need to overrate the difficulties of training a hunting dog. Most boys can teach their dogs any number of tricks by the simple method of showing the pupil what is wanted, practicing it until well learned, and rewarding the dog's progress with praise. The amateur trainer who stresses the development of companionship with his dog, and encourages his inborn desire to do things to please his master, paves the way for progress in training.

The man who likes hunting dogs and dog work and who is willing to acquaint himself with the fundamentals of training can usually do at least a fairly good job of training his own dog. The development of a good hunting companion will amply reward him for his work. Moreover, the skill in handling acquired during the training period will serve the hunter well in the field. Obviously, good dog work is in large measure dependent on good handling.

Training Systems

Various systems are used in training bird dogs. Some owners do little yard training and confine their programs largely to a few field trips before the hunting season, and then take the dog

Int. Ch. Tula II Jagersbo pointing woodcock. This beautiful orange belton bitch was the mother of Rackets Rummey Jagersbo. Owned by Mr. Erik Bergishagen of Birmingham, Michigan.

along on hunting trips. If the owner works frequently with his dog, the animal can eventually become a useful hunting companion, but he will make mistakes, some of which might have been avoided with more yard work and other preliminary training.

A program that combines yard training and field training over an extended period of time seems to give best results.

Training Classes

A program that combined yard training and field training over an extended period was used successfully by a group of spaniel owners in northern Illinois. They began a training class in April and continued until October. Yard (obedience) training was given first. When this was thoroughly mastered, the dogs were taken to the field and put through an intensive course of quartering, finding and flushing game, remaining steady to flush and shot, and retrieving. In the autumn a field trial was held.

Observation of the methods of a successful trainer was particularly helpful to the beginners, who had a good man to act as instructor and coach. A class met for instruction every other Sunday. At each meeting progress was checked, mistakes were straightened out, and questions were answered. Then each amateur trainer was given a mimeographed sheet of the next lesson and told to work at home.

Sound instruction of this kind is helpful in all phases of dog training, particularly in the more difficult tasks, such as training to retrieve.

Planted Game

The use of planted birds is of great assistance in training dogs for hunting and retrieving. Barn-loft or pen-reared pigeons, game-farm pheasants and guineas are used for this purpose.

Planting or hiding a dizzied bird in cover, where its exact location is known, enables the trainer to control his dog on the approach or on point.

Flushing and shooting planted birds in flight provides the means of training a dog to retrieve under conditions that approximate actual hunting.

176

Photograph showing how to dizz a bird. The pheasant is held with both hands and swung around fast in a circular motion five or six times.

The Young Dog

The dog makes most of his physical and mental growth during the first year of life. At six months most dogs have developed only to the stage of simple yard training, finding and chasing game, and other relatively easy tasks. To adapt training to the mental development of the young dog, most trainers delay the start of intensive yard training until the puppy is at least eight months old or even a year or more. Some trainers, however, believe it does no harm, and may be beneficial, to do a limited amount of hunting with a puppy five or six months old before he has had advanced yard training. However, Martin Hogan warns that a young dog, even one that has been trained to the firing of a gun, can easily be made gun-shy if several hunters shoot at once when the dog is in the immediate vicinity. A young dog that seems fully trained to field hunting can be ruined by being taken into cover where there is heavy shooting.

English Setters are trained to remain steady to wing and shot in standing position, and also to "Whoa" in the same position.

The following brief training outline, based on steps followed and methods recommended by well-known professional trainers and authorities on hunting dogs, may be helpful to the amateur trainer in planning his program. Numerous variations in the sequence of steps of training are employed successfully by different trainers.

PUPPY TRAINING

First Lessons. The puppy from the age of about three to eight months can be taught a few simple lessons. In addition to being housebroken, he can be taught to know his name well and the meaning of "No," and he can be given simple yard training, for example, to lead, to stand, to "Fetch," and a few other easy lessons such as those outlined below. During this period, like a child, he learns how to learn, and how to mind. He learns the meaning of a number of words (sounds to him). This preliminary training, based largely on the desire of the puppy to do things with his master, paves the way for future progress.

During this time, the young dog is usually given a period of freedom in the field, which is continued until he learns to recognize game and to handle himself well afield.

The pheasant's head is then tucked under one wing.

Name. Whenever you call the puppy speak to him, make a point of using his name. He should learn always to associate the sound of his name with himself. Later, when you teach him to stand, you should be able to call him by a dozen different names, without having him move from position. He should not move until you use his own name.

Lead. The puppy should be taught to lead early and the owner should exercise care in this training. Any good dog of any breed can be cowed by an owner who handles it too roughly on a leash. You can make pups leash shy by being too rough with them at first. At the age of four months or so, a pup should have a short leash snapped on his collar so he can trail it around. Then you gradually exert pressure on the leash and guide him. He can then be taught to follow readily at the pull of the leash.

"No." When the puppy does something wrong, give the command "No" in a firm tone, and make every effort to show him what he has done wrong. His knowledge of the meaning of "no" will be very useful throughout his training.

Pointing Game. As a means of introducing the English Setter to game, one professional trainer uses the following device. A pheasant wing is tied to a piece of twine about ten feet long attached to a long stick. The wing is placed on the lawn close to the puppy's nose, where he will get the scent. As the puppy tries to pick up the wing, it is pulled along, just out his reach. When he learns that he cannot quite catch the quarry he will usually begin to point instead of chase. This pastime develops pointing at an early age, but it should not be continued more than a month or it may form the habit of "false pointing" of moving objects.

Natural Retrieving. Most English Setter puppies possess a natural tendency to retrieve that can be developed by practice. Carlton points out that the puppy's inclination to pick up and carry things is present much earlier than his desire to hunt. Similar stages of development are evident in young foxes; for example, around the entrance of a fox den will usually be found dead ground squirrels or other prey animals, which serve as playthings for the young. Vixens have been observed to give to their young parts of prey animals, to carry during their first hunting trips.

Early training of puppies in retrieving is partially summarized on the next page:

180

1. Do not begin until you have gained the puppy's confidence so that he is eager to race up to you whenever he sees you.

2. When you begin his retrieving lessons, take him to a place where he will not be distracted by dogs, other animals, traffic or people. This may be on the lawn, if it is not his regular playground, or it may be in some area where the grass is not close cut, but where he will have no difficulty seeing a thrown object.

3. Get him interested in a knotted handkerchief or a similar easily seen, soft object that is to be used as a dummy. When he is watching the movement of your hand and moving in the same direction, throw the dummy underhand a yard or two away, at the same time telling him to "Fetch."

4. If he has seen the dummy leave your hand, the chances are he will race out to it, pick it up, and run back to you. If he does not go to it, he probably has not seen it leave your hand, in which case pick it up and throw it again.

5. If the puppy does not come directly back to you, try to get him to do so by sitting down, or by turning your back, or by walking away from him. When he comes to you with the dummy, your object is to get it directly back in your hand. However, do not snatch it or engage in a tug-of-war with the puppy. To do so tends to develop a "hard mouth," that is, a habit of biting down hard on what is being retrieved. Place your hand under the puppy's lower jaw, so that he will not duck his head or drop the dummy, and press the dummy up and toward the back of his mouth as you remove it. If necessary, place your fingers in his mouth and open it gently.

6. When the dummy is back in your hand, reward the puppy with a bit of food or by making much of him. Probably food is the best reward for the first two or three lessons. Following these lessons, rely on praise, reserving additional food until he shows a disinclination to return to you after he picks up the dummy.

While the puppy is very young, limit the practice periods to four or five minutes at a time, and once or twice a day. He should always consider these lessons play; whenever his interest wanes, take away the dummy and discontinue the lesson.

After a week or two of practice, begin to substitute larger dummies, such as a stuffed canvas glove, a short piece of garden hose, or some other soft object that the puppy likes to pick up. For later lessons, a good practice dummy is one made of a piece

The bird is then gently placed in some thick grass cover, lying on the side so that the body, head, and wing are toward the ground. The planter should carefully but quickly walk away. The bird should stay where planted from fifteen to thirty minutes.

of soft wood, eight or ten inches long, rounded off to a diameter of about two inches, with a number of pigeon, pheasant, or other bird feathers attached to it.

As your puppy grows and becomes proficient at picking up and returning the dummy, you must vary lessons gradually in the direction of retrieving in the field. As early in his schooling as possible, begin to throw the dummy where he will have to use his nose to find it but not at first, in thick cover. He should return it to you in the same way as in the earlier lessons.

Another variation is to get the puppy to find the dummy without having seen you throw it. When you are walking downwind with him, drop the dummy when he is not looking. After you have gone fifty feet or so, turn and walk back into the wind toward the dummy, encouraging him to hunt for it. If he is familiar enough with it to recognize the scent, he should be able to draw up to it for a distance of several yards. He will thus learn to look for and retrieve something he has not seen fall.

Later, under hunting conditions, the training of natural retrievers must be extended to include retrieving of shot birds. Methods of field training vary among trainers. One of the most useful methods of teaching the dog to retrieve birds is by releasing pigeons to be shot in flight and retrieved by the dog.

If the puppy will not retrieve in play, the practice should be discontinued, and he can be force broken to retrieve after he has had some hunting experience.

Force Breaking to Retrieve. There is some difference of opinion as to the merits of natural and force-broken retrievers. It is generally agreed, however, that if the dog has been thoroughly force broken he can be depended on to retrieve, while a natural retriever may refuse to retrieve and the owner will be unable to enforce the command. Nevertheless, force breaking is one of the most difficult and time-consuming tasks of training, especially for the amateur. Unless the job is done thoroughly, it is better not attempted. If the dog shows indications of being at least a fair natural retriever, it may be questioned whether it is worth while for the nonprofessional to attempt force breaking. The amateur trainer who plans to force break his hunting dog to retrieve can find descriptions of methods in the books on the subject.

Freedom in the Field. Getting your young dog into the field

Ch. Jiggs Mallwyd D was a smart pheasant dog. He knew their tricks and usually pointed them so that the pheasant was in between. He was an all-day, tireless hunter and a natural retriever.   He was the most satisfactory shooting dog that I ever had the pleasure of hunting over.   Owned by Mr. C. S. Schneck, Allentown, Pa. Bred by Dr. Daw of Vancouver, B. C.

and allowing him to learn to hunt by himself is an important part of his training. By the time the puppy is five or six months old you will probably find it profitable to get him into the field to gain experience in finding wild things as often as possible. Although some trainers favor delaying this period of freedom in the field until advanced yard training is begun (eight months to a year), it seems better in most cases for amateur trainers to begin to take their dogs to the field at an earlier age. Generally, the more preliminary field training and experience on game your puppy receives, the better hunter he will become.

On these trips allow him to find and chase rabbits, squirrels, birds, anything he finds, to his heart's content. Four or five field trips a week where he will have a chance to find game provide excellent training. This is his time to get acquainted with the field and to develop independence in finding likely spots for game.

The dog should be allowed plenty of freedom to learn things for himself. His early attempts at hunting may be supervised, but not too obviously. Frequent directions may take away his initiative, or give him the idea he is doing something wrong, which is likely to lead to disobedience later.

Usually a good shooting dog can be made from one that likes to hunt. The period of freedom in the field is his time to learn thoroughly to enjoy hunting. He can be got under control with obedience training after his hunting instinct is developed.

Since he needs to gain self-confidence, it is well for him to be without other dogs on at least most trips; many successful trainers believe a young dog will learn to hunt faster if taken out a few times with an older, experienced dog. If he shows a tendency to point, he should be encouraged, but no attempt should be made to enforce pointing at this time. Sooner or later he will start making points.

Accustoming to Firing of Gun. Field trips offer you good opportunities to accustom the young dog to the report of a gun. Previously you may have introduced him to a report by firing a cap pistol (not close at first) as you approach him with his food. He will thus come to associate a report pleasurably with food. In the field, begin by occasionally firing .22 blanks, at first when the dog is some distance away and **only when he is intent on chasing something he has flushed.** He will probably pay no

This eight week old puppy delights in locating the quail box. Puppies can be tested for natural field ability at a young age.   *B. Kline*

Notice the natural stance as the puppy finds his first bird. Building rapport between handler and dog is an important step in early training.   *B. Kline*

attention to the report. Gradually you may fire the gun nearer to him, **always when he is chasing.** If he shows no nervousness, you may use a .410 or larger gauge, firing it **only when he is chasing,** and at first when he is some distance away. Do not try to kill the game during this early training. The strict observance of this lesson may easily mean the difference between a gun-shy dog and a dog steady to shot.

Fourth of July. Under no circumstances allow fireworks to be shot near your kennel, as it is the cause of many gun-shy dogs. Young stock as well as untrained grown dogs can be made permanently gun-shy by the slightest infringement of this iron-bound rule. No English Setter was ever born gun-shy, as acquired characteristics are not hereditary. It is no fault of a dog that he is gun-shy, and this condition can always be blamed on man's inconsideration, stupidity, or selfishness.

Teaching "Whoa." Another lesson that you can give the dog during field trips is the meaning of "Whoa." When the dog is ready to start his romp in the fields, but before you have unsnapped the leash, grasp him by the collar and tail, putting him in pointing position, at the same time giving the command "Whoa." Since he will be anxious to be off, he will probably stiffen to a point. Repeat this procedure at the start of each trip until he has learned to remain quiet in this position; then try stepping back a few paces, restraining him with the leash. Whenever he moves, go back and straighten him to a point. Soon he will stop on point at "Whoa" with only occasional restraint by the leash.

"Heel." In teaching a dog to heel, carry a very light, willowy switch. When you start to walk with the dog on leash give the command "Heel" and a hand signal to indicate he is to stay behind. He will not know what is wanted and will probably try to go ahead. Call him back, giving the command and hand signal, and repeat these until he understands he is to walk behind. If he is still hard to keep back, flick (not whip) him lightly with the switch, repeating the command. This will cause him to get back in position quickly. Practice with this method will teach him to walk in position at command.

Coming Promptly to Call. One of the most important lessons involves teaching the young dog to come to you when you call him. If you are having difficulty in this respect, you may use

An excellent action photograph taken at a recent Shooting Dog Trial sponsored by the English Setter Club of New England. The pheasant has just been flushed by the handler. Photograph by William Joli.

a twenty-five foot clothesline rope as a lead. If the dog does not come at once when you call, use the lead to start him to you. When he comes promptly, praise him. After he learns to come promptly when called, mistakes in other phases of his training can be corrected at once. It may be questioned seriously, however, whether it is ever good handling, or fair to a dog, to call him to you to punish him. If punishment is necessary for willful infraction of rules (when your dog is old enough and well enough trained to know the rules and to know that he must obey them), you should go to him. He should not have the idea he is likely to be punished when he comes to you.

Hand Signals. Dogs learn the meaning of hand signals more readily than they learn words. During yard training, use hand signals along with commands as often as possible. For example, when you give the command to "Whoa" or "heel," also give an appropriate hand signal. The dog should learn to respond to hand signals in the field whether he hears the command or not.

Advanced Yard Training. By the time your dog is eight to twelve months old he will probably have developed mentally to the point where he is ready for advanced yard training. We will assume that he has had preliminary lessons in most phases of yard work, and that the series of lessons has progressed gradually from the easier to the most difficult tasks.

The advanced yard training program should perfect by degrees his performance of the earlier yard lessons, or any new ones given him. Later when further freedom in the field will do no good and teaching control will do no harm, these lessons may be applied to initiate control of your dog in the field.

I have successfully practiced the yard training lesson in the living room, using an easy chair for the "kennel." At the command "kennel," the dog jumps in the chair, and upon being called by name comes to me. The advantage of house training over yard training is that it can be done at night and during bad weather, thereby saving time.

Field Training

Teaching Dog to Quarter. Eventually, in the field, you will bring your hunting dog's yard lessons into play in teaching him

Steadying a young English Setter bitch on point by the use of a check-cord. She is on a stiff point and was lifted up several times by the tail and stroked to keep her steady.

to remain steady to flush and shot, and in bringing him under control while working ahead of you. Do not be in a hurry to enforce control, however, until he has gained field experience. You should teach him to quarter the ground ahead of you, but he will have to learn for himself to work the birdy spots and to skirt the unlikely places. Proper working of the cover requires experience on his part.

A dog that finds and flushes game fifty yards ahead gives little chance for a killing shot. A pheasant will be at least sixty and perhaps seventy yards away before it is safe to shoot (because of the dog). From twenty-five years' hunting experience, I know that most game is shot under thirty yards. It is my opinion that most hunters and even top wing shots can't even cripple a bird at seventy yards, much less kill one. Also, a dog fifty yards in front of the gun will flush a moving bird far out of range if it is necessary to follow the line any distance before flushing. A dog ranging or quartering over a seventy- to eighty-yard front with the gun in the middle of that front is covering enough ground, even though he is crossing in front of the gun at a distance of five yards.

In training the dog to quarter, you may use hand signals to advantage to indicate that he is to turn and quarter in the opposite direction. Some trainers use their dog whistles for no other purpose than to turn the dogs. Perhaps the most useful device you can use in training your young dog to quarter properly is to follow a zigzag course over the field, always working into the wind in early lessons. When the puppy sees you change your course he will usually swing back to keep ahead. Occasionally you may find it necessary to start to run to arouse his interest in what lies ahead of you. After the dog has learned to quarter properly, you may reserve whistle signals or voice signals for special occasions when it is necessary to get his attention.

Steadiness on Point and to Wing and Shot. The well-trained dog should hold in pointing position until the hunter flushes the game and shoots; then remain steady in this position until sent to retrieve or to resume hunting.

Achieving steadiness in the young dog requires patience on the part of the trainer as well as frequent rehearsals of the lesson. It is probably better not to strive for complete steadiness early in the dog's hunting experience. The first impulse of the

Aspetuck's Red Sumac

dog when game is flushed seems to be to leap after the quarry. The strong tendency found in all breeds of dogs to chase moving objects is undoubtedly inherited from their wild hunting ancestors.

Some dogs learn with experience that it is useless to chase birds, but most dogs, if not given careful training, repeated when necessary, are likely to develop persistent habits of breaking and chasing.

When the setter begins to point game, make a special effort to get to him when he is on point. Hold him there for five minutes or more, stroking him and straightening him to a good pointing position; let him know you are well pleased with him. Repeat "Whoa" several times to associate this command with pointing game. Pushing the dog gently toward the pointed game tends to make him lean back. This is a good way to make some dogs more staunch.

Methods of teaching steadiness to wing and shot vary among trainers. Many trainers rely on a check cord (twenty-five to fifty feet of clothesline attached to collar) to steady the dog on point or to wing or shot. Stopping the dog with enough force to cause him to turn end-for-end after he has broken point and started to chase is frequently recommended to cure these faults. Nevertheless, in most cases it seems better for the amateur to teach steadiness without the use of a check cord if possible. The check cord ruins more dogs than any other thing; it makes blinkers out of them. Many bird-shy dogs are caused by a check cord, even in the hands of a good trainer.

The following method of teaching steadiness without a check cord is recommended by a nationally known professional trainer. When the dog has been taught to "Whoa," is accustomed to the firing of a gun, and is undergoing advanced training in the field, the trainer begins the steadiness training by firing a gun at an opportune time. The dog is probably accustomed to associate the report with the fun of chasing, and his impulse will be to be off, but in this lesson the command "Whoa" is given immediately after the report. If the dog has been sufficiently trained, and all goes well, he will stop and hold the pointing position.

If the dog does not obey the command, the trainer usually (under some circumstances it may be preferable to let the dog

F.T. Ch. Johnny Crockett, winner of the annual Purina Award for the Top Field Trial Bird Dog in the United States during the 1969-1970 season. Owned by H.P. Sheely, Dallas, Texas, and trained by W.C. Kirk.

194

get his chase out) goes to him and carries him back to the exact spot where he should have stopped. The dog is put in correct position, kept there a few minutes, and allowed to think over his mistake. This procedure is repeated until the dog learns to stop at the shot and command, and finally to the shot alone.

The author believes that training a shooting dog to be steady to wing and shot is an unnecessary detail, as it serves no practical purpose. Such training is a left-over from field trials, where it may serve a definite purpose to keep these wide-ranging dogs under control at the important moment. It is against a dog's nature not to chase, which is the reason it is so difficult to break them of it. Moreover, in real hunting it is a decided advantage to have the dog under the bird when it comes down in case it is wounded. Not so many wounded birds would be left in the field if the dog were allowed to retrieve them at once. In case of a missed shot the dog can have the bird located and be on point again when you come up with him. I can see no good reason for keeping the rule of steady to wing and shot in our shooting dog trials (not field trials), and would attach more importance to the dog's being under control at all times than his being steady to wing and shot. I have discussed this subject with several trainers and have yet to be offered a sensible reason for training to be steady to wing and shot. One well-know trainer said, "Without the dog's being steady to wing and shot he lacks a finished performance," which of course is an unsatisfactory explanation.

Training the Pheasant Dog. Training an English Setter to hunt pheasants presents special problems because of the cock pheasant's habit of running ahead of the hunter and dog. Dogs must learn by experience to follow the pheasant, rather than to keep on pointing while the bird runs away. Occasionally, one of these dogs learns by himself to circle the pheasant, thus probably causing it to lie to a point between the dog and hunter.

Instead of pursuing the cock from the rear (trailing) it is best for the dog to move out and around the bird, thereby either changing its course or causing it to lie to a point or to flush within shot of the gun. There are several methods for training the dog to handle the wily cock in this manner.

1. Keep the dog's head off the ground; never let him develop into a trailer. The best method found by the author has been to

Let the young dogs find and chase birds to their hearts' content. They cannot catch them, and it offers you the best possible opportunity of firing light loads in the air to accustom them to the noise. An English setter will never be gun-shy if introduced to the gun while chasing a bird. Photograph by William Joli.

take the dog out of short cover at the first indication of ground trailing and put him down in a dense vegetation that he can best traverse with his head held high.

2. Never permit the young dog to trail the bird from behind. Train him to move around the bird. This may be done by teaching him to respond to a command. I personally like to locate a pheasant in a narrow draw with but two normal escapes, one at either end; then when it is known that the bird is there the dog is put down so that he has the advantage of the wind. When he has his bird well located, force him to leave it completely and circle around, approaching the bird from the opposite side. After he has learned to do this efficiently from command, he may be encouraged to make the same move without command. Time and much patience will eventually result in an automatic response which seems to increase with age.

3. By tethering a cock bird in dense cover, or by attaching to it a light stick, one has almost a complete control over the training. By repeatedly controlling the dog's movements when the exact location of the bird is known, the approach and the point can be steadied. This is probably the best method of training the pheasant dog.

4. Once the idea takes hold, it is advisable to give the dog plenty of opportunity to develop all of the fine technique which the particular dog is capable of developing through plenty of self-hunting, or better still through loose control when the trainer is present.

This seems to be about the only way the dog has of learning the characteristic behavior of pheasants under varying conditions.

Overhandling Undesirable. It should be the objective of the hunter to train his dog thoroughly in the essential points of working to the gun; then to allow him to work with a minimum of direction. Frequent directions will distract the dog and retard the development of initiative in finding and skill in handling game, both marks of the good hunting dog.

Ch. Ms. Devon of Hollycrest C.D. owned by J. & A. Lawson and handled by Trainer Mike Fletcher displays the style which has earned her field points.

10

Breeding

In creative work, that which is first must survive
the spotlight of criticism and so becomes a target for
the malicious tongues of the envious. The charlatan,
the mountebank, the phony, unable to equal or better
the best, tries to depreciate and destroy, thereby con-
firming the superiority of that which he degrades. The
best is advertised by the clamor of envy by the jackals.

BREEDING ENGLISH SETTERS requires a
clear picture of the type of dog you want to produce, some
knowledge of genetics, and a lot of luck. Only the surface has
been covered in the study of dog genetics. With the exception of
the work of the late Davis Tuck, whose list of undesirable
English Setter Traits is shown in this work, no organized
research has been done on inheritance in English Setters.

In the past, there were several large English Setter kennels that housed as many as one hundred dogs at a time. Choosing the best specimen to show would be a relatively easy task, i.e., a mass selection process. However, often limited by lack of space and more certainly by the tremendous increase in the cost of food, veterinary care and help, today's breeder is no longer apt to be a mass producer. He is more likely to be a hobby breeder who is limited to one or two litters a year at most. He must select the best brood bitch possible and choose his stud dogs very carefully in the hope of complementing what good traits his dogs have in order to produce the desired quality on a limited scale. While he strives for perfection of the standard, he must also realize that there will never be a perfect dog.

Genetics

Mendel's Laws of Heredity are relatively simple to understand. He determined that most traits occur in contrasting pairs. We now know that they consist of genes which are lined up on chromosomes like towns on a highway. They occur in the same order on every like chromosome in every dog. If the gene for coat color is the third "town" on the "highway" on the number six chromosome in one dog, coat color will be in the same place on the same chromosome in all other normal dogs.

Dogs have 78 chromosomes in each of their body cells. Thirty-nine come from the egg and thirty-nine come from the sperm. Thirty-eight pairs of these chromosomes control the physical characteristics of the individual dog. The other pair determines the sex of the dog. The sex determiners are known as the X and Y chromosomes. A male has XY and the female XX sex chromosomes. When eggs and sperm are formed it becomes obvious that the 78 chromosome number must be halved in order to produce sex cells containing only one of each of the original set so that when fertilization occurs the normal number of chromosomes will be maintained from generation to generation. This reduction process is known as meiosis. Each time meiosis occurs there is first a pairing of like chromosomes followed by a separation process. In this process the chromosomes from each parent are thoroughly shuffled.

Each time meiosis occurs the laws of probability operate and

200

new combinations of chromosomes occur in the eggs or sperms produced. This explains the reason there is usually considerable variation of type within a single litter and why repeat breedings do not guarantee duplicate offspring. It is obvious also that males produce sperm with either X or Y sex chromosomes in equal number while the bitch can only produce eggs with X chromosomes. The sperm then determine the sex of the offspring.

When an egg is fertilized there is a 50-50 chance that the offspring will be a male and an equal chance that it will be a female. Since the laws of chance are again operating and their effect can be seen only when large numbers are involved it follows that a single litter may be all males or all females. In the long run, things will even out and about equal numbers can be expected.

Many people tend to think of inheritance in terms of simple dominant and recessive genes. When this is the case only one dominant gene of a pair is necessary to cause that trait to show up. The recessive gene remains inactive in its presence. The resulting individual is termed a hybrid for that trait. In order for a recessive trait to show up it must be pure. Each parent must contribute a recessive gene. Blue coat color in English Setters seems to be dominant and orange recessive which is why breeding orange to orange can be expected to produce all orange pups. If a stud dog is pure dominant for a trait that trait could be expected to show up in his offspring even if the bitch is recessive or vice versa.

Orange belton puppies are usually more evenly marked than either blue beltons or tricolors. Blue beltons bred to blue beltons produce blue, orange and sometimes tricolor puppies depending on the genetic make up of the sire and dam. One of the disappointing results of breeding blue belton to blue belton is the large number of poorly marked puppies resulting, which in effect reduces the size or value of the litter.

A tricolor bred to an orange belton will give a mixed litter of all three colors while a tricolor bred to a tricolor will usually produce all tricolor puppies.

Eye Color

Evidence seems to point to the conclusion that few traits in dogs are determined by a single gene pair. Many traits are controlled by several different genes on several different chromosomes and this produces great variations in expression of the trait. Eye color and height are good examples of this. Color of eyes being a continuous type of variation, some puppies, even from parents having genetic dark eyes, will have lighter eyes than the parents.

Eye color occurs in variation from light yellow to very dark brown, with the average being a medium brown. It is not known how many genes are involved to produce eye color, but if there were only four pairs on four different chromosomes one can illustrate how this great variation can result. A medium eye color would be caused by the presence of four genes for light and four for dark eye color. During meiosis only four of these genes would go to any egg or sperm, again determined at random. Differing numbers of genes from dark to light could be contributed by the two individuals and they could produce great variation in eye color. Probability would tend to keep medium eye color in the majority of the puppies.

By consistently breeding only dark eyed individuals to each other one could push the average color toward the dark side. But breeders know that whole animals must be considered. Using a stud dog which complements your bitch in more important aspects but which might not have the exact eye color you prefer would be the better choice.

Mutation

There are many reasons why the unexpected happens in a breeding program and not all of these can be blamed on heredity. When mutations, sudden changes in genes, occur during the formation of eggs and sperms those changes, for example an unusual coat color, will be passed on to the offspring. The overwhelming number of these mutations are recessive and will not show up again until the gene involved happens to pair with a similar gene in some future generation. Many times mutations occur after fertilization as the new organism is developing. Since the sex cells are not affected and the change occurs only in the body cells such a mutation will not be passed on. One example of this type of mutation is an animal having two different color eyes. The mutation occurred on one side of the body only. The

202

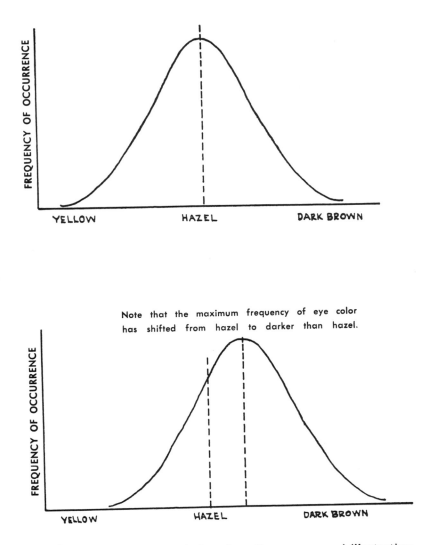

Note that the maximum frequency of eye color has shifted from hazel to darker than hazel.

Typical curves showing variations from the average, and illustrating how by long selection the average color of eyes may be pushed from hazel toward dark brown.

problem is that there is really no way to tell just what type of mutation has taken place in most cases without entering into breeding experiments which are both costly and time consuming. It is vastly more sensible not to breed an animal with an unfavorable mutation.

There are some mutations that are actually lethal to the recipient and cause death and reabsorption before birth causing smaller than normal litters. Lethal genes can cause stillbirths and early death of puppies.

Deafness

Genes can interact with other genes on the same or other chromosomes. Even dominant genes may fail to act because of the presence of a repressor gene which keeps the dominant one from being expressed. There are also modifying genes which can alter normally dominant or recessive expectations. Deafness could fall into one of these categories.

In a Swedish experiment on genetic hearing impairment in the Dalmatian, two pairs of deaf dogs were crossed. One of each pair was totally deaf and the other had little hearing. If this were a normal recessive trait all of the progeny would have been deaf. However, of the 49 puppies resulting, three has some reduction in hearing and thirty-eight were normal.*

It is obviously not worth the risk to breed a deaf dog and add more such genes to the existing gene pool. If a deaf puppy is identified it should be destroyed. To live with such an animal takes an unusual amount of understanding because of the lack of normal interaction that exists. Deaf dogs are prime targets for automobile accidents and other problems brought about by lack of hearing. Deafness shows up at times in most English Setter lines. It is sometimes not recognized by the breeder because such animals often react rather normally while in the company of their littermates. They become adept in substituting sight and smell for their missing sense.

Veterinarians have reported that some owners complain about extreme stubbornness in dogs whose problem proves to be

---

* Frederick B. Hutt, GENETICS FOR DOG BREEDERS, W.H. Freeman and Company, San Francisco, 1979, p. 162.

deafness. The puppy in a litter that always seems to be a sound sleeper even when his littermates awaken deserves to be tested. Having such a puppy is one of the heartaches of breeding. Fortunately, deafness, unlike other problems such as hip dysplasia and PRA, can be recognized by three or four weeks of age.

Hip Dysplasia

Hip dysplasia is a common problem in English Setters. The condition exists in degrees from normal hip formation through subluxation of the head of the femur from the hip socket. It is thought to be an hereditary defect which is influenced by an undetermined number of genes. Movement alone cannot always determine the degree of dysplasia. One affected animal may show no evidence of the problem in his movement while another animal having the same degree of dysplasia may become a virtual cripple.

The outward symptoms may be stiffness in hindquarter action, a desire to sit most of the time, straightening of the stifle joint, lack of muscle development in the thigh, and evidence of pain. However, only one or two or none of these symptoms may be present in certain afflicted dogs. Usually some evidence of lameness or stiffness is apparent at one or more stages in the animal's development. Since so many puppies are sold as pets before HD manifests itself, the quantitative incidence among English Setters is unknown. The inexperienced owners of pets only slightly affected are often unaware of its presence. Fortunately, in time most cases of HD compensate by themselves, and though the dogs cannot now be cured they may live happy, useful lives as companions.

As with deafness experimenters have crossed dysplastic animals and have produced some dysplastia free puppies. The inverse also holds true. Two certifiably normal animals can and do produce dysplastic progeny. In Europe where breeding experiments have been done it has definitely been shown that generations of judicious breeding of certified animals does show results in the lessening of the number of dysplastic animals produced. The issue is still clouded on the possible environmental influence on the development of the condition. Diet, limiting exercise, and keeping puppies off slippery surfaces have all had their adherents, but there has been no real evidence either pro or con for such treatment. It all seems to come back to heredity.

Veterinarians often grade dysplasia according to the degree of severity from near normal to badly dysplastic. In this country The Orthopedic Foundation for Animals, University of Missouri-Columbia, Columbia, MO 65201, has been set up as a clearing house for grading x-rays sent to them. The OFA provides a kit for taking the pelvic radiograph which includes instructions for the veterinarian, application card, fee requirement, and mailer. The dog's registered name, registration number, date of birth, owner's name, breed, date taken, veterinarian's name, and animal hospital's identification number must all be permanently fixed to the 14" x 17" x-ray. The best argument for using the services of the OFA is that each x-ray is read by panel of three experts and a consensus judgment is given. Since they review hundreds of x-rays, they have developed a standard of comparison that is fair.

There is never a reason to use a badly dysplastic animal for breeding. There seems to be little reason, however, for an outstanding example of the breed which is rated near-normal to be eliminated from a breeding program. At one time OFA passed on x-rays taken at one year of age or over. It was then discovered that animals which had excellent hip joint conformation at one year could develop a marked degree of dysplasia by the age of two. At the present time OFA will only accept radiographs taken of a dog two years old or older. If this evaluation indicates the dog is free of hip dysplasia, the OFA mails the owner a certificate so stating and bearing an OFA number.

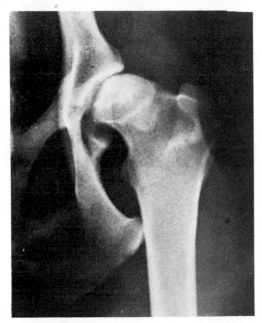

Severe hip dysplasia at 24 months.

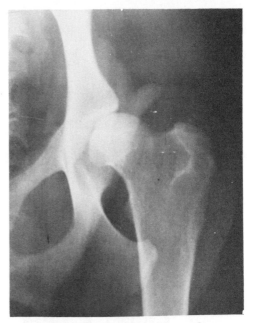

Moderate hip dysplasia at 24 months.

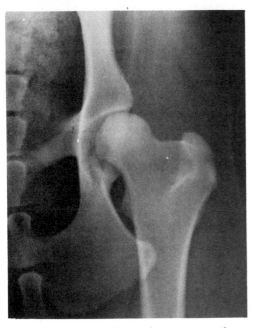

Good hip joint conformation at 24 months.

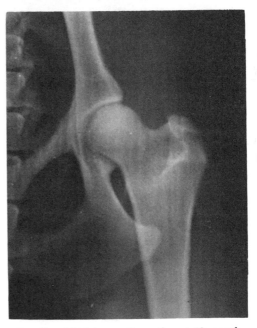

Excellent hip joint conformation at 42 months.

"Keep in mind that the classifications are associated with age at the time the radiograph is taken and the breed of dog. That is; a dog classified as good at 24 months of age with the same radiographic appearance at 10 years would be classified as excellent. Also there is a range of radiographic appearances within each classification. If a person is 'hung up' on one appearance then they will be disappointed as they have forgotten that we are dealing with a biological system." E.A. Corley, D.V.M., Ph.D OFA Project Director

Progressive Retinal Atrophy PRA

PRA is a retinal eye disease that seems to be expressed differently in different breeds of dogs. It has been shown to exist in English Setters only recently and is not as yet a major problem.

According to a Veterinary Opthalmologist the affected animal may have night blindness or trouble marking specific points. The disease may lead to blindness, but it does not always. An English Setter should be tested annually from the age of two until the age of six by an opthalmologist. If the animal remains free of the disease at that time one can safely assume the complete absence of the disease. An animal that does have PRA should never be used for breeding because it has been shown to be caused by a single recessive gene. If two affected animals are crossed all of their offspring will inherit the disease. If two normal animals are carriers 25 percent of their progency can be expected to show it and another 50 per cent will be carriers. Remember that these predictions pertain when large numbers of animals are involved. In a single litter there can be great variation from the predicted numbers.

Inbreeding and Linebreeding

The difference between inbreeding and linebreeding is one of degree. Inbreeding is the crossing of brother to sister, or of father to daughter, or mother to son. Linebreeding, which is a more generally accepted practice is the mating of half brother with half sister or more distantly related members of the same line. Inbreeding can be considered only when one has animals of such outstanding quality that one hopes to fix these traits and do it quickly. Provided no undesirable recessive genes have remained hidden there is no reason why this cannot be attempted. Because the undesirable qualities are also more likely to appear this type of breeding is done with the realization that puppies having these faults should be destroyed.

Linebreeding is generally accepted practice once one has approached the type he finds most pleasing and closest to his conception of the English Setter standard. It is good practice to breed into another line every couple of generations in order to bring in new genes and overcome the effects of recessive muta-

GENERATION (N)	1	2	3	4
NUMBER OF ANCESTORS IN GENERATION	2	4	8	16
INFLUENCE OF AN INDIVIDUAL IN GENERATION $(\frac{1}{2})^n$	25%	6.25%	1.56%	0.39%
INFLUENCE OF THE GENERATION $(\frac{1}{2})^n$	50%	25%	12.50%	6.25%

Illustration of Galton's Law, showing relative importance of ancestors in four generations.

tions. The resulting animals should then be bred back into one of the two lines crossed. If this is not done, consistency in the line will be lost and the resulting puppies will lack uniformity of type.

The Stud Dog

There are few truths, proven by long practice, that may well be a primer for English Setter breeders:

In selecting a stud, do not look at his show record and pedigree alone. Rather find out how many of his get have been able to make the grade at shows. The questions that should be answered are: 1. Is he a good specimen? 2. Is he able to reproduce his good points in his get? 3. Is he only fairly good but has the proven ability to sire outstanding specimens? Obviously 2 or 3 would make a better stud than 1. An outstanding example of 3 was Rummey Stagboro who never finished his championship but was responsible for a large number of outstanding dogs and bitches. Many of yesterday's top winners descended from Rummey Stagboro.

The Brood Bitch

When buying a bitch for breeding purposes, it is not necessary to buy a top flight show specimen. A bitch with a few outstanding faults of the type that are not common in English Setters, from a uniform litter that were all as good or better than she is, is a better buy from a breeding standpoint than an outstanding bitch who is the pick of a poor litter. It would be much better to buy the poorest in an outstanding litter. The late Leon Whitney* states: "The finest bit of common sense ever produced by any method for studying heredity is that which is so ably summed up by the Norwegian proverb. It gets at the very truth of the whole matter. 'Marry not the maid who is the only good maid in the clan.'"

Before Breeding

Breeding dogs is both expensive and time consuming. The owner of the bitch must be prepared to hold onto puppies, in

---

* *How To Breed Dogs*, Leon F. Whitney, Howell Book House, New York

sanitary facilities, as long as necessary in order to sell them to responsible homes. The newcomer tends to think that breeding dogs is pure profit and makes the false assumption that if one puppy in a litter is sold for $300.00 and there are eight puppies in the litter that the breeder has made over $2,000.00. One must be aware of and ready to meet the out-of-pocket expenses which go into each mating. An examination of the cost of raising a litter of eight English Setter puppies to 12 weeks of age will make it clear that it is difficult to make a profit on the sale of puppies. Profits from puppies are best left to the pet shops which as the name implies, deal in pets for profit.

From the tabulation of cost it will be noted that the stud fee is a relatively small item, compared with the cost of food for the bitch and puppies. It follows, therefore, that it is false economy to try to save money on the stud service at the risk of using an inferior stud. The best is none too good. The English Setter breeder who tries to make his kennel pay a profit or break even will never become one of our top breeders because he is tempted to sacrifice the ideal for dollar. You will find such a profit-minded person drifting from one breed to another, trying to cash in on the popular breed of the day.

It is readily seen that to market healthy puppies requires careful and often expensive veterinary care as well as excellent food and the expenditure of enormous amounts of time. No breeder is ever reimbursed for the late night vigils and hundreds of day-time hours spent in the care of the litter.

Cost of Raising a Litter of Eight English Setter Puppies to 12 Weeks of Age

Cost of a good brood bitch at $800 (amortized over 5 years) . $	160.00
Feeding bitch for one year @ $1.00 per day	365.00
Inoculations against Parvo (2), Rabies, DHL, Parainfluenza .	72.00
Dog license	12.00
PRA examination	25.00
Hip dysplasia x-ray under anesthesia	60.00
OFA certification	12.50
Brucellosis test	10.00
Heartworm test	10.00
Fecal on bitch	5.00
Health certificate	16.00
Stud service to a good stud	250.00
Shipping or other transportation (varies)	125.00
Veterinary fee after whelping	16.00
Dew claw removal	43.00
Composite fecals on puppies @ 6,8,12 weeks	15.00
Worming (price varies depending on weight and medication)	add on
Shots (measles shot @ 6 weeks, parvo shot @ 4,8,12 weeks, DHL Parainfluenza shot @ 12 weeks)	310.00
Feeding for 12 weeks	150.00
Labor @ $3.20 per hour, three hours per day	806.40
Litter registration	9.00
Futurity nomination	8.00
Advertising	50.00
TOTAL	$2,529.90

NOTE: Each puppy would cost $316.13. This list covers normal expenses including a normal delivery with healthy puppies. Expenses increase drastically for Caesarean section, hand raising puppies, and veterinary care of mother and puppies if illness occurs.

Anyone who wishes to breed English Setters with the ideal of improving the breed must have certain personal characteristics. They are listed as follows, and unless you are strong on the ones marked (*), you had better stay out of English Setters.

*Self-control.	Don't take it out on your dogs.
*Perseverance.	Don't quit in the face of adversity, hard luck, sickness in your dogs, etc.
*A good sport.	Don't crab when you lose. If your dog is good, he will win eventually.
Good natured.	A smile does not cost anything.
*Love for animals.	All kinds, and have an eye for them.
*Energetic.	Not lazy.
*Early riser.	Not a late sleeper. Do it now. Don't procrastinate and invent excuses.
*Honest.	
*Truthful.	Don't lie about your own or the other fellow's dog.
Helpful.	Try to help the other breeder.

The conscientious breeder produces litters out of love for English Setters; and the desire to improve the breed through wise mate selection and excellent care.

Before breeding a bitch careful consideration must be paid to the physical well being, structural quality, and disposition of that individual. She should be x-rayed to determine the invisible hip joint conformation and checked for hereditary eye disease. The bitch must also be tested and found free of heartworm and other internal parasites. All shots must be up-to-date before the breeding as there is suspected danger to the unborn puppies if the bitch is inoculated while she is in whelp.

Each animal used for breeding must be kept in outstanding physical condition. This depends on proper diet, exercise and weight control. An overweight bitch often has difficulty conceiving and whelping. An overweight stud dog may not perform.

Before breeding both the stud dog and the brood bitch should be checked for Brucellosis. Brucellosis is a canine bacterial, venereal disease which causes spontaneous abortion, stillborn puppies, newborn deaths, and reproductive failure. The test requires drawing a vial of blood which is submitted to a laboratory for screening. The owner of a stud dog usually requires a certificate from the owner of the bitch certifying the animal is free from this disease before the time of service.

The terms of any breeding should be agreed upon in advance of the service. Will the stud dog owner require "pick of the litter" or a stud fee? If "pick of the litter" is agreed upon it should be made clear at what age it will be chosen. Is the fee to be paid at the time of the breeding or time of whelping? If the bitch is to be shipped to the stud dog will the owner of the bitch be required to pay board or airport pick-up and delivery charges? If the bitch fails to conceive will she be entitled to a return service during her next heat cycle? If she whelps fewer than three puppies is there a guarantee of another breeding at no additional charge? In other words, be sure you understand the terms under which you are entering a verbal or written breeding contract.

A male dog is usually sexually mature and able to sire puppies by ten months of age although he may not be interested in breeding until after he is a year old. It is not advisable to use a very young dog at stud unless he has been screened for HD and PRA.

Being the owner of a stud dog carries with it tremendous responsibility. Introducing a young inexperienced dog to its first mate can try the patience of even the most relaxed individual. There are many excellent books which discuss the details of breeding dogs. If you lack the knowledge it is always best to have someone who has the experience of handling successful matings supervise the breeding.

While a bitch can conceive at her first season she is usually not physically or psychologically mature enough to handle a litter until her second. Some breeders prefer to breed a bitch at a young age because they think it will develop spring of rib and mature her.

Breeding Cycle

It is often difficult to determine the best time to breed a maiden bitch. The owner should keep accurate records from the first day color shows and note physical changes which occur that signal when the bitch should be bred. By keeping a calendar of each season it is easier to know when a bitch will most readily accept the stud dog.

214

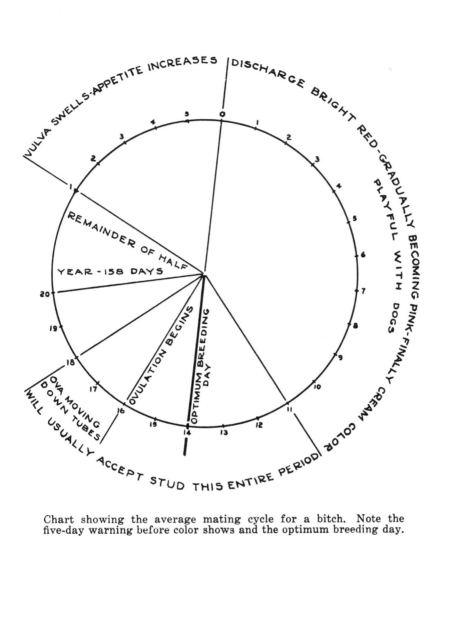

Chart showing the average mating cycle for a bitch. Note the five-day warning before color shows and the optimum breeding day.

Some bitches fail to conceive. There are many possible reasons for infertility. The leading cause is improper timing of a breeding. Poor physical condition and obesity are two other common causes. It is all too easy to blame the stud dog if the bitch does not conceive when in reality there are many factors to investigate in order to determine the cause.

What signals when observed determine the proper day for breeding? One sign is observing the change in color of the discharge from red to pale pink to straw color. Use a white tissue daily to monitor the color. Another sign is when the congestion of the vulva begins to lessen, feels soft to the touch, and the swelling appears to decrease slightly. A veterinarian can also take a smear of vaginal secretions which are examined under a microscope for cellular changes. When the red cell count decreases the bitch is close to ovulating.

The typical heat cycle lasts 21 days and occurs every six to eight months. The bitch's heat can be divided into three stages: rejection, acceptance, then rejection of the stud. Most females will not accept a male during the beginning or end of her season. At either of these stages the bitch will probably sit down, growl or snap at the dog. During the middle phase the bitch becomes receptive to the dog. She stands and flags her tail to the side and becomes aggressive and willing to be bred. This standing heat can last one day to 12 days. Bitches have been known to conceive as early as the 5th day or as late as the 21st day of heat. Simply counting the days of the heat cycle is an inaccurate method to determine when to breed. Watch the bitch for the signs discussed. If possible breed the bitch at the 2nd, 4th and 6th day of the standing heat. Sperm live for up to seven days which allows fertilization to occur over an extended period of time. Skipping days between breedings allows a healthy stud dog time to raise his sperm count for the next service.

An experienced stud is usually the most accurate indicator of the best time to service the bitch. Little failure can be expected when all the breeding indicators are observed and followed.

The chart shows the heat cycle of the average bitch. Remember, that not all bitches can be average. Information concerning the fertility record and time of breeding of other bitches of similar bloodlines can also be a helpful guide to the owner.

When shipping a bitch for breeding it is wise to send her

before she reaches the standing heat cycle to allow her time to adjust to new surroundings, people and routine.

Do not use drugs to stimulate the production of a heat cycle or fertility drugs to increase the chances of a large litter. There have been many examples of severe problems resulting. It is thought that the onset of heat can be accelerated naturally by providing additional hours of artificial light.

Determining Pregnancy

When the bitch is about 26 days in whelp a veterinarian can palpate the uterus to determine pregnancy. At that time the puppies are the size of walnuts and feel like lumps in the uterus. A dog's uterus is Y shaped and the puppies mature in the uterine horns. Sometimes it is not possible to determine pregnancy by palpation because the puppies are carried up in the horns behind the ribs.

There are other visible signs that a bitch is in whelp. The nipples turn bright pink and enlarge; the swelling of the vulva does not return to normal; and some have morning sickness and refuse to eat or vomit. False pregnancy is not uncommon.

Whelping

On the whelping chart the large type shows the date the bitch was bred. She will be due to whelp on the date shown in small type immediately below. Dates are based on the normal gestation period of sixty-three days. Variations in date of birth of two to three days either way are not unusual.

A well balanced diet is essential to the health and well being of the dam and her unborn puppies. Supplements are unnecessary if the bitch is fed a good high protein commercial kibble. Do not increase the amount of feed during the first four weeks of pregnancy. As the puppies grow they begin to demand more nourishment from the bitch. During the latter half of her pregnancy the food ration is increased by one half or more. As the abdomen swells the internal organs are pushed aside making it difficult to feed the daily ration in one feeding. Divide the food into two or more feedings at this time. Loss of appetite in the later stage is often due to lack of internal space.

217

WHELPING CHART

JANUARY

1	2	3	4	5	6	7
Mar.5	Mar.6	Mar.7	Mar.8	Mar.9	Mar.10	Mar.11
8	**9**	**10**	**11**	**12**	**13**	**14**
Mar.12	Mar.13	Mar.14	Mar.15	Mar.16	Mar.17	Mar.18
15	**16**	**17**	**18**	**19**	**20**	**21**
Mar.19	Mar.20	Mar.21	Mar.22	Mar.23	Mar.24	Mar.25
22	**23**	**24**	**25**	**26**	**27**	**28**
Mar.26	Mar.27	Mar.28	Mar.29	Mar.30	Mar.31	Apr.1
29	**30**	**31**				
Apr.2	Apr.3	Apr.4				

FEBRUARY

1	2	3	4	5	6	7
Apr.5	Apr.6	Apr.7	Apr.8	Apr.9	Apr.10	Apr.11
8	**9**	**10**	**11**	**12**	**13**	**14**
Apr.12	Apr.13	Apr.14	Apr.15	Apr.16	Apr.17	Apr.18
15	**16**	**17**	**18**	**19**	**20**	**21**
Apr.19	Apr.20	Apr.21	Apr.22	Apr.23	Apr.24	Apr.25
22	**23**	**24**	**25**	**26**	**27**	**28**
Apr.26	Apr.27	Apr.28	Apr.29	Apr.30	May1	May2
29						
May3						

MARCH

1	2	3	4	5	6	7
May3	May4	May5	May6	May7	May8	May9
8	**9**	**10**	**11**	**12**	**13**	**14**
May10	May11	May12	May13	May14	May15	May16
15	**16**	**17**	**18**	**19**	**20**	**21**
May17	May18	May19	May20	May21	May22	Ma23
22	**23**	**24**	**25**	**26**	**27**	**28**
May24	May25	May26	May27	May28	May29	May30
29	**30**	**31**				
May31	June1	June2				

APRIL

1	2	3	4	5	6	7
June3	June4	June5	June6	June7	June8	June9
8	**9**	**10**	**11**	**12**	**13**	**14**
June10	June11	June12	June13	June14	June15	June16
15	**16**	**17**	**18**	**19**	**20**	**21**
June17	June18	June19	June20	June21	June22	June23
22	**23**	**24**	**25**	**26**	**27**	**28**
June24	June25	June26	June27	June28	June29	June30
29	**30**					
July1	July2					

MAY

1	2	3	4	5	6	7
July3	July4	July5	July6	July7	July8	July9
8	**9**	**10**	**11**	**12**	**13**	**14**
July10	July11	July12	July13	July14	July15	July16
15	**16**	**17**	**18**	**19**	**20**	**21**
July17	July18	July19	July20	July21	July22	July23
22	**23**	**24**	**25**	**26**	**27**	**28**
July24	July25	July26	July27	July28	July29	July30
29	**30**	**31**				
July31	Aug.1	Aug.2				

JUNE

1	2	3	4	5	6	7
Aug.3	Aug.4	Aug.5	Aug.6	Aug.7	Aug.8	Aug.9
8	**9**	**10**	**11**	**12**	**13**	**14**
Aug.10	Aug.11	Aug.12	Aug.13	Aug.14	Aug.15	Aug.16
15	**16**	**17**	**18**	**19**	**20**	**21**
Aug.17	Aug.18	Aug.19	Aug.20	Aug.21	Aug.22	Aug.23
22	**23**	**24**	**25**	**26**	**27**	**28**
Aug.24	Aug.25	Aug.26	Aug.27	Aug.28	Aug.29	Aug.30
29	**30**					
Aug.31	Sept.1					

JULY

1	2	3	4	5	6	7
Sept.2	Sept.3	Sept.4	Sept.5	Sept.6	Sept.7	Sept.8
8	**9**	**10**	**11**	**12**	**13**	**14**
Sept.9	Sept.10	Sept.11	Sept.12	Sept.13	Sept.14	Sept.15
15	**16**	**17**	**18**	**19**	**20**	**21**
Sept.16	Sept.17	Sept.18	Sept.19	Sept.20	Sept.21	Sept.22
22	**23**	**24**	**25**	**26**	**27**	**28**
Sept.23	Sept.24	Sept.25	Sept.26	Sept.27	Sept.28	Sept.29
29	**30**	**31**				
Sept.30	Oct.1	Oct.2				

AUGUST

1	2	3	4	5	6	7
Oct.3	Oct.4	Oct.5	Oct.6	Oct.7	Oct.8	Oct.9
8	**9**	**10**	**11**	**12**	**13**	**14**
Oct.10	Oct.11	Oct.12	Oct.13	Oct.14	Oct.15	Oct.16
15	**16**	**17**	**18**	**19**	**20**	**21**
Oct.17	Oct.18	Oct.19	Oct.20	Oct.21	Oct.22	Oct.23
22	**23**	**24**	**25**	**26**	**27**	**28**
Oct.24	Oct.25	Oct.26	Oct.27	Oct.28	Oct.29	Oct.30
29	**30**	**31**				
Oct.31	Nov.1	Nov.2				

SEPTEMBER

1	2	3	4	5	6	7
Nov.3	Nov.4	Nov.5	Nov.6	Nov.7	Nov.8	Nov.9
8	**9**	**10**	**11**	**12**	**13**	**14**
Nov.10	Nov.11	Nov.12	Nov.13	Nov.14	Nov.15	Nov.16
15	**16**	**17**	**18**	**19**	**20**	**21**
Nov.17	Nov.18	Nov.19	Nov.20	Nov.21	Nov.22	Nov.23
22	**23**	**24**	**25**	**26**	**27**	**28**
Nov.24	Nov.25	Nov.26	Nov.27	Nov.28	Nov.29	Nov.30
29	**30**					
Dec.1	Dec.2					

OCTOBER

1	2	3	4	5	6	7
Dec.3	Dec.4	Dec.5	Dec.6	Dec.7	Dec.8	Dec.9
8	**9**	**10**	**11**	**12**	**13**	**14**
Dec.10	Dec.11	Dec.12	Dec.13	Dec.14	Dec.15	Dec.16
15	**16**	**17**	**18**	**19**	**20**	**21**
Dec.17	Dec.18	Dec.19	Dec.20	Dec.21	Dec.22	Dec.23
22	**23**	**24**	**25**	**26**	**27**	**28**
Dec.24	Dec.25	Dec.26	Dec.27	Dec.28	Dec.29	Dec.30
29	**30**	**31**				
Dec.31	Jan.1	Jan.2				

NOVEMBER

1	2	3	4	5	6	7
Jan.3	Jan.4	Jan.5	Jan.6	Jan.7	Jan.8	Jan.9
8	**9**	**10**	**11**	**12**	**13**	**14**
Jan.10	Jan.11	Jan.12	Jan.13	Jan.14	Jan.15	Jan.16
15	**16**	**17**	**18**	**19**	**20**	**21**
Jan.17	Jan.18	Jan.19	Jan.20	Jan.21	Jan.22	Jan.23
22	**23**	**24**	**25**	**26**	**27**	**28**
Jan.24	Jan.25	Jan.26	Jan.27	Jan.28	Jan.29	Jan.30
29	**30**					
Jan.31	Feb.1					

DECEMBER

1	2	3	4	5	6	7
Feb.2	Feb.3	Feb.4	Feb.5	Feb.6	Feb.7	Feb.8
8	**9**	**10**	**11**	**12**	**13**	**14**
Feb.9	Feb.10	Feb.11	Feb.12	Feb.13	Feb.14	Feb.15
15	**16**	**17**	**18**	**19**	**20**	**21**
Feb.16	Feb.17	Feb.18	Feb.19	Feb.20	Feb.21	Feb.22
22	**23**	**24**	**25**	**26**	**27**	**28**
Feb.23	Feb.24	Feb.25	Feb.26	Feb.27	Feb.28	Mar.1
29	**30**	**31**				
Mar.2	Mar.3	Mar.4				

218

The backbone becomes a good monitor of proper weight. Nature protects the unborn by taking all the vital nutrition a puppy needs from the bitch if she is not receiving it in her daily food intake. If there is a tremendous depletion of the essential nutrients through improper diet the bitch suffers the most. Do not cook for your dog. The dry feeds are scientifically balanced and supply everything your dog needs. Any additives should be recommended by your veterinarian. Keep your bitch well exercised for proper muscle tone and without excess weight. An obese animal can have a difficult delivery.

Most bitches refuse to eat immediately before they whelp. They become very restless, ask to go out frequently, begin to pant, dig up carpets, and search for a place to have their puppies. To reduce anxiety a bitch should be allowed to become familiar with the whelping box for a week or more before her due date. Perhaps she can be encouraged to sleep in the area you have set aside for the event. Give her a thorough bath a week before her due date.

It is important to have a rectal thermometer in order to monitor changes in body temperature. The normal temperature of 101.5 usually drops to less than 99 degrees with 12 hours of delivery. With some the temperature drop is sudden and with others it fluctuates until labor begins.

A plywood box is necessary and convenient for whelping. It is safest to build the box with a recess all the way around so that the puppies have a chance to get out of the way when the bitch lies down to nurse them. Without a guard rail puppies can be crushed against the side. This is a common cause of newborn mortality.

The floor of the box should be covered with clean newspaper for whelping. Continue to use newspaper after whelping but cover it with bath size towels, an old mattress pad or indoor-outdoor carpeting to provide traction for the puppies. Do not leave the bitch unattended with a newborn litter because when scratching the bedding the bitch can cover and smother her puppies. If the bitch cannot be supervised it is better to leave the boards on the bottom of the box uncovered. After the puppies outgrow the whelping box it should be removed, thoroughly scrubbed with a heavily diluted chlorine bleach solution, aired and put away for the next use.

This whelping box is 36 inches square x 6½ inches high with an overhang of 3½ inches. Although it is fine for delivering puppies it will not be appropriate for raising the litter for more than ten days. A larger four foot square box can be built with 12 inch high sides and a 5 inch wide ledge nailed 6 inches above the floor for puppy safety. The addition of the overhang provides a comfortable resting place for the bitch's head.

The whelping area must be warm, draft free, and spotlessly clean. Elevate the room temperature to 80 degrees for the first few days. Have an ample supply of clean terry towels for rubbing puppies dry. It is also important to equip a separate cardboard box with a heating pad covered with a soft cloth. Keep the pad set on the LOWEST setting to warm the newborns while the bitch is actively whelping. Too high a temperature can dehydrate puppies and cause death. Newspapers are used in the whelping box to absorb birth fluid and can be replaced easily as needed.

Most bitches handle labor and delivery with little if any assistance. It is always important to be there in case the bitch has a problem and needs a helping hand or a veterinarian's assistance. An excellent guide for whelping, illustrated with photographs of labor and delivery is the book, *How Puppies Are Born* by Virginia Bender Prine.

Since English Setters are usually born solid white and gain their markings as they grow the breeder will want to know them as individuals as early as possible. As puppies are born and weighed they should be marked by cutting hair in different areas such as left shoulder, right shoulder, neck, mid back and so on. Identification can then be made to chart weekly weight gain or to know specifically which puppy has a problem if one develops.

Always have a veterinarian examine your bitch within 24 hours after the last puppy is born. Palpation of the uterus will usually indicate if one or more puppies have been retained. A shot of oxytocin is given to contract the uterus and expel birth material. Make an appointment to have the puppies' front dew claws removed when they are three days old.

As the puppies grow and demand more milk the bitch's diet needs to be increased substantially. Cottage cheese can be mixed with the dry kibble to supply additional protein and calcium. Always feed a proportion of ¾ or more dry kibble to ¼ or less other food additives. A balanced vitamin-mineral supplement can be given and is essential if the bitch refuses her daily rations. Food can be consumed at three times the normal level during the height of lactation.

Begin the weaning process when the puppies are three to four weeks of age when the teeth have erupted through the gums. A commercial dry puppy food can be used immediately if you allow it to soak in warm water long enough to produce a cereal

221

like consistency. As the puppies mature and gain good chewing ability decrease the amount of water added and the soaking time. Growing puppies should be fed on a schedule either three or four times a day.

Have a composite stool sample tested for worms when the puppies are three to four weeks old. Even if the bitch tested free of parasites before breeding it has been proven that puppies can be born with round worm or hook worm which have encysted in the muscle tissue of the dam and are activated during pregnancy by the change in hormones. These worms migrate through the placental barrier to the puppies before birth or through the mammary glands while the puppies nurse.

Your Role as a Breeder

If we were to breed the very best English Setter bitch in the country to the very best English Setter dog, none of the get would be as good as either of the parents. They represent the very apex of improvement and any change will be downward — they degenerate. This is a most important consideration for a breeder; he must realize that he must continue climbing the ladder, for if he ever reaches the top he can go no farther. There is never a static condition in breeding but rather one of flux — we must go up or down, and can never stand still. If you accidentally breed a hot one, just make up your mind that the get from it will be poorer. It is not necessary to start at the bottom of the ladder each time, as a good breeder will usually be found somewhere about the last three-quarters of the way up the ladder. This is a healthy condition because it gives everyone a chance to be the first to reach the top of the ladder. Do not confuse the breeder with the professional handler who for many years has shown winning dogs; the professional handler often represents the maximum effort of many breeders. He is the jockey who rides the winning horse, but he does not breed the horses.

The law of the drag of the breed is constantly operating. It may be the breeder's best friend or his worst enemy, depending upon whether you make it work for you or you work for it. All English Setters tend toward an average of the breed. Thus, if the average height of English Setter bitches is twenty-four inches, then there must be about as many under twenty-four inches as

222

there are above twenty-four inches, and if you breed a twenty-five inch bitch, her get will average less than twenty-five inches. So it is for most of the desirable points. The only way that we can raise the height of an English Setter bitch as a breed from an average of twenty-four to an average of twenty-five inches (if it is desirable to do this) is by selective breeding. Of course there is a limit in this direction, and the more nearly we approach this limit the more difficult it becomes to force the average upward. There is a tendency in breeding English Setters toward increasing their size. This tendency is an unhealthy one for the breed and should be closely watched, as its long continued practice could eventually harm the breed structurally.

Any breeder, to be successful in the long run, must cooperate with nature and not try to go contrary to her laws or improve on them. Chemicals, machines, money cannot improve on or replace nature. The whole dog is not merely the integration of parts, nor can the parts be mixed, as salt and water, to get the desired concentration, but rather it is an organism with laws of a higher order than the physio-chemical—it is LIFE.

Do not allow yourself to get stocked up with poor specimens of the English Setter. If you look hard enough you can always find some good points in almost any well-bred English Setter. Here again we should go along with nature who, by her law of the survival of the fittest, is constantly destroying the weaklings and the misfits. Do not use undesirable specimens for breeding, for by so doing you are helping the drag of the breed to bring down the degree of excellence that you are striving to bring up.

From a practical standpoint, the law of variation is the drag of the breed which tends to bring all English Setters up or down to the average of the breed. This makes rigid selection of puppies, bitches, and studs necessary if real improvement is desired.

There are still some breeders who disregard nature's laws and work out some elaborate system of breeding that in their mind will produce flyers with mathematical precision. Just because they may accidentally get one or two good ones does not prove that their system works. Where are the many other puppies that were sold cheap or destroyed? If we will assume that Rummey Stagboro was one of the greatest English Setter studs, our faith even in his prepotency may be shaken when we consider that he served one hundred forty-five bitches, and if the average litter were five, then he would have sired seven hundred twenty-five puppies. His owner's records show that of these seven hundred twenty-five puppies only thirty-three, or 4.5 per cent, made their championships. Following this line of reasoning your chances of producing a flyer, even when you have a super stud like Rummey Stagboro, are only about 5 per cent, and you can make your own guess what your chances are without another Rummy Stagboro. The chances that the popular idol of the day in the show ring will sire a dog as good as himself are remote. Where are his brothers and sisters? Where are his many champion sons and daughters?

That breeding bench type English Setters is largely a gamble is the secret of why the confirmed breeder keeps on. He knows the odds are all against him but he keeps on putting in the dimes hoping his will be the luck of hitting the jackpot. Knowing full well that the dogs he exhibits are not his ideal and that they have shortcomings, he shows them at the bench shows so that he can see by comparison with others if he is doing better or worse than his friends.

The only means known of improving the breed of English Setters is to practice selective line breeding which is made possible by nature's laws of variation, which in turn is preponderantly the result of reduction in the germ cells of both dog and bitch at time of breeding.

11

Laverack Type
in America

THE Laverack type English Setters in America are, as we know them, a relatively recent strain dating back to about 1900, or some seventy years ago. Our modern Laverack type English Setter's breeding stock was, for the most part, imported from the Mallwyd, Maesydd, Stylish, Shiplake, Rummey, and Crombie kennels from the United Kingdom, and around 1920 from Swedish imports.

The Mallwyd imports have been by far the greatest influence on our modern Laverack type English Setters, because the imports from the other kennels of the United Kingdom were strong in Mallwyd bloodlines. The introduction of Swedish blood, coming when it did, had an excellent influence by introducing hybrid vigor into the Mallwyd strain without the usual adverse characteristics of out-crossing. Rummey Stagboro was the outstanding result of this Mallwyd-Swedish outcross. A few other

225

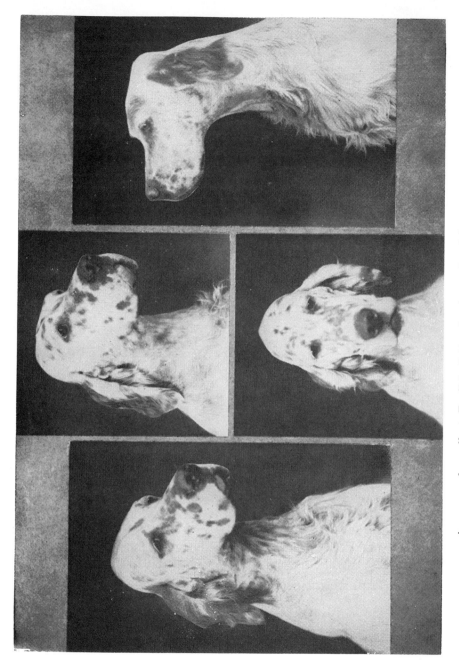

A group of excellent English Setter heads produced by careful breeding having in mind head improvement as being of major importance.

outcrosses were also made to the Llewellin strain, of which Mall-hawk Jeff and Blue Dan of Happy Valley are the best known.

A word of caution at this point is not amiss, lest the reader confuse and take too literally the descriptive words "Laverack" and "Llewellin." As already pointed out, these names that have been tacked on to English Setters, were poorly chosen. Llewellin actually originated the Mallwyd strain, and Statter and others originated the so-called Llewellin strain (so-called in America, but not in England). Regardless of the actual facts, however, common usage in America has placed the Laverack English Setter as the Bench Show type, and the Llewellin English Setter as the Field Trial type, both representing a kind of spectacle in the Dog Show and Field Trial, and having little or no connection with the original purpose for which the English Setter was developed: a facility in the procurement of game birds for meat. (Note the title of the often quoted book, "Hunger's Prevention, or the Whole Art of Fowling, by Water and Land," 1661.)

The Mallwyd strain of English Setters was the property of Thomas Steadman of Merionitshire, Wales, and the very height of his success is exemplified in Ch. Mallwyd Albert in 1916. Mallwyd Albert was genetically sound and prepotent. The Selkirk, Grayland, Southboro, Rowland, Crombie, Shiplake, Happy Valley and other English Setter kennels, were founded on the prepotency of Mallwyd Albert, as were the Maesydd Kennels of D. K. Steadman, the son of Thomas Steadman.

The Mallwyd influence on English Setters of some 50 years ago, which predominated as will be seen by a study of the pedigree section, was due largely to such outstanding and prepotent sires as Ch. Rummey Racket, owned by H. A. Belcher of Somerville, Mass.; Ch. Racket's Rummey, bred by Rees James and owned by Erik Bergishagen of Birmingham, Mich.; and the greatest sire of his time, Rummey Stagboro, bred and owned by H. F. Steigerwald of Auburn, N. Y. Rummey Stagboro traces back to Mallwyd Albert on his dam's side, and was a direct outcross to Swedish blood on the maternal side of his sire.

The major credit for bringing the 20th century English Setter Laverack type, to its present state of excellence, belongs, more or less, in the order named, to Thomas Steadman (Mallwyd), Dr. L. Thurston Price (Crombie), N. P. McConnell (Selkirk), A. J. Kruger (Mallhawk), Wallace Wilgress (Shiplake), Dr. J. F. Daw (D.), J. J. Sinclair (Orkney), Erik Bergishagen (Jagersbo), William F. Gilroy (Gilroy), Richard Jennings

227

(Hearthstone), Henry Hunt (Huntstone), Dr. A. A. Mitten (Happy Valley), J. Raymond Hurley (Kanandarque), William M. Crull (Sturdy), Philip Schwartz (P.S.), Henry D. Myers (Lakelands), E. E. Elderd (Peninsula), C. N. Myers (Blue Bar), Charles Palmer, Priscilla Ryan (Prune's Own), C. H. Allen (Hadceda), Noah Burfoot, Henry Steiger-wald (Stagboro), Ward C. Green (Scyld), Davis H. Tuck (Silvermine), Mary Ann Wadsworth (Vilmar), William T. Holt (Rock Falls), Mr. & Mrs. John W. Brady, Jr. (Frenchtown), Joseph Rotella (Manlove), Mead Hanes (Meadboro), William Sears, Rachael VanBuren (Valley Run), Mr. & Mrs. R. I. Pusey, Jr. (Cabin Hill), Darby Chambers (Mt. Mansfield), Mr. & Mrs. Peter Polley (Skidby), Mr. & Mrs. Andrew Hawn (Margand), Cmdr. Thomas W. Hall, Marsha Hall Brown, Bethny Hall Mason (Stone Gables), Mr. & Mrs. Earl Zamarchi (Zamitz), John A. Stocker (Yorkley), Dorothy Reiter Fouse (Cherry Lane), Mrs. George Rosen (Canberra), Vera & Warren Brewbaker (Chandelle), Jeanne Millet (Candlewood), Jeanne & Lynn Smith (Berriwood), Mr. & Mrs. Robert Ellen (Camelot), Joan Stainer (Lonesome Lane), Mr. & Mrs. J. Brooks Emory (Phantom Brooks), Susan Maire (Penmaen), Mr. & Mrs. Richard Howe and Jane Slosson (Clariho), Harry Kurzrock (Polperro), Mary Beth Nichol (Makepeace), Mrs. Frank Vertulia (Wragge Run), Mr. & Mrs. Ray Parsons (Raybar), Mr. & Mrs. Neal Weinstein and Lloyd & Linda Talbot and Nancy Jenkins (Guys 'n Dolls), Marge O'Connell (Hiddenlane), Dr. & Mrs. Jeffrey Bottrell (Lorien). Shirley Hoeflinger (Seamrog), Dr. & Mrs. John Kilgus (Heljax), Mr. & Mrs. James Hanson (Northwood), Dave & Winnie Baker (Burr Ridge), Fran & Ben Sprecher (Pleasant Point), Barbara Oakes (Five Oakes).

There are a great many others who have given freely of their time, brains, and money to advance the breed, and credit is due them also. Time and perspective will add new names to the list from the generation now carrying on old bloodlines and establishing new ones. The list of great producers and pedigrees in the next chapters will write the future of the breed.

228

12

Great Winners and Producers of the 1930's and 1940's

IN the first edition of this book, Davis Tuck included the pictures and pedigrees of 78 English Setters that had shone in the show ring and/or produced great progeny.

As time passes, any such large compilation as 78 needs to be sifted down to the truly great dogs of the past. Space must be provided for the newcomers, some of which greatly excel their predecessors in performance. In the reviser's judgment, 25 of the dogs appearing in the first edition merit continuation in this new edition. Unfortunately, we had no statistician in the 1930's and 1940's to compile the breeding records which appear in the next chapter for the leading winners and sires and dams of the 1950's, 1960's and 1970's. However, the following list of those retained from the previous edition is representative of the best English Setters of their day. It is historically interesting because many of the dogs pictured in this chapter are the ancestors of the producers pictured in the next chapter titled "The Leading Winners, Sires and Dams of the 1950's, 1960's and 1970's."

Ch. Blue Dan of Happy Valley
Ch. Daro of Maridor
Ch. Dean of Blue Bar
Int. Ch. Gilroy's Chief Topic
Ch. Grayland Racket's Boy
Kanandarque Rackets Boy
Ch. Lakelands Yuba
Ch. Lem of Blue Bar
Ch. Mallhawk's Jeff
Ch. Mallhawk's Rackets Boy
Ch. Maro of Maridor
Ch. Mary of Blue Bar
Ch. Pat II
Ch. Pilot of Crombie of
Happy Valley
Ch. Prune's Own Palmer
Rackets Rummey
Ch. Rip of Blue Bar
Ch. Rhett Butler of
Silvermine
Rummey Stagboro
Ch. Rummey Sam of Stagboro
Ch. Samantha of Scyld
Int. Ch. Silvermine Waga-
bond
Ch. Sir Herbert of Kennel-
worth
Int. Ch. Spiron
Ch. Sturdy Max

(*Note:* The following dogs also appeared in the original edition: Ch. Rock Falls Cavalier, Ch. Rock Falls Colonel, Ch. Rock Falls Racket. Since they were outstanding sires in the 1950's, their pictures, pedigrees and lists of progeny appear in the next chapter.)

CH. BLUE DAN OF HAPPY VALLEY

AKC No. 762757   Whelped April 10, 1926   Dog
Height - 24 inches   Weight - 60 pounds   Blue Belton
Owner: Happy Valley Kennels, Roxborough, Philadelphia, Pa.
Breeder: D. B. LeCompte

Leonidas of Ware
Heather Shot Over
Peg O' My Heart
Gores Blue Pal
Leonidas of Ware
Monte Carlo Topsy
Keatings Nellie

Island Count
Simmon's Count Jack
Yadkin Diana
LeCompte's Queen
Dock
Jones Trixie
Belle's Ghost

Massycromer Mallwyd
Ch. Primley Hesse
Ch. Bachelor Racket
Rowlands Sparkling Beauty
Massycromer Mallwyd
Ch. Primley Hesse
Ch. Bachelor Racket
Keatings Molly
Berkeley Rocket
Shaw's Lady Rose
Dobel B
Baldwins Princess
Dock's Ghost
Lady's Speedy Ghost
Eugene's Ghost
Bell Benstone

231

CH. DARO OF MARIDOR

AKC No. A-231570   Whelped March 18, 1937   Dog
Height - 25¼ inches   Weight - 63 pounds   Orange Belton
Owner: Charles Grayson Diamon, Roxbury, Conn.
Breeder: Maridor Kennels

Spiron Jagersbo
Rummey Stagboro
Selkirk Snooksie
Ch. Sturdy Max
Ch. Pat II
Rummey Girl of Stagboro
Selkirk Snooksie

Spiron Jagersbo
Rummey Stagboro
Selkirk Snooksie
Ch. Lakelands Dawn
Ch. Rackets Rummey
Lakelands Nymph
Lakelands Fascination

Int. Ch. Spiron
Arbu Lala B
Int. Ch. McConnell's Nori
Int. Ch. Selkirk Juliet
Mountain Top Tony
Ch. Lady Rowland
Int. Ch. McConnell's Nori
Int. Ch. Selkirk Juliet
Int. Ch. Spiron
Arbu Lala B
Int. Ch. McConnell's Nori
Int. Ch. Selkirk Juliet
Ch. Mallwyd Ralph
Stylish Pretty Polly
Meadowdale Mallwyd Count
Myers' Blue Bird

CH. DEAN OF BLUE BAR

AKC No. 4311325   Whelped July 14, 1938   Dog
Height - 24¾ inches   Weight - 55 pounds   Orange Belton
Breeder-Owner: C. N. Myers, Blue Bar Kennels, Hanover, Pa.

	Int. Ch. Rackets Rummey	Ch. Mallwyd Ralph
		Stylish Pretty Polly
	Ch. Mallhawk Rackets Boy	
		Ch. Rowlands Pathfinder
	Lady Rowland Racket	Rackets Belle
Ch. Mallhawk Jeff		
		Ch. Mallhawk Rackets Boy
	Int. Ch. Mallhawk Banker	Patsy What
	Flora Mallhawk	
		Int. Ch. McConnell's Nori
	Selkirk Mallhawk Juliet	Int. Ch. Selkirk Juliet
		Int. Ch. Spiron
	Spiron Jagersbo	Arbu Lala B.
	Rummey Stagboro	
		Int. Ch. McConnell's Nori
	Selkirk Snooksie	Int. Ch. Selkirk Juliet
Ch. Lakeland's Peaches		
		Ch. Mallwyd Ralph
	Ch. Rackets Rummey	Stylish Pretty Polly
	Lakeland's Nymph	
		Meadowdale Mallwyd Count
	Lakelands Fascination	Myers' Blue Bird

233

INT. CH. GILROY'S CHIEF TOPIC

AKC No. 799365   Whelped June 30, 1930   Dog
Height - 24 inches   Weight - 58 pounds   Blue Belton
Owner: Mrs. Allan Ryan, Rhinebeck, N. Y.
Breeder: W. F. Gilroy

Ch. Primley Nebo	Beachley Haig
Ch. Gilroy's Speckled Chief	Primley Hesse
Clover Ridge Dottie	Ch. Gilroy's Chase
Gilroy's Speckled Chief II	Ch. Clover Ridge Maid
Ch. Cole's Guess Again	Alberts Sir Allister
Clover Ridge Jane	Dix Girl
Ch. Clover Ridge Rose	Sir Roger's Emma
	Brown's Queen B
	Chase
Ch. Gilroy's Chase	Brown's Colo
Ch. Gilroy's Pal	Ch. Cole's Guess Again
Ch. Clover Ridge Maid	Ch. Sis Boom
Gilroy's Lady Doris	Alberts Sir Allister
Ch. Cole's Guess Again	Dix Girl
Clover Ridge Jane	Sir Roger's Emma
Ch. Clover Ridge Rose	Brown's Queen B

234

CH. GRAYLAND RACKET'S BOY

AKC No. A-310961   Whelped February 16, 1937   Dog
Height - 24½ inches   Weight - 61 pounds   Orange Belton
Owners: Mr. and Mrs. W. T. Holt, Rock Falls Kennel, Richmond, Va.
Breeder: Frank A. Bily

Int. Ch. Spiron
Spiron Jagersbo
Arbu Lala B
Rummey Stagboro
 Int. Ch. McConnell's Nori
Selkirk Snooksie
 Int. Ch. Selkirk Juliet

Ch. Mallwyd Ralph
Int. Ch. Racket's Rummey
Stylish Pretty Polly
Bleheim Violet
 Snowden Ralph
Principe Bonnie
 Graylands Belle

Ch. Pluto Horridoh
Tonny
Quip Cadillac
Ch. Gloria's Peggy B
Int. Ch. Racket's Rummey
Ch. Grayland Snowbird
Ch. Rowlands Pathfinder
Ch. Grayland Snowbird
Ch. Mallwyd Albert
Kell View Nell
Ch. Bachelor Racket
Stylish Kate
Ch. Mallwyd Ralph
Ch. Grayland June
Overland Superfine
Grayland Lassie

235

KANANDARQUE RACKETS BOY

AKC No. 920907   Whelped December 7, 1932   Dog
Height - 25½ inches   Weight - 65 pounds   Orange Belton
Owner: C. N. Myers, Blue Bar Kennels, Hanover, Pa.
Breeder: A. J. Krueger

        Ch. Mallwyd Ralph
     Int. Ch. Rackets Rummey
        Stylish Pretty Polly
Ch. Mallhawk Racket's Boy
        Ch. Rowlands Pathfinder
     Imp. Lady Rowland Racket
        Rackets Belle

        Int. Ch. Rackets Rummey
     Int. Ch. McConnell's Nori
        Grayland Snowbird
Selkirks Mallhawk Juliet
        Ch. Rowlands Pathfinder
     Int. Ch. Selkirks Juliet
        Grayland Snowbird

Ch. Mallwyd Albert
Kell View Nell
Ch. Bachelor Racket
Stylish Kate
Ch. Rowland Credential
Ch. Lady Rowland Sensation
Ch. Bachelor Racket
Kettings Molly
Ch. Mallwyd Ralph
Stylish Pretty Polly
Ch. Mallwyd Ralph
Ch. Grayland June
Ch. Rowlands Credential
Ch. Lady Rowland Sensation
Ch. Mallwyd Ralph
Ch. Grayland June

CH. LAKELANDS YUBA

AKC No. 880734   Whelped March 27, 1932   Dog
Height - 25½ inches   Weight - 64½ pounds   Blue Belton
Owner: Charles Palmer, East Longmeadow, Mass.
Breeder: Henry D. Meyers

Int. Ch. Spiron
Spiron Jagersboro
Arbu Lala B
Rummey Stagboro
Int. Ch. McConnell's Nori
Selkirk Snooksie
Int. Ch. Selkirk Juliet

Ch. Mallwyd Ralph
Ch. Rackets Rummey
Stylish Pretty Polly
Lakeland's Nymph
Meadowdale Mallwyd Count
Lakeland Fascination
Myers' Blue Bird

Ch. Pluto Horridoh
Tonny
Quip Cadillac
Ch. Gloria's Peggy B
Int. Ch. Racket's Rummey
Ch. Grayland Snowbird
Ch. Rowlands Pathfinder
Ch. Grayland Snowbird
Ch. Mallwyd Albert
Kell View Nell
Ch. Bachelor Racket
Stylish Katie
Junedale Prince
May Fairbanks
Cook's Blue Prince
Lad Rodney's Doll

237

CH. LEM OF BLUE BAR

AKC No. A-495250   Whelped May 19, 1941   Dog
Height - 25¼ inches   Weight - 62 pounds   Orange Belton
Owner: C. N. Myers, Blue Bar Kennels, Hanover, Pa.
Breeder: J. Raymond Hurley

Ch. Mallhawk Rackets Boy
Ch. Mallhawks Jeff
Flora Mallhawk
Lone Ace of Kanandarque
Ch. Esterada Blue Haze
Esterada's White Flyer
Miss Whitey Flyer

Ch. Mallhawk Rackets Boy
Kanandarque Racket Boy
Selkirks Mallhawk Juliet
Lovely Dawn of Kanandarque
Ch. Mallhawk Banker
Dawn of Stagboro
Ch. Fly of Stagboro

Int. Ch. Rackets Rummey
Lady Rowland Racket
Int. Ch. Mallhawk Banker
Selkirk Mallhawk Juliet
Rackets Rummey
Keatings Belle
Ch. Kanandarque Chief
Ch. Miss Grey Flyer
Int. Ch. Rackets Rummey
Lady Rowland Racket
Int. Ch. McConnell's Nori
Int. Ch. Selkirk Juliet
Ch. Mallhawk Rackets Boy
Int. Ch. Patsy What
Inglehurst Rock
Selkirk Snooksie

238

CH. MALLHAWK'S JEFF

AKC No. A-1910   Whelped May 22, 1935   Dog
Height - 25½ inches   Weight - 60 pounds   Orange Belton
Owner: C. N. Myers, Blue Bar Kennels, Hanover, Pa.
Breeder: Earl C. Kruger

                                   Ch. Mallwyd Albert
     Ch. Mallwyd Ralph   Kell View Nell
  Int. Ch. Rackets Rummey   Ch. Bachelor Racket
    Stylish Pretty Polly   Stylish Katie
Ch. Mallhawk Rackets Boy   Ch. Rowland Credential
   Ch. Rowlands Pathfinder   Ch. Lady Rowland Sensation
  Lady Rowland Racket   Ch. Bachelor Racket
    Rackets Belle   Keatings Molly
                              Int. Ch. Rackets Rummey
    Ch. Mallhawk Rackets Boy   Lady Rowland Racket
  Int. Ch. Mallhawk Banker   Leonidas of Ware
    Int. Ch. Patsy What   Queen Mohawk Girl
Flora Mallhawk   Int. Ch. Rackets Rummey
   Int. Ch. McConnell's Nori   Grayland Snowbird
  Selkirk Mallhawk Juliet   Ch. Rowlands Pathfinder
    Int. Ch. Selkirk's Juliet   Grayland Snowbird

CH. MALLHAWKS RACKETS BOY

AKC No. 595867   Whelped March 26, 1926   Dog
Height - 26 inches   Weight - 73 pounds   Orange Belton
Owner: A. J. Kruger, Mallhawk Kennels, Troutdale, Oregon
Breeder: G. Vanaken

	Ch. Mallwyd Albert	Mallwyd Markham
Ch. Mallwyd Ralph		Mallwyd Violet
	Kell View Nell	Smut of Hest
Int. Ch. Rackets Rummey		Bob White Killview Meg
	Ch. Bachelor Racket	Prince Charming II
Stylish Pretty Polly		Stylish Katie
	Stylish Katie	Mallwyd Prince
		Gypsy Girl II
	Ch. Rowlands Credential	Ch. Mallwyd Rowland
Ch. Rowlands Pathfinder		Woodsmore Peggy
	Ch. Lady Rowland Sensation	Ch. Bachelor Racket
Lady Rowland Racket		Snowden Lady Rowland
	Ch. Bachelor Racket	Prince Charming II
Rackets Belle		Stylish Katie
	Keatings Molly	Arbutus Sirdar
		Count's Molly Whitestone

240

CH. MARO OF MARIDOR

AKC No. A-231572	Whelped March 18, 1937	Dog
Height - 25 inches	Weight - 60 pounds	Orange Belton

Owner: Wilfred Kennedy, Detroit, Mich.
Breeder: Maridor Kennels

Spiron Jagersbo	Int. Ch. Spiron
Rummey Stagboro	Arbu Lala B
Selkirk Snooksie	Int. Ch. McConnell's Nori
Ch. Sturdy Max	Int. Ch. Selkirk Juliet
Ch. Pat II	Mountain Top Tony
Rummey Girl of Stagboro	Ch. Lady Rowland
Selkirk Snooksie	Int. Ch. McConnell's Nori
	Int. Ch. Selkirk Juliet
	Int. Ch. Spiron
Spiron Jagersbo	Arbu Lala B
Rummey Stagboro	Int. Ch. McConnell's Nori
Selkirk Snooksie	Int. Ch. Selkirk Juliet
Ch. Lakeland's Dawn	Ch. Mallwyd Ralph
Ch. Rackets Rummey	Stylish Pretty Polly
Lakeland's Nymph	Meadowdale Mallwyd Count
Lakeland's Fascination	Myers' Blue Bird

241

CH. MARY OF BLUE BAR

AKC No. S-109320   Whelped November 13, 1946   Dog
Height - 24 inches   Weight - 54 pounds   Orange Belton
Breeder-Owner: C. N. Myers, Blue Bar Kennels, Hanover, Pa.

<table>
<tr><td></td><td>Ch. Mallhawk Rackets Boy</td></tr>
<tr><td>Ch. Mallhawk's Jeff</td><td></td></tr>
<tr><td>Ray of Blue Bar</td><td>Flora Mallhawk</td></tr>
<tr><td>Kanandarque Lovelyness</td><td>Kanandarque Rackets Boy</td></tr>
<tr><td>Ch. Jesse of Blue Bar</td><td>Dawn of Stagboro</td></tr>
<tr><td>Rummey Stagboro</td><td>Spiron Jagersbo</td></tr>
<tr><td>Ch. Lovely Lady of Stucile</td><td>Selkirk Snooksie</td></tr>
<tr><td>Ch. Modern Maid of Stucile</td><td>Ch. Sir Orkney Wilgress, Jr.</td></tr>
<tr><td></td><td>Wilgress Lady Luck</td></tr>
<tr><td>Ch. Mallhawk's Jeff</td><td>Ch. Mallhawk Rackets Boy</td></tr>
<tr><td>Sammy of Blue Bar</td><td>Flora Mallhawk</td></tr>
<tr><td>Kanandarque Lovelyness</td><td>Kanandarque Rackets Boy</td></tr>
<tr><td>Ch. Lola of Blue Bar</td><td>Dawn of Stagboro</td></tr>
<tr><td>Kanandarque Rackets Boy</td><td>Ch. Mallhawk Rackets Boy</td></tr>
<tr><td>Faith of Blue Bar</td><td>Selkirk Mallhawk Juliet</td></tr>
<tr><td>Saga Oakholm II</td><td>Ch. Rackets Rummey</td></tr>
<tr><td></td><td>Ch. Mallhawk Sister</td></tr>
</table>

242

CH. PAT II

AKC No. A-609965   Whelped September 7, 1926   Dog
Height - 25 inches   Weight - 63 pounds   Orange Belton
Owner: Captain Thomas W. Reilly, Newfoundland, N. J.
Breeder: C. H. Stewart

Bob Lynk
Thorn Lake Tony
Lady Lemon Molly
Mountain Top Tony
Ch. Sir Roger de Coverly II
Cute of Playmore
Beck's Peg O' My Heart

Ch. Mallwyd Rowland
Ch. Rowland's Credential
Woodsmore Peggy
Ch. Lady Rowland
Ch. Bachelor Racket
Ch. Lady Rowland's Sensation
Snowden Lady Rowland

Mallwyd Edward
Rodger Blue Bell
Meadowview Bob Roy
Meadowview Vassar
Sir Roger de Coverly
Blue Girl Janie
Mallwyd Invader
Wyoming Valley Valma
Mallwyd John
Mallwyd Rose
Ch. Mallwyd Albert
Mallwyd Margot
Prince Charming II
Stylish Katie
Ch. Mallwyd Rowland
Woodsmore Peggy

243

CH. PILOT OF CROMBIE OF HAPPY VALLEY

AKC No. 881743	Whelped February 21, 1930	Dog
Height - 25½ inches	Weight - 60 pounds	Blue Belton

Owner: Happy Valley Kennels, Roxborough, Philadelphia, Pa.
Breeder: Prof. L. Turton Price, Dundee, Scotland

O' By Jingo	Fosters Double
Maesydd Poy of Ardagh	Fleda
Maesydd Pansy	Beachley Haig
Albert of Crombie	Rufflyn Fickle
Ch. Crossfell	Tarnside Major
Maesydd Monica	Grouse of Crossfell
Nan of Crombie	Rufflyn Clansman
	Glaisnock Kate
	Mallwyd Foster
Fosters Double	Myrtle Connie
O' By Jingo	Glaisnock Haig
Fleda	Glaisnock Nannie
Patch of Crombie	Glaisnock Jim
Beachley Haig	Craigielands Madge
Maesydd Pansy	Ch. Mallwyd Albert
Rufflyn Fickle	Rufflyn Fanela

244

CH. PRUNE'S OWN PALMER

AKC No. A-853935   Whelped July 4, 1944   Dog
Height - 26 inches   Weight - 70 pounds   Lemon Belton
Owner: N. Burfoot, Elizabeth City, N. C.
Breeder: Albert K. Thommen

Ch. Sturdy Max
Ch. Prune's Own Sensation
Ch. Desire of Maridor
Ch. San Marino P. S.
Orkney Master Key
Fern Hill Trigger P. S.
Fern Hill Gee Gee

Ch. Sturdy Max
Ch. Maro of Maridor
Ch. Lakeland Dawn
Prune's Own Duchess
Rummey Stagboro
Ch. Roger Dale Flirtation
Queen of Stagboro

Rummey Stagboro
Rummey Girl of Stagboro
Rummey Stagboro
Lakeland Nymph
Ch. Sir Orkney Willgress
Orkney Masterpiece
Ch. Sturdy Max
Hi Nellie P. S.
Rummey Stagboro
Rummey Girl of Stagboro
Rummey Stagboro
Lakeland's Nymph
Ch. Spiron Jagersbo
Selkirk Snooksie
Ch. Kanandarque Chief
Ch. Smile of Stagboro

RACKETS RUMMEY

AKC No. 428961 Whelped December, 1922 Dog
Height - 26 inches Weight - 70 pounds Orange Belton
Owner: Erik Bergishagen, Birmingham, Mich.
Breeder: Rees Jones

	Mallwyd Markham	Mallwyd Major
Ch. Mallwyd Albert		Mallwyd Evelyn
	Mallwyd Violet	Ch. Mallwyd Diamond
Ch. Mallwyd Ralph		Mallwyd Rose
	Smut of Hest	Bolton Simon
Kell View Nell		Bolton Katie
	Kell View Meg	Mallwyd Blue Prince
		Juno
	Prince Charming II	Ch. Mallwyd Bob
Ch. Bachelor Racket		Rockline Ladybird
	Stylish Katie	Mallwyd Prince
Stylish Pretty Polly		Gypsy Girl II
	Mallwyd Prince	Mallwyd Bob
Stylish Katie		Victoria
	Gypsy Girl II	Mallwyd Major
		Arbutus Pearl

246

CH. RIP OF BLUE BAR

AKC No. A-749742   Whelped July 1, 1943   Dog
Height - 26 inches   Weight - 68 pounds   Orange Belton
Breeder-Owner: C. N. Myers, Blue Bar Kennels, Hanover, Pa.

Ch. Mallhawk Rackets Boy
Ch. Mallhawk Jeff
Flora Mallhawk
Ch. Dean of Blue Bar
Rummey Stagboro
Ch. Lakeland's Peaches
Lakeland's Nymph

Ch. Mallhawk Jeff
Roy of Blue Bar
Kanandarque Lovelyness
Ina of Blue Bar
Inglehurst Rock
Ch. Fly of Stagboro
Selkirk Snooksie

Int. Ch. Rackets Rummey
Lady Rowland Racket
Int. Ch. Mallhawk Banker
Selkirk Mallhawk Juliet
Spiron Jagersbo
Selkirk Snooksie
Ch. Rackets Rummey
Lakeland's Fascination
Ch. Mallhawk Rackets Boy
Flora Mallhawk
Kanandarque Rackets Boy
Dawn of Stagboro
Ch. Fernbank Blue Rock
Inglehurst Patches
Int. Ch. McConnell's Nori
Int. Ch. Selkirk Juliet

CH. RHETT BUTLER OF SILVERMINE

AKC No. A-236797   Whelped January 26, 1938   Dog
Height - 25½ inches   Weight - 70 pounds   Orange Belton
Breeder-Owner: Davis H. Tuck, Silvermine, Redding Ridge, Conn.

Int. Ch. Spiron
Spiron Jagersbo
Arbu Lala B
Rummey Stagboro
   Int. Ch. McConnell's Nori
Selkirk Snooksie
   Int. Ch. Selkirk Juliet

Gilroy's Speckled Chief II
Int. Ch. Gilroy's Chief Topic
Gilroy's Lady Doris
Lady Dian of Silvermine
   Int. Ch. Racket's Rummey
Racket's Nell
   Keating's Nellie

Ch. Pluto Horridoh
Tonny
Quip Cadillac
Ch. Gloria's Peggy B
Int. Ch. Racket's Rummey
Ch. Grayland Snowbird
Ch. Rowlands Pathfinder
Ch. Grayland Snowbird
Ch. Gilroy's Speckled Chief
Clover Ridge Jane
Ch. Gilroy's Pal
Clover Ridge Jane
Ch. Mallwyd Ralph
Stylish Pretty Polly
Ch. Bachelor Racket
Keating's Mollie

248

RUMMEY STAGBORO

AKC No. 746120   Whelped August 31, 1929   Dog
Height - 26 inches   Weight - 65 pounds   Orange Belton
Breeder-Owner: Henry F. Steigerwald, Stagboro Kennels, Auburn, N. Y.

			Brush
Ch. Pluto Horridoh			Ch. Hera
Int. Ch. Spiron			Ch. White Noirhat
Tonny			Sussan
Spiron Jagersbo			Ch. A Real Beau
Quip Cadillac			Brightfield Good Fairy
Arbu Lala B			Linwood Spot
Ch. Gloria's Peggy B			Ch. Watlands Gloria
			Ch. Mallwyd Ralph
Int. Ch. Racket's Rummey			Stylish Pretty Polly
Int. Ch. McConnell's Nori			Ch. Mallwyd Ralph
Ch. Grayland Snowbird			Grayland June
Selkirk Snooksie			Ch. Rowlands Credential
Ch. Rowlands Pathfinder			Ch. Lady Rowlands Sensation
Int. Ch. Selkirk Juliet			Ch. Mallwyd Ralph
Ch. Grayland's Snowbird			Grayland June

CH. RUMMEY SAM OF STAGBORO

AKC No. A-411011   Whelped February 20, 1939   Dog
Height - 25¼ inches   Weight - 65 pounds   Orange Belton
Owner: M. L. Hanes, Buffalo, N. Y.
Breeder: Stagboro Kennels

Spiron Jagersbo
Rummey Stagboro
Selkirk Snooksie
Rummey II Stagboro
Kanandarque Racket's Boy
Ch. Ladybelle of Stagboro
Ch. Fly of Stagboro

Kanandarque Racket's Boy
Ch. Mark of Stagboro
Ch. Fly of Stagboro
Kate of Stagboro
Rummey Stagboro
Racket Mary Ann
Lakeland Nymph

Int. Ch. Spiron
Arbu Lala B.
Int. Ch. McConnell's Nori
Int. Ch. Selkirk Juliet
Ch. Mallhawk Racket's Boy
Selkirk Mallhawk Juliet
Ch. Inglehurst Rock
Selkirk Snooksie
Ch. Mallhawk Racket's Boy
Selkirk Mallhawk Juliet
Ch. Inglehurst Rock
Selkirk Snooksie
Spiron Jagersbo
Selkirk Snooksie
Int. Ch. Racket's Rummey
Lakeland Fascination

250

CH. SAMANTHA OF SCYLD

AKC No. A-408376   Whelped March 27, 1940   Bitch
Height - 25¾ inches   Weight - 51 pounds   Orange Belton
Breeder-Owner: Ward C. Green, South Norwalk, Connecticut

Int. Ch. Spiron
Spiron Jagersbo
Arbu Lala B.
Rummey Stagboro
Int. Ch. McConnell's Nori
Selkirk Snooksie
Ch. Selkirk Juliet

Rummey Stagboro
Ch. Sturdy Max
Rummey Girl of Stagboro
Jane of Maridor
Ch. Phar Lap P. S.
Hi Nellie P. S.
Ch. Highlight Lady

Ch. Pluto Horridoh
Tony
Quip Cadillac
Ch. Gloria's Peggy B.
Int. Ch. Racket's Rummey
Ch. Grayland's Snowbird
Ch. Rowland's Pathfinder
Ch. Grayland's Snowbird
Spiron Jagersbo
Selkirk Snooksie
Ch. Pat II
Selkirk Snooksie
Ch. Gilroy's Speckled Chief
Double Bronx P. S.
Ch. Highlight P. S.
Ch. Post Road Peggie

INT. CH. SILVERMINE WAGABOND

AKC No. A-837082   Whelped August 14, 1944   Dog
Height - 26 inches   Weight - 70 pounds   Blue Belton
Owner: Davis H. Tuck, Silvermine, Redding Ridge, Conn.
Breeder: Augustus Kellog

Spiron Jagersbo
Rummey Stagboro
Selkirk Snooksie
Ch. Rhett Butler of Silvermine
Int. Ch. Gilroy's Chief Topic
Lady Dian of Silvermine
Racket's Nell

Ch. Lakeland Yuba
Fox Flame
Duchess of Dixmont
Keyfield Judy
Rummey Stagboro
Lavender Lady
Blue Diana

Int. Ch. Spiron
Arbu Lala B.
Int. Ch. McConnell's Nori
Int. Ch. Selkirk Juliet
Gilroy's Speckled Chief II
Gilroy's Lady Doris
Int. Ch. Racket's Rummey
Keating's Nellie
Rummey Stagboro
Lakeland's Nymph
Ch. Sturdy Max
Lakeland's Nymph
Spiron Jagersbo
Selkirk Snooksie
Dusty D
Betsy D

252

CH. SIR HERBERT OF KENNELWORTH

AKC No. S-242571   Whelped October 12, 1947   Dog
Height - 26 inches   Weight - 65 pounds   Orange Belton
Owner: C. N. Myers, Hanover, Pa.
Breeder: David Ross Scott

	Ch. Mallhawk Jeff	Ch. Mallhawk Racket's Boy
Ch. Dean of Blue Bar		Flora Mallhawk
	Ch. Lakeland Peaches	Rummey Stagboro
Ch. Rip of Blue Bar		Lakeland Nymph
	Roy of Blue Bar	Ch. Mallhawk's Jeff
Ina of Blue Bar		Kanandarque Loveliness
	Ch. Fly of Stagboro	Inglehurst Rock
		Selkirk Snooksie
	Int. Ch. Maxie of Stagboro	Rummey Stagboro
Banker of Fallondale		Kate of Stagboro
	Ch. Grayland Orange Blossom	Rummey Stagboro
Vivacious Doll of Vilmar		Mallhawks Lady Daine
	Ch. Sturdy Max	Rummey Stagboro
Delta of Larana		Rummey Girl of Stagboro
	Ch. Lakeland Dawn	Rummey Stagboro
		Lakeland's Nymph

INT. CH. SPIRON

AKC No. 509949 Whelped April 19, 1916 Dog
Height - 26 inches Weight - 70 pounds Blue Belton
Owner: Eric Bergishagen, Birmingham, Michigan
Breeder: Herr Wilhelm Carlberg

```
        Dan
      Brush
        Windi
Ch. Pluto Horridoh
        Boy                     Ponto
      Ch. Hera Jaegerhus        Bella av Harndrup
        Dora av Jaegerhus       Ponto
                                Cora
        Ch. Noirhat Monk II     Blue Monk
      Ch: White Noirhat         Lize
        White Frigg             Odd
Tonny                           Beauty E
        Leader of Salop         Duke
      Sussan                    Belle
        Gitta                   Compton Ben
                                Gerda av Stavanger
```

254

CH. STURDY MAX

AKC No. 944324   Whelped October 12, 1932   Dog
Height - 25¾ inches   Weight - 65 pounds   Orange Belton
Owner: Dr. L. T. Rogers, Roger Dale Kennels, Stamford, Conn.
Breeder: Sturdy Dog Food Company

Int. Ch. Spiron
Spiron Jagersbo
Arbu Lala B
Rummey Stagboro
    Int. Ch. McConnell's Nori
Selkirk Snooksie
    Int. Ch. Selkirk Juliet

Mountain Top Tony
Ch. Pat II
    Ch. Lady Rowland
Rummey Girl of Stagboro
    Int. Ch. McConnell's Nori
Selkirk Snooksie
    Int. Ch. Selkirk Juliet

Ch. Pluto Horridoh
Tony
Quip Cadillac
Ch. Gloria's Peggy B.
Int. Ch. Racket's Rummey
Ch. Grayland Snowbird
Ch. Rowland's Pathfinder
Ch. Grayland Snowbird
Thorn Lake Tony
Cute of Playmore
Ch. Rowland's Credentials
Ch. Lady Rowland's Sensation
Int. Ch. Racket's Rummey
Ch. Grayland Snowbird
Ch. Rowland's Pathfinder
Ch. Grayland Snowbird

255

13

The Leading Sires
Dams of the
1950's, 1960's and 1970's

THE following compilation represents an unequalled contribution to the future of the English Setter. It is the labor of love of Mrs. Peter C. Polley and Mrs. John Dillon, former secretaries of the English Setter Association of America, and Judy Graef who is the principal revisor of this new edition.

They poured thousands of hours of painstaking effort into this list. It is priceless because it offers the breeders of today and tomorrow a **blueprint for breeding** unique in the annals of pure-bred dog lore. From it, any breeder may prepare and accumulate a chart of interesting combinations to research and plan his own breeding program.

To qualify for entry herein, the minimum number of champions produced was set at eight for sires and at four for dams.

256

The reader may extend this compilation by adding new champions as produced by the listed dogs. The champion progeny listed are up to date through the November 1980 issue of **Purebred Dogs—The American Kennel Gazette**, published monthly by the American Kennel Club, 51 Madison Avenue, New York, N. Y. Reference to later issues of this publication will extend and amplify this listing as long as the official AKC magazine publishes the names of new champions. These continuing studies can be a pleasurable, creative and rewarding activity.

The wise breeder will keep in mind that sheer numbers of champions produced are not necessarily the only criteria for considering a sire or dam a "great" producer. Frequency of matings, outstanding show records, accessibility to certain sires and dams, and other factors often have a bearing on the records. A sire or dam may produce several champions from only one litter, and never produce another champion; or it may "nick" successfully with one mate but not others. Even repeated matings of the same sire and dam may not duplicate the high quality of progeny born of the first mating; gene influences may vary from mating to mating of the same parents. The **quality** of champions, preferably from more than one mate, is the best measure of a stud or dam.

The reader is strongly advised to temper his statistical study with a sound knowledge of breeding principles, good judgment and the fruits of his own experience.

As an author and editor, the publisher of this book is painfully aware of the occasional error that inevitably creeps into any such complex compilation as follows. While every effort has been made to insure accuracy — even to the point of correcting an owner's information by reference to AKC records — the publisher will welcome notice of errors providing, however, that the correction has been verified by the AKC. The publisher hereby absolves the compilers from any errors which may appear. They have the most meticulous minds he has ever encountered. But several other minds — of editors, typesetters, proofreaders — have worked on the compilation since it was prepared.

(IMPORTANT!—The following abbreviations, designations and information should be reviewed by the reader for proper understanding of the compilation.)

Am. & Can. Ch. indicates dog has been awarded championship certificates by the American and Canadian Kennel Clubs.

If **Am.** does not appear before **Ch.**, dog is an American champion only. If **Can.** only appears before **Ch.**, dog is a Canadian champion only.

Ch. is omitted before names of American champion progeny of listed sires and dams, to save space and eliminate needless repetition.

Numbers following dogs' names, such as **S-454627**, represent registrations in the American or Canadian Kennel Clubs.

Pedigrees are given for the most outstanding sires and dams. In some cases, where pedigrees appear elsewhere for sires and dams of outstanding producers, no pedigrees are shown for the latter, and the reader may construct such pedigrees to the fifth generation. In fact, the reader will find the construction of pedigrees, from the data given herein, to be a fascinating exercise, all the more informative because he is doing it himself. The influence of such studs as Rummey Stagboro, Sturdy Max, Rock Falls Cavalier, Dean of Blue Bar, Rip of Blue Bar, Rock Falls Colonel, Rock Falls Racket, Ludar of Blue Bar, Margand Lord Baltimore, Ben-Dar's Winning Stride, Buff's Pride, Guys 'N Dolls Onassis, Guys 'N Dolls Shalimar Duke and Sir Kip of Manitou can be readily traced by analysis of the pedigrees in this and the preceding chapters. An absorbing game may be played by predicting the prepotent and winning lines of the future from the backgrounds of living champions listed under the leading sires and dams of the 1950's, 1960's and 1970's.

Note that pictures of some champion progeny appear after their respective sires or dams. In other cases, the progeny themselves have produced sufficient champions to warrant special listings of their own.

258

Rummey Stagboro
Ch. Lakeland's Yuba
Lakeland's Nymph
Sturdy Max II
   Ch. Sturdy Max
Ch. Dora of Maridor
   Ch. Lakeland's Dawn

   Ch. The Snark of Scyld
Ch. Silvermine Showman
Silvermine Story
Aspetuck's Red Sumac
   Can. & Am. Ch. Sig of Blue Bar
Ch. Suzette of Setterfield
   Trim of Blue Bar

Spiron Jagersbo
Selkirk Snooksie
Can. & Am. Ch. Rackets Rummey
Lakeland's Fascination
Rummey Stagboro
Rummey Girl of Stagboro
Rummey Stagboro
Lakeland's Nymph
Ch. Sturdy Max
Ch. Samantha of Scyld
Can. & Am. Ch. Maro of Maridor
Melanie of Silvermine
Kanandarque Rackets Boy
Inglehurst Matchless
Int. Ch. Pilot of Crombie of Happy Valley
Inglehurst Matchless

Dam of 7 Champions:

		Sired by:
Chatterwood Hot Toddy	S-696509	
Chatterwood on the Rocks	S-696508	
Chatterwood Lyric	S-824737	
Aspetuck's Golden Touch	S-696515	Ch. Rock Falls Racket
Chatterwood Marmalade	S-824735	
Aspetuck's Shadow	S-957593	
Aspetuck's Red Satin, C. D.	S-915777	

Ch. Aspetuck's Shadow

259

AM. & CAN. CH. BEN-DAR'S WINNING STRIDE, S-689327

Ch. Rip of Blue Bar
Ch. Sir Herbert of Kennelworth
Vivacious Doll of Vilmar
Can. & Am. Ch. Ludar of Blue Bar
Ch. Dean of Blue Bar
Ch. Manlove's Goldie
Ch. Manlove's Goldie of Stagboro

Ch. Commander Rickey
Ch. Sunny Jim
Prune's Own Patricia
Yorkley Wisp O' Heather
Tom of Merrie Sherwood
Ch. Southern Lady of Aragon
Orange Empress of Aragon

Ch. Dean of Blue Bar
Ina of Blue Bar
Banker of Fallondale
Delta of Larana
Ch. Mallhawk's Jeff
Ch. Lakeland's Peaches
Ch. Rummey Boy of Stagboro
Viola of Stagboro
Can. & Am. Ch. Maro of Maridor
Meadow's Penny
Ch. Dean of Blue Bar
Ch. Prune's Own Sunbeam
Rummey Stagboro
Lady Bell of Stagboro
Ch. Sturdy Max
Ch. Pride of Arthurlie

AM. & CAN. CH. BEN-DAR'S WINNING STRIDE, S-689327

Sire of 22 Champions:

		Out of:
Oaklynn's Top Brass	S-922031	Oaklynn's Lakeland Robby
Hidden Lane's Penelope	S-834221 ⎤	Notice-Me of Carylane
Hidden Lane's Winning Pride	S-834219 ⎦	
Am. & Can. Ch. Winifred of Cherry Lane	S-957334	Bunnydale's Daisy Belle
Hidden Lane's Bridget	SA-35451	Linda
Susie Chubb	S-893365	Dag Mar Little Lady
Can. Ch. Hidden Lane's Blue Symphony	409644	Notice-Me of Carylane
Windsor of Cherry Lane	S-967333	Bunnydale's Daisy Belle
Hidden Lane's Sindy-Lou	S-943135	Ch. Lady Marco
Wallis of Cherry Lane	S-957332	Bunnydale's Daisy Belle
End O' Maine White Rock	SA-35816	Notice-Me of Carylane
Anne of Sherwood	SA-101993	Ch. Manlove's Anna Lee
Cynthia Darbella	S-967392	Linda
Goldie of Meadboro	SA-83374	Hasty Miss of Meadboro
Chandelle's Folly	S-996226	Ch. Parpoint Precarious
Flirtation of Meadboro	SA-83375	Hasty Miss of Meadboro
Hidden Lane's Barnstormer	SA-117113	Enid of Cherry Lane
Hidden Lane's Mark Me	SA-122414	Enid of Cherry Lane
Saber of Mardego	SA-976776	Ch. Lady Marco
Buff's Pride	SA-68293	Bunnydale's Daisy Belle
Brandy of Bloomfield	SA-65743	Bambi of Bloomfield
James of Cherry Lane	SA-312329	Ch. Pretty Maid of Cherry Lane

Am. & Can. Ch. Winifred of Cherry Lane

CH. BLUE DIAMOND MIST

AKC No. SA-234932   Whelped September, 1963   Bitch
Height - 24 inches   Weight - 55 pounds   Blue Belton
Owner: Dr. R. S. Freeman, Salina, Ks.
Breeder: Gordon M. Parham

Kirket Kerryboy	Sh. Ch. Ripleygae Mallory
Ernford Kingfisher	Kirket Karmina
Ch. Ernford Evening Flight	Ernford Easter Parade
Ch. Ernford Oriole	Teal of Yarsyde
Grouse of Capard	Ir. Ch. Peter of Beechmount
Ch. Ernford Cilldapa Felicity	Nan of Beechmount
Minx of Medeshamstede	Rombalds Furious
	Blue Belle
Ch. Ludar of Blue Bar	Ch. Sir Herbert of Kennelworth
Ch. Darby of Carylane	Ch. Manlove's Goldie
Ch. Silvermine Chambray	Ch. The Snark of Scyld
Ch. Parpoint Precarious	Silvermine Wanita
Int. Ch. Silvermine Wagabond	Ch. Rhett Butler of Silvermine
Ch. Silvermine Matchless	Keyfield Judy
Ch. Silvermine Swift	Ch. The Snark of Scyld
	Silvermine Story

262

CH. BLUE DIAMOND MIST

Dam of 10 Champions:

		Sired by:
Blue Diamond's Benedictine	SA-545218	
Blue Diamond's Beau Geste	SA-545215	
Blue Diamond's Babette By Law	SA-556486	Ch. Bucket of Bolts by Law
Blue Diamond's Brandy And Soda	SA-545219	
Blue Diamond's Bit O'Tarragon	SA-560513	
Blue Diamond's Abner Yokum	SA-344912	
Blue Diamond's Abbiegirl, C. D.	SA-344913	Ch. Dover's Blue Sky
Blue Diamond's Alice Blue Gown	SA-344915	
Blue Diamond's Drambuie	SA-772831	Ch. Hiddenlane's Merry Max
Blue Diamond's Digby	SA-344915	

CH. BRIARPATCH OF BRYN MAWR

AKC No. SA-724673   Whelped October 14, 1968   Dog
Height - 26 inches   Weight - 70 pounds   Tricolor
Owner: Ralph & Mary Wendels. Fond du Lac, Wi.
Breeder: Ralph & Mary Wendels   OFA # ES-71

263

Winberts' Blue Moon
Heldons' Black Knight Winbert
Ch. Sue-Lin's Golden Spur
Heldons' Sturdy Knight
Oak Lynn's Beau Geste
Heldons' Debutante of Oak Lynn
Oak Lynn's Lady Wendy

Diamondale's Delight
Winberts' Sharon
Ch. Ben-Dar's Carbon Copy
Sue-Lin's Shooting Star
Ch. Oak Lynn's Top Brass
Stridette of Mardego
Oak Lynn's Jet Pilot
Pleasant Point's Belle

Phantom Brooks' Briar
Phantom Brooks' Clarence
Phantom Brooks' Nell Gwynn
Idlenot's Dancers' Daughter
Ch. Margand Man About Town
Idlenot's Gypsy
Marre's Blue Feather

Phantom Brooks' Cholmondley
Ch. Phantom Brooks' Popcorn
Ch. Phantom Brooks' Thunderbolt
Phantom Brooks' Tattersal
Ch. Ernford Oriole
Ch. Margand Mary Jane
Luke's Royal Count
Luke's Lady Luck

Sire of 21 Champions:

		Out of:
Patchwork of Bryn Mawr	SB-893378	
Mcmichael Misty Sunset	SB-937060	Win-Mawr of Bryn Mawr
The Stonehenge of Bryn Mawr	SB-958665	
Redrah Sockeye of Hillock	SA-960237	
Abramson's Blue Patch	SB-105614	Ch. Margand Artemis
Redrah's Prince	SA-933121	
Skagerrak's Young Mortimer	SB-682443	
Skagerrak's Crackerjack	SB-673450	Ch. Manlove's Leka
Solheim's Starlet of Merimac	SB-845928	
Solheim's Diana of Merimac	SB-771320	Ch. Solheim Razzle Berry
Happyday's Blazon Banyon	SB-347418	
Happyday's Candy Man Can	SB-312701	Rossmoor's Lady Gwendolyn
Happyday's Tapestry	SB-325456	
Garson's Extra Special 'N Orange	SB-636751	
Garson's Extra Special	SB-433315	Ch. Excalibur's Exctacy Of Garson
Sunstone's Sturdy Patch	SC-79450	Fantail's Copper Tjanting
Redrah's Feathered Fleck	SB-344133	Ch. Redrah's Gay Feather
Abbyroad My Sunshine	SC-596307	Ch. Penmaen Here Comes The Sun
Esquire's Foxy Lady	SB-908918	Ch. Esquire's Kalico Kid
Prince Charles of Devonshire	SB-811979	Zuercher's Village Gossip
Redrah's Rachel Ann of Engl-I	SC-409061	Ch. Redrah's Bluebonnet

CH. BUFF'S PRIDE

AKC No. SA-68293   Whelped July 18, 1958   Dog
Owner: Mrs. Sydney J. Smith   Orange Belton
Breeder: Dorothy Reiter

	Ch. Rip of Blue Bar
Ch. Sir Herbert of Kennelworth	Vivacious Doll of Vilmar
Ch. Ludar of Blue Bar	Ch. Dean of Blue Bar
Manlove's Goldie	Ch. Manlove's Goldie of Stagboro
Ch. Ben-Dar's Winning Stride	Ch. Commander Rickey
Ch. Sunny Jim	Prune's Own Patricia
Yorkley Wisp O'Heather	Tom of Merrie Sherwood
Ch. Southern Lady of Aragon	Orange Empress of Aragon
	Ch. Dean of Blue Bar
Ch. Rip of Blue Bar	Ina of Blue Bar
Ch. Dill of Blue Bar	Banker of Fallondale
Schoolgirl Sue of Havertown	Belle's Queen
Bunnydale's Daisy Belle	Rummey II Stagboro
Ch. Rummy Sam of Stagboro	Kate of Stagboro
Martie of Blue Bar	Ch. Dean of Blue Bar
Kanandarque Goldie	Ch. Gem of Blue Bar

Sire of 12 Champions: **Out of:**

Vicar of Cherry Lane	SA-289885	⎤
Viscount of Cherry Lane	SA-289884	
Can. & Am. Ch. Viking of Cherry Lane	SA-289882	Enid of Cherry Lane
Can. & Am. Ch. Browning of Cherry Lane	SA-351094	
Bridget of Cherry Lane	SA-351094	⎦
Yankee Clipper of Makepeace	SA-397049	⎤
Calumet of Makepeace	SA-511775	Valley Run Dinah's Damoselle
Makepeace Thunder of Delta	SA-413619	⎦
Bayonet Point Preakness	SA-272218	⎤ Heljax Black Eyed Susan
Heljax Just Call Me Mister	SA-332431	⎦
Valley Run's Beau Barbu	SA-369688	Ch. Valley Run Dixie Barbu
Manlove's All American	SA-435974	Ch. Manlove's Cover Girl

Ch. Calumet of Makepeace   265

CH. CALUMET OF MAKEPEACE

AKC No. SA-511775   Whelped August 30, 1967   Bitch
Height - 24 inches   Weight - 52 pounds   Orange Belton
Owner: Janet E. Miner, Ashford, Ct.
Breeder: Gladys T. Nichol

     Ch.Ludar of Blue Bar
   Ch. Ben-Dar's Winning Stride
     Yorkley Wisp O'Heather
Ch. Buff's Pride
     Ch. Dill of Blue Bar
   Bunnydales Daisy Belle
     Martie of Blue Bar

     Ch. English Accent of Valley Run
   Ch. Merry Rover of Valley Run
     Wamley's Merry Minx
Valley Run Dinah's Damoselle
     Ch. Pirate of Polperro
   Ch. Valley Run Dinah-Mite
     Ch. Panthorn Valley Run
     Samantha

Ch. Sir Herbert of Kennelworth
Ch. Manlove's Goldie
Ch. Sunny Jim
Ch. Southern Lady of Aragon
Ch. Rip of Blue Bar
Schoolgirl Sue of Havertown
Ch. Rummey Sam of Stagboro
Kanandarque Goldie
Ch. Rock Falls Racket
Ch. Starbright of Valley Run
Ch. Mike of Meadboro
Cinderella of Oak Valley
Ch. Ernford Highflier
Ch. Betsworth Gold Flake
Silvermine Skychief
Ch. Panthorn Gold of Pleasure

Dam of 6 Champions: **Out of:**

Penuche of Meadowset	SB-787454 ⌉	
Sir Woody of Meadowset	SB-266991	
Ms Plantagenet of Meadowset	SB-298046	Ch. Clariho Major of Meadowset
Wesmar Meadowset's Top Son of B	SB-814709 ⌋	
Meadowset's Touch of Class	SB-523707	Ch. Clariho Kristofer of Critt-Du
Meadowset's Smooth Sailing	SA-961250	Ch. Clariho Rough Rider

266   Ch. Canberra's Carbon Copy

CH. CANBERRA'S CARBON COPY

AKC No. SA-513171   Whelped June 24, 1967   Bitch
Height - 25 inches   Tricolor
Breeder-Owner: Dr. & Mrs. George M. Rosen, Plantation, Fl.

      Ch. Rock Falls Racket   Ch. Rock Falls Cavalier
    Ch. Aspetuck's Shadow   Ch. Rock Falls Belle
      Ch. Aspetuck's Diana   Sturdy Max II
Ch. Canberra Blue Shadow   Aspetuck's Red Sumac
      Ch. The Rock of Stone Gables   Ch. Mike of Meadboro
    Blue Mist of Stone Gables   Ch. Vivacious Sally of Vilmar
      Blue Bess   Ch. Raskalus Raff of Stone Gables
            Ch. Prize Par-Sal of Stone Gables

      Ch. Rock Falls Racket   Ch. Rock Falls Cavalier
    Ch. Aspetuck's Shadow   Ch. Rock Falls Belle
      Ch. Aspetuck's Diana   Sturdy Max II
Ch. Canberra's Legend   Aspetuck's Red Sumac
      Ch. Skidby's Sturdy Tyke   Ch. Ben-Dar's Advance Notice
    Gilroy's Dixie   Ch. Hillsdale Susan
      Ch. Charm of Stone Gables   Ch. Raskalus Raff of Stone Gables
            Ch. Prize Par-Sal of Stone Gables

Dam of 6 Champions: **Sired by:**

Canberra's Different Drummer	SB-99229 ⎤	
Canberra's Overlord II	SB-305064 ⎥	
Canberra's Triple Spectrum	SB-97939 ⎥	Ch. Clariho Checkmate of Critt-Du
Storm Haven's Canberra Saga	SB-402403 ⎥	
Canberra Pride of Morningstar	SB-159325 ⎦	
Canberra's Flagmaster	SA-870946	Ch. The Hallmark of Stone Gables

Ch. Chandelle's Anchor Man, SA-95127

CH. CHANDELLE'S ANCHOR MAN

AKC No. SA-95127   Whelped June 7, 1961   Dog
Height - 26 inches   Weight - 70 pounds   Orange Belton
Owner: Joseph A. Kaziny, Minneapolis, Mn.
Breeder: Warren H. Brewbaker

	Margand El Capitan	Ch. Buzz of Haon
Ch. Margand Lord Calvert		Duchess Blue Artemis
	Margand Princess Anne	Ch. Elshar Jake
Ch. Margand Lord Baltimore		Ch. Talphanz Lady Elizabeth
	Ch. Rock Falls Colonel	Ch. Rock Falls Cavalier
Ch. Phantom Brooks' Petticoat		Ch. Rock Falls Belle
	Ch. Phantom Brooks' Deductible	Ch. Ken of Blue Bar
		Ch. Babe of Blue Bar II
	Ch. Rock Falls Colonel	Ch. Rock Falls Cavalier
Ch. Rock Falls Lieutenant		Ch. Rock Falls Belle
	Jacklin O'Rackets	Ch. Jack O'Rackets
Ch. Chandelle Lady		Tyronne Farm Belle
	Rugged Boy	Ch. Mike of Meadboro
Duchess Rugged Honey		Ch. Gloria
	Rubin's Honey Maid	Ch. Sambeauz Rex
		Ch. Betty Grable of Aragon

Sire of 30 Champions: **Out of:**

Black Oak's Brett of Tel-Mo	SA-313786	⎤
Excalibur's Anchors Aweigh	SA-395307	
Gal's Gay Debut of Tel-Mo	SA-542015	Ch. Lynda's Melynda of Tel-Mo, C. D.
Tel-Mo's Lady Debora	SA-348217	
Tel-Mo's Groovy Gidget	SA-590233	⎦
Popkin's Sweet Polly Pure Bred	SA-626370	⎤
Sir James Dickens	SA-626368	
Humble Lovable Shoe Shine Boy	SA-626367	Castleroc Duchess of Popkins
Popkin's Little Nipper	SA-626369	⎦
Sukarla's Samantha Sue	SA-838051	⎤
Sukarla's Sandpiper	SA-802859	Ch. Sukarla's Serendipity
Sukarla's Sorceress	SA-815481	⎦
Chandelle's City Slicker	SA-391403	⎤
Chandelle's Charmin	SA-391405	Ch. Chandelle Lady
Chandelle's Chambray	SA-391404	⎦
Morgental's Arnica	SA-950180	⎤
Morgental's Absinthe	SA-926196	Ch. Gemody's Gidget Goes Hawaiian
Shallegan's Bit O'Honey	SA-615997	⎤
Shallegan's Headmaster	SA-757952	Ch. Parpoint Pretti-Tri
Gypsy Lane's Big Joe	SA-248247	⎤
Redstone's Gypsy Lane Gerry	SA-243524	Zip of Hi-Flight
Excalibrette of Gypsy Lane	SA-221694	⎦
Jubilee's Maggie Mae	SB-67109	Margand Black Opal
Excalibur's Sparkler	SA-910808	Raybar's Solitaire
Excalibur's Shady Lady	SA-392253	Ch. Excalibrette of Gypsy Lane
Hideaway's Miss Moneypenny	SA-699053	Alderlake Pepagena
Sudrok's Honey of Pine Park	SA-379538	Karamel of Berriwood
Pollyanna's Penelope	SA-255200	Ch. Lieutenant's Pollyanna
Plum Creek's Hot Toddy	SA-457453	Ch. Cecily of High Moon
Michigan Slim By Law	SA-433004	Ch. Hidden Lane's Scheherazade

268

CH. CHANDELLE'S FIRST LOVE

AKC No. SB-099232   Whelped March 20, 1972   Bitch
Height - 24 inches   Weight - 52 pounds   Orange Belton
Owner: John M. & Barbara M. Kulstad, Sturgeon Lake, Mn.
Breeder: Vera L. German

	Ch. Margand Lord Calvert
Ch. Margand Lord Baltimore	Ch. Phantom Brooks Petticoat
Ch. Chandelle's Anchor Man	Ch. Rock Falls Lieutenant
Ch. Chandelle Lady	Duchess Rugged Honey
Ch. Chandelle's City Slicker	Am/Can/Cuban Ch. Rock Falls Colonel
Ch. Rock Falls Lieutenant	Jacklin O'Rackets
Ch. Chandelle Lady	Rugged Boy
Duchess Rugged Honey	Rubins Honey Maid
	Am/Can Ch. Ben-Dar's Winning Stride
Ch. Hiddenlane's Mark Me	Enid of Cherry Lane
Ch. Harmony Lane Marquis	Am/Can Ch. Ben-Dar's Carbon Copy
Am/Can Ch. Camelot Candace	Ch. Cynthia Darbella
Thistledown's Lady Amber	Ch. Margand Lord Baltimore
Ch. Chandelle's Anchor Man	Ch. Chandelle Lady
Excalibur Lady Luck	Ch. Chandelle's Anchor Man
Ch. Excalibrette of Gypsy Lane	Zip of High Flight

Dam of 7 Champions: Sired by:

Maraspelle Lady of Belton Bay	SC-168444	
Georgia Luv of Belton Bay	SC-206936	
Barnstormer of Belton Bay	SB-861402	
Beau Brummel of Belton Bay	SB-709785	Ch. Sukarla's Sandpiper
Chandelle's Great Day	SB-520517	
Mr. Chips of Belton Bay	SB-543020	
Luv's Niklgrab'R of Belton Bay	SC-438364	

CH. CHANDELLE LADY

AKC No. S-925916   Whelped March 13, 1958   Bitch
Height - 25½ inches   Weight - 64 pounds   Orange Belton
Owner: Warren H. Brewbaker, Minnetonka, Mn.
Breeder: Ethel Hawkins

Ch. Rock Falls Cavalier   Ch. Grayland Racket's Boy
Am/Can/Cuban Ch. Rock Falls Colonel   Ch. Linda Lou of Blue Bar
Ch. Rock Falls Belle   Ch. Grayland Racket's Boy
Ch. Rock Falls Lieutenant   Nocturne of Crowlcroft
Ch. Jack O'Rackets   Ch. Grayland Racket's Boy
Jacklin O' Rackets   Ch. Linda Lou of Blue Bar
Tyronne Farm Belle   Ch. Cedric of Delwed
     Blondie Bell

Ch. Mike of Meadboro   Thelan Sir Rocklyn
Rugged Boy   Lady McBeth
Ch. Gloria   Ch. Captain Jenks
Duchess Rugged Honey   My True Blue
Ch. Sambeaux Rik   Ch. Prunes Own Yukon
Rubin's Honey Maid   Dusk of Devon
Ch. Betty Grable of Aragon   Ch. Prunes Own Yukon
     Prunes Own New Moon

Dam of 11 Champions: **Sired by:**

Chandelle's Anchor Man	SA-95127	
Chandelle's Air Mail, C.D.	SA-95126	Ch. Margand Lord Baltimore
Chandelle's Allspice	SA-95130	
Chandelle's Littlest Angel	SA-95128	
Chandelle's Bambi	SA-250902	
Chandelle's Bittersweet	SA-250905	Ch. Margand Lord Baltimore
Chandelle's Billet Doux	SA-250904	
Chandelle's Butterscotch	SA-250903	
Chandelle's City Slicker	SA-391403	
Chandelle's Charmin	SA-391405	Ch. Chandelle's Anchor Man
Chandelle's Chambray	SA-391404	

CH. CLARIHO BLUE HORIZON

AKC No. SL-271545   Whelped August 24, 1967   Bitch
Owner: Mrs. Sheila Stotyn, Calgary, Alberta   Blue Belton
Breeder: Alice Fay Grannon

Can. Ch. Wamlay Mike Chism	Int. Ch. Mike of Meadboro
Ch. Skidby's Bosun of Stone Gables	Chism's Queenie
Royal Blue of Stone Gables	Ch. Raskalus Raff of Stone Gables
Ch. Sir Kip of Manitou	Tower Hill To And Again
Ch. Cinnabar of High-Tor	Sycamore Lodge Lord
High-Tors Spicy Lady	Sycamore Lodge Champagne
Blue Mountain Plain Jane	Ch. Silvermine Messenger
	Mariners Blue Imp
	Int. Ch. Mike of Meadboro
Can. Ch. Wamlay Mike Chism	Chism's Queenie
Ch. Skidby's Bosun of Stone Gables	Ch. Raskalus Raff of Stone Gables
Royal Blue of Stone Gables	Tower Hill To And Again
Druid's Brew of Stone Gables	Ch. Raskalus Raff of Stone Gables
Gunner of Stone Gables	Ch. Wamlay Lollypop
Blue Lisa of Stone Gables	Ch. Raskalus Raff of Stone Gables
My Mimi of Stone Gables	Rock's Ann of Stone Gables

Dam of 6 Champions: **Sired by:**

Arundel's Orange Fire	SA-813874	
Arundel's Mighty Warrior	SC-38508	
Arundel's Blue Barron	SB-264459	Ch. Tom Terrific of Stone Gables
Arundel's Duke of Norfolk	SB-214400	
Arundel's Highwayman of B	SB-388901	
Westward Ho of Stone Gables	SA-813874	Ch. Prince of Deerfield

271

CH. CLARIHO CHECKMATE OF CRITT-DU

AKC No. SA-816573   Whelped October 2, 1969   Dog
Owner: Mrs. R.S. Howe & Mrs. T.C. Slosson, Jr., Chester, N.J.   Orange Belton
Breeder: Philip Crittenden & Joan Duda   OFA # ES-109

Ch. Skidby's Sturdy Tyke	Ch. Ben-Dar's Advance Notice
Am/Can. Ch. Hillsdale Sentinel	Ch. Hillsdale Susan
Ch. Hillsdale Sparkle	Am/Can. Ch. Ludar of Blue Bar
Ch. Guys 'N Dolls Shalimar Duke	Can. Ch: Pollyanna
Ch. Sir Guy of Ellendale	Ch. Manlove of Ellendale
Ch. Guys 'N Dolls Bridget O'Shea, C.D.	Ch. Manlove's Mona
Lady Jill of Ellendale	Ch. Skyline of Stone Gables
	Ch. Manlove's Mona
Ch. The Rock of Stone Gables	Ch. Mike of Meadboro
Ch. Prince of Deerfield	Ch. Vivacious Sally of Vilmar
Ch. Frosty of Stone Gables	Ch. Raskalus Raff of Stone Gables
Ch. Clariho Pell of Stone Gables	Tower Hill To and Again
Ch. The Rock of Stone Gables	Ch. Mike of Meadboro
Candy of Clariho	Ch. Vivacious Sally of Vilmar
High-Tors Spicy Lady	Ch. Cinnabar of High-Tor
	Blue Mountain Plain Jane

Sire of 25 Champions: **Out of:**

Canberra Pride O'Morningstar	SB-159325 ⌐	
Canberra Different Drummer	SB-99229	
Canberra's Overlord II	SB-305064	Ch. Canberra Carbon Copy
Canberra's Triple Spectrum	SB-97939	
Storm Haven's Canberra Saga	SB-402403 ⌐	
Rossmoor's Patent Pending	SB-816849 ⌐	
Rossmoor's Some Pumpkin	SB-770542	
Rossmoor's Lovebug	SB-732966	Ch. Rossmoor's Captivatin Carrie
Rossmoor's Razzamatazz	SB-727555 ⌐	

272

Blue Chip of Stone Gables	SB-264269 ⎤	
My She Was Coy of Stone Gables	SB-264275 ⎬	Flirtations of Stone Gables
Stone Gables Miss Elodie	SB-264273 ⎦	
Clariho Blue Admiral	SC-33331 ⎤	
Clariho Johnny Come Lately	SB-597966 ⎦	Clariho My Gal's A Corker
Seafield's Sandcastle	SB-711789 ⎤	
Seafield's Catamaran of Teplr	SB-327310 ⎦	Ch. Stone Gables Seafield Romany
Clariho Seafield's Comeabout	SB-354724	Ch. Clariho Moonlight Cocktail
Clariho Royal Flush	SB-879898	Clariho Paprika
Sunstorm of Kimba	SB-891288	Ch. Brinor Mayfair Miss
Guyline's Artemis of Cymbria	SB-110134	Guyline's Jet Setter
Clariho Cornelian George	SB-882631	Ch. Clariho Moonlight Melanie
Shelly of Lansdowne	SB-816849	Ch. Elizabeth of Lansdowne
Kenrobs Piccadilly of Lazy F	SC-080572	Ch. Lazy F Two For The Show
Clariho Basil of Stillwood	SC-303844	Manlove's Ginger
Tristan of Spring Hill	SC-083872	Panda Splendens

CH. CLARIHO CONVERSATION PIECE, SA-872175

(Ch. Sir Kip of Manitou x Ch. Lemon Delight of Carowa)

Dam of 7 Champions: **Sired by:**

Fern Rocks Jandal's Claribel	SB-639200 ⎤	
Fern Rocks First Edition	SB-379901 ⎥	
Fern Rocks Ross Charlin	SB-630958 ⎬	Ch. Highland's Whip of Penmaen
Fern Rocks Whipper Snapper	SB-557978 ⎦	
Fern Rocks Orangeade	SB-927571 ⎤	
Fern Rocks Princess Sherry	SB-742073 ⎥	Penmaen Peter
Fern Rocks Music Man	SB-948814 ⎦	

Am. Can. Ch. Clariho Kristofer of Critt-Du

273

AM. CAN CH. CLARIHO KRISTOFER OF CRITT-DU

AKC No. SA-731148   Whelped October 2, 1969   Dog
Owner: Vicki Darling Wilder   Orange Roan
Breeder: Philip Crittenden & Joan Duda   OFA # ES-72

(Pedigree same as litter mate, Ch. Clariho Checkmate of Critt-Du)

Sire of 16 Champions: **Out of:**

Seafield Tickle My Fancy	SB-695746 ⎤	
Seafield's Virginia Storm	SB-597986 ⎟	Ch. Stone Gables Seafield Romany
Seafield's Holiday Mystique	SB-701975 ⎦	
Clariho Jubal Troop	SB-255088 ⎤	
Clariho Warpaint	SB-397396 ⎟	Clariho Moonlight Magic
Clariho Knight Rider	SB-252483 ⎦	
Wildpalm's Sir Lancelot	SB-830782 ⎤	Clariho Luck Be A Lady
Wildpalm's Sweet Gypsy Rose	SB-855201 ⎦	
Wileire Taylor Made	SC-257135	Ch. Guys'N Dolls Elizabeth Taylor
Maidstone's Brookview Sprite	SB-741417	Ch. Clariho Social Butterfly
Belset Cassanova	SB-823514	Ch. Amberil Wish of Lonesome Lane
Wildpalm's Free Spirit	SC-150234	Ch. Clariho Sweet Sue
Meadowset's Touch of Class	SB-523707	Ch. Calumet of Makepeace
Lomar's Tropical Son	SB-251526	Ch. Clariho Brandy Belle
Clariho The Good Life	SB-530723	Andover's Moonlight Mirage
Clariho Rough 'N Ready	SB-19401	Ch. Clariho Annie Laurie

274

CH. CLARIHO MAJOR OF MEADOWSET

AKC No. SA-866405   Whelped May 25, 1970   Dog
Height - 25½ inches   Orange Belton
Owner: Janet Miner, Ashford, Ct.
Breeder: Sally Howe & Jane Slosson

Can. Ch. Wamlay's Mike Chism
Ch. Skidby's Bosun of Stone Gables
Royal Blue of Stone Gables
Am/Bda/Can. Ch. Sir Kip of Manitou
Ch. Cinnebar of High-Tor
High-Tor's Spicy Lady
Blue Mountain Plain Jane

Ch. Skidby's Bosun of Stone Gables
Am/Bda/Can. Ch. Sir Kip of Manitou
High-Tor's Spicy Lady
Ch. Clariho Bit O'Candy
Ch. Prince of Deerfield
Clariho Piper of Stone Gables
Candy of Clariho

Ch. Mike of Meadboro
Chism's Queenie
Ch. Raskalus Raff of Stone Gables
Tower Hill To and Again
Sycamore Lodge Lord Geoffrey
Sycamore Lodge Champagne
Ch. Silvermine's Messenger
Mariner's Blue Imp
Can. Ch. Wamlay's Mike Chism
Royal Blue of Stone Gables
Ch. Cinnabar of High-Tor
Blue Mountain Plain Jane
Ch. The Rock of Stone Gables
Ch. Frosty of Stone Gables
Ch. The Rock of Stone Gables
High-Tor's Spicy Lady

Sire of 19 Champions:

Out of:

Penuche of Meadowset	SB-787454	
Sir Woody of Meadowset	SB-266991	
Ms Plantagenet of Meadowset	SB-298046	Ch. Calumet of Makepeace
Wesmar Meadowset's Top Son of B	SB-814709	
Fairhaven Emmie of Goldenlea	SC-253251	
Goldenlea Sir Adam Meadowset	SB-293625	
Anastasia of Goldenlea	SB-198737	Meadowset Gay Melodie Belle
Meadowset's Rhapsody In Blue	SB-855804	
Meadowset's Dauntless	SB-854841	Ch. Meadowset Blue Velvet

Clariho Spinnaker	SB-970464	⎤ Ch. Clariho Caper of Critt-Du
Clariho Happy Go Lucky	SB-959112	⎦
Andover's Silver Shadow	SB-739672	⎤ Clariho Garnet Hills Am I Blue
Andover's Satin Doll	SB-73967	⎦
Terry's Tonto of Whitehouse	SB-641022	⎤ Patience of Whitehouse
Windem's Sarad of Whitehouse	SB-652857	⎦
Rocky Ridge Play It Again Sam	SB-995969	Ch. Clariho Lady Godiva
Daw Anka's Danny Boy	SB-806264	Daw Anka's Devil's Doin's
Whitehouse Mr. Kissinger	SB-542964	Wisdom of Whitehouse
Tamara Run's Priscilla	SB-796160	Ch. Meadowset Patience of Tamara

CH. CLARIHO MOONRAKER

AKC No. SA-565238   Whelped August 3, 1968   Dog
Owner: Mrs. Richard Howe & Mrs. Fred Valtin   Orange Belton
Breeder: Sally M. Howe & Jane C. Slosson   OFA # ES-36

Can. Ch. Wamlay's Mike Chism
Ch. Skidby's Bosun of Stone Gables
Royal Blue of Stone Gables
Am/Bda/Can. Ch. Sir Kip of Manitou
Ch. Cinnabar of High-Tor
High-Tors Spicy Lady
Blue Mountain Plain Jane

Ch. Mike of Meadboro
Ch. Robin Boy of Stone Gables
Ch. Prize Par-Sal of Stone Gables
Clariho's Once In A Blue Moon
Ch. The Rock of Stone Gables
Navy Blue of Stone Gables
Blue Bess

Ch. Mike of Meadboro
Chism's Queenie
Ch. Raskalus Raff of Stone Gables
Tower Hill To and Again
Sycamore Lodge Lord Geoffrey
Sycamore Lodge Champagne
Ch. Silvermine's Messenger
Mariner's Blue Imp
Thelan Sir Rocklyn
Lady McBeth
Ch. Prunes Own Parade
Ch. Vivacious Sally of Vilmar
Ch. Mike of Meadboro
Ch. Vivacious Sally of Vilmar
Ch. Raskalus Raff of Stone Gables
Ch. Prize Par-Sal of Stone Gables

CH. CLARIHO MOONRAKER

Sire of 14 Champions: **Out of:**

Clariho Mame of Garnet Hill	SB-351493 ⌉	
Clariho Orbit of Garnet Hill	SB-386701	Ch. Dolce
Garnet Hills Miss Solitaire	SB-675329 ⌋	
Madrigal's Madame Butterfly	SB-817563 ⌉	Madrigal's Scarborough Fair
Madrigal's Man of La Mancha	SB-483974 ⌋	
Clariho Moonlight Melanie	SB-145427 ⌉	Ch. Clariho Bit of Candy
Clariho Moonrocket	SB-176877 ⌋	
Geronimo's Caleb	SB-558387	Canterfield's Lady McDuff
Clariho Sugar Moon	SB-208086	Ch. Clariho Candy Bar
Clariho's Auld Sod Scirocco	SB-712050	Somerset Clariho Sassafras
Lorien's Sarah of Auld Sod	SB-895652	Ch. Lorien's Lady Arwen
Friar Tuck's Mark of Meadowset	SB-113018	Ch. Clariho Souvenir
Clariho Comfort of Valley Run	SB-288130	Ch. Pinney Paige of Valley Run
Seafield's Tidal Wave	SB-190258	Ch. Stone Gables Seafield Romany

CLARIHO PELL OF STONE GABLES, SA-292347

(Ch. Prince of Deerfield x Candy of Clariho)

Dam of 6 Champions: **Sired by:**

Surrey's Charm of Stone Gables	SA-563193 ⌉	
Stone Gables's Seafield Romany	SA-537798	Ch. Sir Kip of Manitou
Ye Country Boy of Stone Gables	SA-605377 ⌋	
Clariho Checkmate of Critt-Du	SA-816573 ⌉	
Clariho Kristofer of Critt-Du	SA-731138	Ch. Guys 'N Dolls Shalimar Duke
Clariho Caper of Critt-Du	SA-738515 ⌋	

CLARIHO PIPER OF STONE GABLES, SA-296427

(Ch. Prince of Deerfield x Candy of Clariho)

Dam of 8 Champions: **Sired by:**

Clariho Luck Be A Lady	SA-781259 ⌉	
Clariho Zuercher Aristocrat	SA-781675	
Clariho Candy Bar	SA-393185	
Clariho Encore of Critt-Du	SA-806253	Ch. Sir Kip of Manitou
Clariho Bit O'Candy	SA-410611	
Clariho Rough Rider	SA-402848	
Tom Terrific of Stone Gables	SA-411562	
The Hallmark of Stone Gables	SA-411561 ⌋	

CH. CLARIHO ROUGH RIDER

AKC No. SA-402848   Whelped October 25, 1965   Dog
Owner: Mrs. R.S. Howe & Mrs. Fred Valtin, Sanibel Island, Fl.   Orange Belton
Breeder: Sally M. Howe & Jane C. Slosson   OFA # ES-40

	Can. Ch. Wamlay's Mike Chism	Ch. Mike of Meadboro
Ch. Skidby's Bosun of Stone Gables	Chisms Queenie
Royal Blue of Stone Gables	Ch. Raskalus Raff of Stone Gables
Am/Can/Bda. Ch. Sir Kip of Manitou	Tower Hill To and Again
Ch. Cinnabar of High-Tor	Sycamor Lodge Lord Geoffrey
High-Tors Spicy Lady	Sycamore Lodge Champagne
Blue Mountain Plain Jane	Ch. Silvermine Messenger
	Mariners Blue Imp

Ch. The Rock of Stone Gables   Ch. Mike of Meadboro
Ch. Prince of Deerfield   Ch. Vivacious Sally of Vilmar
Ch. Frosty of Stone Gables   Ch. Raskalus Raff of Stone Gables
Clariho Piper of Stone Gables   Tower Hill To and Again
Ch. The Rock of Stone Gables   Ch. Mike of Meadboro
Candy of Clariho   Ch. Vivacious Sally of Vilmar
High-Tors Spicy Lady   Ch. Cinnabar of High-Tor
  Blue Mountain Plain Jane

Sire of 16 Champions: **Out of:**

Valley Run's Barrymore	SB-15442	
Clariho Easy Rider	SA-924988	Ch. Pinney Paige of Valley Run
Clariho Whimsy of Valley Run	SB-19684	
Clariho Annie Laurie	SA-520261	
Clariho Conflict	SA-520261	Meadowset's Caprice
Clariho Souvenir	SA-520264	
Yankee Pacesetter	SA-623229	
Leelynn's Jetsetter	SA-520361	Ch. Leelynn's Pacesetter
Leelynn's Lancer of Erinway	SA-895866	

Clariho Rough Rider (continued)

Brinor's Mayfair Miss	SA-915114	Ch. Clariho Treble Chance
Clariho Triumph	SA-949414	
Clariho Perhaps	SA-877165	Ch. Clariho Precisely
Meadowset's Smooth Sailing	SA-961250	Ch. Calumet of Makepeace
Wesley Molly Coddle	SA-634912	Ch. Blessed of Lonesome Lane
Heatherhope Gussy Dancer	SA-729932	Clariho April Dancer
Heldon's Purdy Corrie, C. D.	SA-542596	Jinny Pepper

CH. CLARIHO WARPAINT, SB-397396

(Ch. Clariho Kristofer of Critt-Du x Clariho Moonlight Magic)

Sire of 10 Champions:		**Out of:**

Seamrog Gold Streak	SC-52289	
Gold Rush Gold Miner Blues	SC-46323	Ch. Guyline's Artemis of Cymbria
Gold Rush Gold Digger Blues	SC-046322	
Pickwick Canis Major	SB-847524	
Pickwick Cafe Au Lait	SB-847523	Ch. Pickwick Flying Nun
Windem's Noble Chieftain	SB-905029	Wisdom of Whitehouse, C.D.
Tra-Bon's Love of Penfield	SC-239233	Ch. Tra-Bon's Orange Sunshine
Seafield's Moontide	SB-910808	Ch. Clariho Perhaps
Lady Jennifer B of Torcon	SB-593369	Daw-Anka's Bit O'Holly
Lorien's Blue Sapphire	SB-861855	Ch. Lorien's Lady Galadriel

AM. & CAN. CH. CRAWFIE OF BLUE BAR, S-461515

(Ch. Sir Herbert of Kennelworth x Ch. Enid of Blue Bar)

Dam of 6 Champions:		**Sired by:**

Sunridge Antiphon	S-883546	Ch. Rock Falls King Charles
Halfback of Button Ball	S-832549	Al-Kay's Lar Sonny
Javelin of Button Ball	S-868833	
Vaulter of Button Ball	S-868839	
Discus of Button Ball	S-868838	Ch. Thelan Mark of Distinction
Al-Kay's Sky Watch	S-868836	

CH. DIONE DUTCHESS OF DOGSTAR, SA-198187

(Ch. Faneal's Blue Danube x Ch. Golden Dawn of Dogstar)

Dam of 8 Champions:		**Sired by:**

Gemody's Danny Boy	SA-457261	
Gemody's Star Dust	SA-457263	
Gemody's Gidget Goes Hawaiian	SA-457266	
Gemody's Ina Darling	SA-457267	
Gemody's Barbara Gal	SA-457270	Ch. Margand Meteor of Dogstar
Gemody's Rambling Laddie	SA-457260	
Gemody's Gemini of Dogstar	SA-460394	
Gemody's Sophisticated Lady	SA-457268	

CH. CONFETTI OF CALAMITY LANE, S-792633

(Ch. Bullet of Calamity Lane x Ch. Rock Candy of Calamity Lane)

Dam of 10 Champions: **Sired by:**

Dover's Wall Street	S-946627 ⎤	
Dover's Replica of Ludar	S-949336 ⎟	
Dover's Ticker Tape	S-924006 ⎬ Am. & Can. Ch. Ludar	
Dover's Par Value	S-939358 ⎟ of Blue Bar	
Dover's Sir-Plus, C.D.	S-925080 ⎦	
Dover's Robert E. Lee	SA-82716 Ch. Derringer of Calamity Lane	
Dover's Molly Pitcher	SA-253022 ⎤	
Can. Ch. Dover's Betsy Ross	609235 ⎦ Can. Ch. Wamlay's Mike Chism	
Dover's Blue Sky	SA-187369 ⎤	
Dover's Blue Velvet	SA-195052 ⎦ Mt. Mansifled's Spruce Peak	

Ch. Dover's Ticker Tape

280

CH. DOVER'S BLUE SKY

AKC No. SA-187369   Whelped January 22, 1963   Dog
Height - 25¾ inches   Blue Belton
Owner: Dennis A. Ronyak, Chardon, Ohio
Breeder: Lois & S. Jack Staples

Thelan Sir Rocklyn	Ch. Jack O'Rackets
Ch. Mike of Meadboro	Rock Falls Lady Marilyn
Lady McBeth	Ch. Honor's Even Marksman
Mt. Mansfields Spruce Peak	Royal Whirl
Ch. Silvermine Wagabond	Ch. Rhett Butler of Silvermine
Revielle's Pandora	Keyfield Judy
Gwen Du Hameau	Ch. Randy of Blue Bar
	Dean's Cricket
Ch. Yorkley's Ensign Roberts	Ch. Wag of Blue Bar
Ch. Bullet of Calamity Lane	Ch. Southern Lady of Aragon
Ch. Candy of Blue Bar	Ch. Eric of Blue Bar
Ch. Confetti of Calamity Lane	Lisa of Blue Bar
Ch. Rock Falls Lieutenant	Ch. Rock Falls Colonel
Ch. Rock Candy of Calamity Lane	Ch. Jacklin O'Rackets
Ch. Candy of Blue Bar	Ch. Eric of Blue Bar
	Lisa of Blue Bar

Sire of 11 Champions: **Out of:**

Sukarla's Sundance Kid	SA-912362 ⎤	
Sukarla's Sweet Bippy 'O Kaynor	SA-718917	Ch. Chandelle's Bambi
Sukarla's Sock It To Me	SA-717826 ⎦	
Blue Diamond's Abner Yokum	SA-344912 ⎤	
Blue Diamond's Abbigirl, C.D.	SA-344913	Ch. Blue Diamond Mist
Blue Diamond's Alice Blue Gown	SA-344915 ⎦	
Eliza Doolittle of Kaynor	SA-351802 ⎤	
Kaynor's Aces Over	SA-383418 ⎦	Kaynor's Samantha of Mayhew
Sunswept Mack of Kaynor	SA-592196 ⎤	
Sunswept Misty of Kaynor	SA-594900 ⎦	Mirock's Missy
Blue Lupine of Berriwood	SA-346028	Kopper Penny of Berriwood

CH. ENGLISH ACCENT OF VALLEY RUN, S-893847

Ch. Grayland Rackets Boy
Ch. Rock Falls Cavalier
Ch. Linda Lou of Blue Bar
Ch. Rock Falls Racket
Ch. Grayland Rackets Boy
Ch. Rock Falls Belle
Nocturne of Crowlcroft

Ch. Lakeland's Yuba
Sturdy Max II
Ch. Dora of Maridor
Ch. Starbright of Valley Run
Ch. Dean of Blue Bar
Silvermine Confection
Silvermine Wanita

Rummey Stagboro
Blenheim Violet
Ch. Blue Bar Limited
Gretta of Blue Bar
Rummey Stagboro
Blenheim Violet
Ch. Blaze of Fallondale
Romance of Crowlcroft
Rummey Stagboro
Lakeland's Nymph
Ch. Sturdy Max
Ch. Lakeland's Dawn
Ch. Mallhawk's Jeff
Ch. Lakeland's Peaches
Int. Ch. Silvermine Wagabond
Ch. Rackets Gene of Silvermine

Sire of 10 Champions:

		Out of:
Gentleman Jim of Valley Run	SA-86980 ⎤	
Valley Run's Miss Cassandra	SA-119254	
Prince Charlie of Valley Run	SA-104105	Posie of Blue Bar
Valley Run Dixie Barbu	SA-58256 ⎦	
Merry Rover of Valley Run	SA-116098	Wamlay's Merry Minx
Phantom Brook's Oliver	SA-129431 ⎤	
Betsworth Judy Van Buren	SA-142534 ⎦	Ch. Phantom Brook's Pinafore
Valley Run's Accent's Finale	SA-163061 ⎤	
Valley Run's Cinnamon Cindy	SA-88582	Posie of Blue Bar
Valley Run's Sabrina Fair (1)	SA-119253 ⎦	

282

Ernford Easter Parade
Ernford Apollo
Ernford Cilldara Silver
Ch. Ernford Highflier
Ensign of Remor
Teal of Yaresyde
Tarnock Fiona of Remor

Ch. Rip of Blue Bar
Dill of Blue Bar
Schoolgirl Sue of Havertown
Bunnydale's Daisy Belle
Ch. Rummey Sam of Stagboro
Martie of Blue Bar
Kanandarque Goldie

Fluellen of Fermara
Celandine of Haverbrack
Grouse of Capard
Minx of Medeshamstede
Irish Ch. Banner of Crombie
Pretty Maid of Ketree
Irish Ch. Banner of Crombie
Penelope of Ketree
Ch. Dean of Blue Bar
Ina of Blue Bar
Banker of Fallondale
Belle's Queen
Rummey II of Stagboro
Kate of Stagboro
Ch. Dean of Blue Bar
Ch. Gem of Blue Bar

Dam of 14 Champions:		**Sired by:**
Pretty Maid of Cherry Lane	SA-159968	Ch. Bunnydale's Orange Vulcan
Rip of Cherry Lane	SA-183529	Ch. End O'Maine White Rock
Hidden Lane's Barnstormer	SA-117113 ⎤	
		Can. & Am. Ch. Ben-Dar's
Hidden Lane's Mark Me	SA-122414 ⎦	Winning Stride
White Cap of Cherry Lane	SA-219126	Ch. End O'Maine White Rock
Can. & Am. Ch. Viking of Cherry Lane	SA-289882 ⎤	
Vicar of Cherry Lane	SA-289885	Ch. Buff's Pride
Viscount of Cherry Lane	SA-289884 ⎦	
Can. & Am. Ch. Pilot of Cherry Lane	SA-380969 ⎤	
Portia of Cherry Lane	SA-380973 ⎦	Ch. Bayonet Point Preakness
Douglas of Cherry Lane	SA-243094	Ch. End O'Maine White Rock
Can Ch. Browning of Cherry Lane	SA-351094	Ch. Buff's Pride
Rebecca of Cherry Lane (2)	SA-183528	Ch. End O'Maine White Rock
Bridget of Cherry Lane	SA-351090	Ch. Buff's Pride

283

CH. ERNFORD ORIOLE, S-997572

	Sh. Ch. Ripleygae Mallory	Archdale Corncrake of Haverbrack
Kirket Kerryboy		Heatherdrake Diane
	Kirket Karmina	Sh. Ch. Rombalds Sentinal
Ernford Kingfisher		Sh. Ch. Kirket Marinette
	Ernford Easter Parade	Fluellen of Fermanar
Ch. Ernford Evening Flight		Celandine of Haverbrack
	Teal of Yarsyde	Ensign of Remor
		Tarnock Fiona of Remor
	Ir. Ch. Peter of Beechmount	Balmuto Gamble
Grouse of Capard		Leonora of Langlea
	Nan of Beechmount	Ir. Ch. Banner of Crombie
Ch. Ernford Cilldara Felicity		Poppy of Beechmount
	Rombalds Furious	Bayldone Breeze
Minx of Medeshamstede		Rombalds Rovigo
	Blue Belle	Rombalds Tempest
		Dolly Daydreams

Sire of 10 Champions: **Out of:**

Margand Wildcatter	SA-77804 ⎤	
Margand Captain Dan	SA-85616 ⎬	Ch. Margand Mary Jane
Margand Man About Town	SA-77803 ⎦	
Par-point Pretti-Tri	SA-118747	Ch. Parpoint Precarious
Margand Magnolia Blossom	SA-132797	Ch. Margand Mary Jane
Robinwood's Freckles	SA-208831 ⎤	
Candy Chips of Hathaway	SA-197092 ⎦	Ch. Robinwood's Dot
Adam of Lonesome Lane	SA-124846	Ch. Clementine of Calamity La
Chandelle's Sixpence, C.D.	SA-208754	Ch. Chandelle's Folly
Blue Diamond Mist	SA-234932	Ch. Parpoint Precarious

AM. CAN CH. FIVE OAKES SNOW FLAKE

AKC No. SA-847719   Whelped April 9, 1970   Bitch
Breeder-Owner: Barbara Oakes, Scotia, N.Y.   Orange Belton

Ch. Buff's Pride
Ch. Bayonet Point Preakness
Heljax Black-Eyed Susan
Am. Can. Ch. Heljax Top Hat
Ch. Aspetuck's Shadow
Bilmar's Orphan Annie
Winickset Lady Gwendolyn

Ch. Manlove's Colonel
Ch. Flecka's Flash of Cabin Hill
Ch. Princess De Rancho Tranquilla
Tansy of Five Oaks
Anchors Away of Stone Gables
Brunhilda of High Tor
Bows

Ch. Ben-Dar's Winning Stride
Bunnydale's Daisy Belle
Heljax Cye
Ch. Heljax Sweet Lady
Ch. Rock Fall's Racket
Ch. Aspetuck's Diana
Raymond of Blue Bar
Sycamore Lodge Lydibelle
Ch. Rock Fall's Colonel
Ch. Manlove's Patsy Girl
Ch. General Lee Jones
Ch. Kiko Kiko of Lua Lua Lei
Ch. The Rock of Stone Gables
Blue Bess
Ch. Cinnebar of High-Tor
Blue Mountain Plain Jane

Dam of 10 Champions: **Sired by:**

Five Oakes Penny Ante	SB-896558	
Lord Regent of Five Oakes	SB-859396	Ch. Tra Bons Orange Haze
Five Oakes Sno Sprite of Heljax	SB-925900	
Five Oakes Sno Queen of Heljax	SB-925957	
Five Oakes Pistol Pete	SB-4990787	
Five Oakes William of Orange, C.D.	SB-462718	Ch. Canberra's Flagmaster
Five Oakes Snow Bird	SB-499076	
Five Oakes Snow Signal	SB-562237	
Five Oakes Saucy Lass	SC-198394	Ch. Pride's Handsome Boy
Five Oakes Penny Royal	SC-220777	

CH. FRENCHTOWN CALICO BUTTON, S-334742

Ch. Mallhawk's Jeff
Roy of Blue Bar
Kanandarque Lovelyness
Ch. Jesse of Blue Bar
Rummey Stagboro
Ch. Lovely Lady of Stucile
Ch. Modern Maid of Stucile

Bickerton's Monarch
Pendlemar Dan
Squirrel Run Speckled Rose
Frenchtown Blue Feather
Clown of Barleymill
Brandy's Barmaid
Brandy D

Ch. Mallhawk's Rackets Boy
Flora Hallhawk
Kanandarque Rackets Boy
Dawn of Stagboro
Spiron of Jagersbo
Selkirk Snooksie
Ch. Sir Orkney Willgress, Jr.
Willgress Lady Luck
Explorer of Stucile
Bickerton's Lady Gene
Can. & Am. Ch. Gilroy's Chief Topic
Gilroy's Queen B
Happy Valley Helmsman
Happy Valley Colleen Chloe
Freckles D (C.D.)
Autumn's Lady Betty

Dam of 6 Champions:

		Sired by:
Frenchtown Calico Flower	S-550935	
Frenchtown April Dawn	S-507100	
Frenchtown Main Copy	S-579153	Ch. Frenchtown Main Topic
Frenchtown Peter Paul	S-550934	
Frenchtown Topaz	S-579152	
Can. Ch. Frenchtown Chocolate Soldier		

286

AM/CAN. CH. GALAHAD OF POLPERRO

AKC No. SA-415462   Whelped May 9, 1966   Dog
Height - 26 inches   Orange Belton
Owner: James Hanson, Haddam, Ct.   OFA # ES-18
Breeder: Harry B. & Leona N. Kurzrok

             Ted of Thornhurst
         Gilroy's Spot
             Gilroy's Snowey
     Ch. Gilroy's Chancellor
             Ch. Skidby's Sturdy Tyke
         Gilroy's Dixie
             Ch. Stone Gables Charm

             Ch. Ernford Highflyer
         Ch. Pirate of Polperro
             Ch. Betsworth Goldflake
     Ch. Lady Jane of Polperro
             Silvermine Skychief
         Ch. Panthorn Valley Run Samantha
             Ch. Panthorn Gold of Pleasure

Mac's Rummey Valley of Vilmar
Blue Larkspur of Forest Knoll
Gilroy's Jingle
Gilroy's Ava
Ch. Ben-Dar's Advance Notice
Ch. Hillsdale Susan
Ch. Raskalus Raff of Stone Gables
Ch. Prize Par-Sal of Stone Gables
Ernford Apollo
Teal of Yaresyde
Ch. Rock Falls Racket
Aspetuck's Red Sumac
Silvermine Friar Tuck
Silvermine Wanita
Ch. Silvermine Whipcord
Ch. Silvermine Decal

Sire of 13 Champions: **Out of:**

Penmaen Petunia of Northwood	SA-775372	
Northwood Rebel Rouser	SA-955928	
Lady Shea of Northwood	SB-129981	
Northwood's Lancelot	SA-729650	Ch. Penmaen Wandering Home
Valiant of Northwood	SA-738203	
Northwood's Prodigal Son	SA-797399	
Northwood's Miss Poise 'N Ivy	SB-66526	
Lord Jeffrey of Hemlock Lane	SB-4995	
Sir Robin Hood of Hemlock Lane	SA-960350	Ch. Social Climber of Lazy F
Hemlock Lane Social Event	SB-85890	
Meadowset's Blue Velvet	SA-785158	Domino of Meadowset
Northwood's Deb of Belle Nance	SB-192215	Ch. Queen Sheba of Setter Hill
Dolce	SA-685065	Penmaen My Lady Cullen

CH. FRENESSA OF CALAMITY LANE, SA-122679

(Dover's Doc Holiday x Ch. Calamity of Calamity Lane)

Dam of 7 Champions: **Sired by:**

Brooks of Lonesome Lane	SA-248024	
Beloved of Lonesome Lane	SA-201597	
Blessed by Lonesome Lane	SA-20156	Ch. Phantom Brook's Blue Spruce
Bradley of Lonesome Lane	SA-220074	
Dolly of Lonesome Lane	SA-312928	Ch. Adam of Lonesome Lane
Raybar Wisp of Lonesome Lane	SA-418085	
Raybar Ain't She Sweet	SA-408241	Ch. Spark II of Cherry Lane

GORGEOUS GOLDIE OF ORKNEY, S-461808

(Special Agent of Orkney x Sperry's Happy Landing)

Dam of 6 Champions: **Sired by:**

Iverlee Fortune Hunter	S-690255	
Orkney Bob	S-709645	
Memory of Orkney	S-658281	Ch. Rock Falls Troubadour
Laguna Honda Gold Flake	S-701933	
Bem's Sir Christopher	S-740421	
Bem's Sir James	S-845480	Ch. Flecka's Andy

Ch. Iverlee Fortune Hunter

288

CH. GUYLINES'S FLYING TIGER

AKC No. SA-731942   Whelped August, 1969   Dog
Height - 26½ inches   Weight - 70 pounds   Orange Belton
Owner: Margaret Mecleary, Medford, N.J.   OFA # ES-57
Breeder: Sheila & David Ben-Hur   OFA #ES-271

Wamlay's Mike Chism
Ch. Skidby's Bosun of Stone Gables
Royal Blue of Stone Gables
Am/Bda/Can. Ch. Sir Kip of Manitou
Ch. Cinnebar of High-Tor
High-Tor's Spicy Lady
Blue Mountain Plain Jane

Ch. Manlove of Ellendale
Ch. Sir Guy of Ellendale
Ch. Manlove's Mona
Ch. Guyline's Lady Chatterley
Thenderin Aztec of Welwind
Harlequin Heather CDX
Harlequin Harmony CD

Ch. Mike of Meadboro
Chism's Queenie
Ch. Raskalus Raff of Stone Gables
Tower Hill To and Again
Sycamore Lodge Lord Geoffrey
Sycamore Lodge Champagne
Ch. Silvermine Messenger
Mariner's Blue Imp*
Ch. Rock Falls Colonel
Ch. Manlove's Dawn
Ch. Rock Falls Colonel
Ch. Rip's Miss Dusky of Havertown
Ch. Skyline of Stone Gables
Ch. Autumaura Cheery Miss
Ch. Autumaura Corporal Chet
Tom's Queen

Sire of 14 Champions:

		Out of:
Leelynn's Jollymuff Lisa	SB-815281	
Kaydon's Flying High	SB-496936	
Leelynn's Sean of Pickwick	SB-544550	Ch. Leelynn's Jetsetter
Pickwick's Liliput of Leelynn	SB-459748	
Leelynn's Miz Pacesetter	SB-727955	

289

Fern Rock's Royal Tigress	SB-926022	Fern Rock's First Edition
Out West's Muffin of Fernrock	SB-897954	
Guyline's Diabolique	SB-634679	Guyline's Artistry
Pickwick Fantasy	SC-102164	Pickwick's Beloved
Pickwick's Flying Nun	SB-139686	Dariabar Tennessee Rockandy
Seafield's Pride of Brooklawn	SB-981197	Ch. Stone Gables Seafield Romany
Guyline's Belle Of The Ball	SB-144542	Guys 'N Dolls Miss Mindy
Northwood's Follow Me Home	SB-481528	Northwood's Notorious Nell
Northwood Miss Patch of Ivy	SC-66211	Ch. Northwood's Miss Poise 'N Ivy

CH. GUYLINE'S LADY CHATTERLEY

AKC No. SA-565734   Whelped January, 1968   Bitch
Height - 25½ inches   Orange Belton
Owner: Shirley Hoeflinger, Verdes, Ca.
Breeder: David Ben-Hur

	Ch. Rock Falls Cavalier
Ch. Rock Falls Colonel	Ch. Rock Falls Belle
Ch. Manlove of Ellendale	Ch. Rock Falls Colonel
Ch. Manloves Dawn	Ch. Manloves Goldie
Ch. Sir Guy of Ellendale	Ch. Rock Falls Cavalier
Ch. Rock Falls Colonel	Ch. Rock Falls Belle
Ch. Manloves Mona	Ch. Rip of Blue Bar
Ch. Rips Miss Dusky of Havertown	Schoolgirl Sue of Havertown
	Ch. The Rock of Stone Gables
Ch. Skyline of Stone Gables	Ch. Pleiades Electra of Deer Run
Thenderin Aztec of Welwind	Ch. The Rock of Stone Gables
Ch. Autumaura Cherry Miss	Ch. Elaine of Elm Knoll
Harlequin Heather, CDX	Ch. The Rock of Stone Gables
Ch. Autumaura Corporal Chet	Ch. Elaine of Elm Knoll
Harlequin Harmony, CD	Christie's Don
Tom's Queen	Christie's Peggy Sue

Dam of 6 Champions: **Sired by:**

Seamrog Johnny Appleseed	SB-49310	Ch. Guys 'N Dolls Shalimar Duke
Seamrog Apple Annie	SB-36286	
Guyline's Seamrog Shaman	SA-931301	

Guyline's Flying Tiger	SA-731942	Ch. Sir Kip of Manitou
Guyline's Jet Setter	SA-731940	
Seamrog Northern Star	SB-729612	Ch. Camelot's Merlyn The Great

CH. GUYS 'N DOLLS ANNIE O'BRIEN

AKC No. SB-18903   Whelped October 31, 1971   Bitch
Height - 24 inches   Orange Belton
Owner: Lloyd & Lynda Talbot & Neal Weinstein, Stockton, Ca.
Breeder: Neal & Harron Weinstein

        Ch. Hillsdale Sentinel
  Ch. Guys 'N Dolls Shalimar Duke
        Ch. Guys 'N Dolls Bridget O'Shea CD
Ch. Guys 'N Dolls Onassis
        Ch. Manlove of Ellendale
  Ch. Lady Dana of Ellendale
        Duchess of Ellendale

        Ch. Merry Rover of Valley Run
  Ch. Guys 'N Dolls Society Max
        Ch. Guys 'N Dolls Miss Adelaide
Guys 'N Dolls Maidstone Annie
        Ch. Hillsdale Sentinel
  Ch. Guys 'N Dolls Miss Adelaide
        Ch. Guys 'N Dolls Bridget O'Shea CD

Ch. Skidby's Sturdy Tyke
Ch. Hillsdale Sparkle
Ch. Sir Guy of Ellendale
Lady Jill of Ellendale
Ch. Rock Falls Colonel
Ch. Manlove's Dawn
Manlove's Gay Cavalier
Greenbriar's Princess
Ch. English Accent of Valley Run
Wamlay's Merry Minx
Ch. Hillsdale Sentinel
Ch. Guys 'N Dolls Bridget O'Shea CD
Ch. Skidby's Sturdy Tyke
Ch. Hillsdale Sparkle
Ch. Sir Guy of Ellendale
Lady Jill of Ellendale

Dam of 6 Champions: **Out of:**

Guys 'N Dolls Barrister Beau	SC-501724	
Guys 'N Dolls Educated Ed	SC-505797	
Guys 'N Dolls Paleface Kid	SC-555174	Ch. Seamrog Tyson of Palomar
Guys 'N Dolls Delancey Street	SC-509235	
Guys 'N Dolls Sentimental Lady	SC-384720	Ch. Guys 'N Dolls Onassis
Guys 'N Dolls Dream Boat Annie	SC-384719	

AM/MEX. CH. GUYS 'N DOLLS BIG BUTCH

AKC No. SC-18906   Whelped October 31, 1971   Dog
Height - 27½ inches   Weight - 80 pounds   Orange Belton
Owner: Linda Carroll, Whittier, Ca.
Breeder: Neal & Harron Weinstein

             Ch. Hillsdale Sentinel
      Ch. Guys 'N Dolls Shalimar Duke
         Ch. Guys 'N Dolls Bridget O'Shea CD
Ch. Guys 'N Dolls Onassis
         Ch. Manlove of Ellendale
      Ch. Lady Dana of Ellendale
         Duchess of Ellendale

             Ch. Merry Rover of Valley
      Ch. Guys 'N Dolls Society Max
         Ch. Guys 'N Dolls Miss Adelaide
Guys 'N Dolls Maidstone Annie
         Ch. Hillsdale Sentinel
      Ch. Guys 'N Dolls Miss Adelaide
         Ch. Guys 'N Dolls Bridget O'Shea CD

Ch. Skidby's Sturdy Tyke
Ch. Hillsdale Sparkle
Ch. Sir Guy of Ellendale
Lady Jill of Ellendale
Ch. Rock Falls Colonel
Ch. Manlove's Dawn
Manlove's Gay Cavalier
Greenbrier's Princess
Ch. English Accent of Valley Run
Wamlay's Merry Minx
Ch. Hillsdale Sentinel
Ch. Guys 'N Dolls Bridget O'Shea CD
Ch. Skidby's Sturdy Tyke
Ch. Hillsdale Sparkle
Ch. Sir Guy of Ellendale
Lady Jill of Ellendale

Sire of 14 Champions: **Out of:**

Rimrock's Midnight Cowboy	SB-930652	
Rimrock's Clockwork Orange	SB-859532	
Rimrock's Chanting Warrior	SC-149405	Ch. Sunburst Buttons 'N Bows
Rimrock's Collector's Item	SB-958791	
Rimrock's Color Scheme	SC-78776	
Piccadilly Aspin of Buckwood	SC-219646	
Piccadilly Moon Mist	SC-327700	Piccadilly Cinnamon Candy
Piccadilly Moonshadow	SC-315487	
Storybook Clover Dancer	SC-247157	
Storybook's Roustabout	SC-130752	Storybook Spring Bouquet
Annandale Maximum D'Lite	SC-293122	Siobahan's Moonshadow
Annandale California Flash	SC-111366	Guys 'N Dolls Anniversary Ali
Edwardian American Dream	SC-450299	Ch. Edwardian Gibson Girl, C.D.
Sunrose Special Blend	SC-629628	Ch. Limehouse Six Million, C.D.

CH. GUYS 'N DOLLS HONEY GROVE

AKC No. SA-493239   Bitch
Height - 25 inches   Orange Belton

Sire: Ch. Merry Rover of Valley Run — see page 322
Dam: Ch. Guys 'N Dolls Miss Adelaide — see page 295

Dam of 8 Champions: Sired by:

Lorien's Fire Brand	SB-73406	
Lorien's Marigold	SB-57486	
Lorien's Master Meriadoc	SB-81453	
Lorien's Lady Arwen	SB-166050	
Lorien's Lady Galadriel	SB-75762	Ch. Guys 'N Dolls Shalimar Duke
Lorien's Fire Music	SB-734808	
Guys 'N Dolls Lady Lorien	SA-935096	
Guys 'N Dolls Taste of Honey	SA-936164	

CH. GUYS 'N DOLLS MARIE ANTOINETTE

AKC No. SA-720416　　　　Whelped September 12, 1969　　　　Bitch
Owner: Jane J. Bragg,
Macon, Ga.　　　　　　　　　　　　　　　　　　　　　　Orange Belton
Breeder: Neal Weinstein　　　　　　　　　　　　　　　　　OFA # ES-116

Ch. English Accent of Valley Run	Ch. Rock Falls Racket
Ch. Merry Rover of Valley Run	Ch. Starbright of Valley Run
Wamlay's Merry Minx	Ch. Mike of Meadboro
Ch. Guys 'N Dolls Society Max	Cinderella of Oak Valley
Ch. Hillsdale Sentinel	Ch. Skidby's Sturdy Tyke
Ch. Guys 'N Dolls Miss Adelaide	Ch. Hillsdale Sparkle
Ch. Guys 'N Dolls Bridget O'Shea	Ch. Sir Guy of Ellendale
	Lady Jill of Ellendale
	Ch. Ben-Dar's Advance Notice
Ch. Skidby's Sturdy Tyke	Ch. Hillsdale Susan
Ch. Hillsdale Sentinel	Ch. Ludar of Blue Bar
Ch. Hillsdale Sparkle	Can. Ch. Pollyanna
Ch. Guys 'N Dolls Miss Adelaide	Ch. Manlove of Ellendale
Ch. Sir Guy of Ellendale	Ch. Manlove's Mona
Ch. Guys 'N Dolls Bridget O'Shea	Ch. Skyline of Stone Gables
Lady Jill of Ellendale	Ch. Manlove's Mona

Dam of 11 Champions:　　　　　　　　　　　　　　**Sired by:**

Guys 'N Dolls Nathan Detroit	SB-717942	
Guys 'N Dolls Elizabeth Taylor	SB-691767	
Guys 'N Dolls Got 'Em Again	SB-717948	
Guys 'N Dolls Easy Money	SB-709431	Ch. Guys 'N Dolls Onassis
Guys 'N Dolls Miss Somebody	SB-693564	
Guys 'N Dolls Foxie Lady	SB-881962	
Guys 'N Dolls Rhett Butler	SB-882616	
Guys 'N Dolls Spanish Moss	SB-18910	
Duke's Tale of Westerly	SB-266655	
Duke's Tale of Westerly	SB-266652	Ch. Guys 'N Dolls Shalimar Duke
Duke's Challenge of Westerly	SB-266652	
Guys 'N Dolls Westerly Wind	SB-577008	

CH. GUYS 'N DOLLS MISS ADELAIDE

AKC No. SA-342336   Whelped July 31, 1965   Bitch

Height - 24 inches   Weight - 55 pounds   Orange Belton

Breeders-Owners: Neal & Harron Weinstein, Woodland Hills, Ca.

	Ch. Ben-Dar's Advance Notice	Ch. Ludar of Blue Bar
Ch. Skidby's Sturdy Tyke		Ch. Silvermine Chambray
Ch. Hillsdale Susan		Ch. Ludar of Blue Bar
Ch. Hillsdale Sentinel		Ch. Pollyanna
Ch. Ludar of Blue Bar		Ch. Sir Herbert of Kennelworth
Ch. Hillsdale Sparkle		Ch. Manlove's Goldie
Can. Ch. Pollyanna		Rummy Sun Beau of Stagboro
		Pamela
	Ch. Manlove of Ellendale	Ch. Rock Falls Colonel
Ch. Sir Guy of Ellendale		Ch. Manlove's Dawn
Ch. Manlove's Mona		Ch. Rock Falls Colonel
Ch. Guys 'N Dolls Bridget O'Shea		Ch. Rip's Miss Dusky of Havertown
Ch. Skyline of Stone Gables		Ch. The Rock of Stone Gables
Lady Jill of Ellendale		Pleiades Electra of Deer Run
Ch. Manlove's Mona		Ch. Rock Falls Colonel
		Ch. Rip's Miss Dusky of Havertown

Dam of 9 Champions: **Sired by:**

Guys 'N Dolls Hickory Slim	SA-493238	
Guys 'N Dolls Lady Eliza	SA-493240	Ch. Merry Rover of Valley Run
Guys 'N Dolls Society Max	SA-493235	
Guys 'N Dolls Honey Grove	SA-493239	
Guys 'N Dolls Marie Antoinette	SA-720416	
Guys 'N Dolls Madison Avenue	SA-720417	Ch. Guys 'N Dolls Society Max
Guys 'N Dolls Mr. Amboy	SA-720419	
Guys 'N Dolls Bubbles Browning	SB-215534	Ch. Guys 'N Dolls Onassis
Guys 'N Dolls Lemon Drop Kid	SB-18908	Ch. Guys 'N Dolls Shalimar Duke

CH. GUYS 'N DOLLS ONASSIS

AKC No. SA-707532   Whelped August 17, 1969   Dog
Height - 25½ inches   Orange Belton
Owner: Nancy Jenkins, Ontario, Ca.   OFA # ES-77
Breeder: Neal & Harron Weinstein

Ch. Skidby's Sturdy Tyke	Ch. Ben-Dar's Advance Notice
Ch. Hillsdale Sentinel	Ch. Hillsdale Susan
Ch. Hillsdale Sparkle	Ch. Ludar of Blue Bar
Ch. Guys 'N Dolls Shalimar Duke	Can. Ch. Pollyanna
Ch. Sir Guy of Ellendale	Ch. Manlove of Ellendale
Ch. Guys 'N Dolls Bridget O'Shea CD	Ch. Manlove's Mona
Lady Jill of Ellendale	Ch. Skyline of Stone Gables
	Ch. Manlove's Mona
	Ch. Rock Falls Cavalier
Ch. Rock Falls Colonel	Ch. Rock Falls Belle
Ch. Manlove of Ellendale	Ch. Rock Falls Colonel
Ch. Manlove's Dawn	Ch. Manlove's Goldie
Ch. Lady Dana of Ellendale	Ch. Rock Falls Cavalier
Manlove's Gay Cavalier	Ch. Manlove's Dawn
Duchess of Ellendale	Skyman
Greenbriar's Princess	Peerless Lady Hamilton

Sire of 56 Champions: Out of:

Guys 'N Dolls Nathan Detroit	SB-717942	
Guys 'N Dolls Elizabeth Taylor	SB-691767	
Guys 'N Dolls Got 'Em Again	SB-717948	
Guys 'N Dolls Easy Money	SB-709431	Ch. Guys 'N Dolls Marie Antoinette
Guys 'N Dolls Miss Somebody	SB-693564	
Guys 'N Dolls Foxie Lady	SB-88192	
Guys 'N Dolls Rhett Butler	SB-882616	

Charlin Rudolph	SB-41243	
Charlin Eric	SB-41246	
Charlin Valentina	SB-41245	Ch. Thenderin Sarah Brown
Charlin Tiny Tim	SB-41247	
Charlin Christina	SB-41244	
Charlin Billy Jack	SB-382216	
Guys 'N Dolls Hello Dolly	SB-946981	
Guys 'N Dolls Katydid	SC-221488	Ch. Guys 'N Dolls Westerly Wind
Guys 'N Dolls Damon Runyon	SC-95928	
Guys 'N Dolls On The Money	SB-76243	
Guys 'N Dolls Bristol Cream	SB-218056	Ch. Guys 'N Dolls Ziegfield Girl
Seamrog April of Guys 'N Dolls	SB-753078	
Seamrog Seabring Solitaire	SB-721863	
Guys 'N Dolls Spot On	SB-470316	
Guys 'N Dolls Zacharaha	SB-676799	Ch. Marshfield's Lady Ann
Guys 'N Dolls Pretty Boy Floyd	SB-486333	
Guys 'N Dolls Blue Velvet	SB-508719	
Palomar's Best Bette	SB-979407	
Palomar's Orange Marmalade	SB-991363	Ch. Palomar's Abagail of Scotglen
Palomar's Oliver Twist	SC-80120	
Palomar's O'Riely Nell'Son	SC-106776	
Guys 'N Dolls Annie O'Brien	SB-18903	
Guys 'N Dolls Big Butch	SB-18906	Guys 'N Dolls Maidstone Annie
Guys 'N Dolls John The Boss	SB-18905	
Seamrog Carmaleen Savannah, C.D.	SB-294742	
Seamrog Orion	SB-170516	Raybar's Tranquility
Seamrog Shenandoah	SB-292816	
Seamrog Morningstar Beauty	SB-846716	
Seamrog Sweet Freedom	SB-846717	Ch. Seamrog Blue Note
Seamrog Wing Commander	SC-373411	
Morengohills Hello Sunshine	SB-895602	Can. Ch. Countess Carmen
Morengohills Hazel	SB-901751	of Morengohill
Heathrow Winston	SB-770495	Ch. Windmist Bouquet of Heather
Heathrow Triston, C.D.	SB-787221	
Thornbury Fire and Brimstone	SB-848344	Ch. Lady Juliette of Stone Gables
Thornbury Sounding Brass	SB-808973	
Sunburst Hasten Down The Wind	SC-169663	Ch. Solheim's Ginger Snap
Sunburst All Spice	SC-146008	
Jubilee's Goldstrike	SC-477027	Ch. Jubilee's Tambourine Lady
Jubilee's Copperstrike	SC-477028	
Guys 'N Dolls Dream Boat Annie	SC-384719	Ch. Guys 'N Dolls Annie O'Brien
Guys 'N Dolls Sentimental Lady	SC-384720	
Guys 'N Dolls High Flyer	SC-402239	Ch. Guys 'N Dolls Foxie Lady
Edwardian Gibson Girl, C.D.	SB-460734	Marshfield's Edwardian Era
Guys 'N Dolls Solo of Sage Hill	SB-992549	Sage Hill Matchless Molly
Guys 'N Dolls Bubbles Browning	SB-215534	Ch. Guys 'N Dolls Miss Adelaide
Sunburst Lookin' Good	SC-575577	Ch. Sunburst Gingerbread Girl
Colthouse Castlereach	SC-322311	Ch. Colthouse Chelsea
Oblivion of Guys 'N Dolls	SB-716806	Guys 'N Dolls Lotta Dots

CH. GUYS 'N DOLLS SHALIMAR DUKE

AKC No. SA-342335   Whelped July, 1965   Dog
Height - 26½ inches   Orange Belton
Owner: Janice Balme, Richardson, Tx.   OFA # ES-28
Breeder: Neal & Harron Weinstein

Ch. Ben-Dar's Advance Notice	Ch. Ludar of Blue Bar
Ch. Skidby's Sturdy Tyke	Ch. Silvermine Chambray
Ch. Hillsdale Susan	Ch. Ludar of Blue Bar
Ch. Hillsdale Sentinel	Can. Ch. Pollyanna
Ch. Ludar of Blue Bar	Ch. Sir Herbert of Kennelworth
Ch. Hillsdale Sparkle	Ch. Manlove's Goldie
Can. Ch. Pollyanna	Rummy Sun Beau of Stagboro
	Pamela
Ch. Manlove of Ellendale	Ch. Rock Falls Colonel
Ch. Sir Guy of Ellendale	Ch. Manlove's Dawn
Ch. Manlove's Mona	Ch. Rock Falls Colonel
Ch. Guys 'N Dolls Bridget O'Shea CD	Ch. Rip's Dusky of Havertown
Ch. Skyline of Stone Gables	Ch. The Rock of Stone Gables
Lady Jill of Ellendale	Ch. Pleiades Electra of Deer Run
Ch. Manlove's Mona	Ch. Rock Falls Colonel
	Ch. Rip's Dusky of Havertown

Sire of 74 Champions: **Out of:**

Sunburst Gingerbread Girl	SB-825904	
Sunburst Shalimar of R-Lew	SB-907008	
Sunburst Peaches 'N Cream	SB-825905	
Sunburst Rhinestone Cowboy	SB-825906	Ch. Solheim's Ginger Snap
Sunburst Special Edition	SB-337619	
Sunburst Shelly	SB-183943	

Sunburst Buttons 'N Bows	SB-45148	
Solheim's Star Attraction	SB-498069	
Solheim Checkerberry	SB-221635	
Solheim Royal Duke	SB-60119	Ch. Solheim's Ginger Snap
Solheim Ravishing Ruby	SB-348053	
Solheim Razzleberry, C.D.	SB-153134	
Sixpence Kelly of Sunburst	SB-499001	
Captain Jack of Ennistar		
Lorien's Fire Music	SB-734808	
Lorien's Fire Brand	SB-73406	
Lorien's Marigold	SB-57486	
Lorien's Master Meriadoc	SB-81453	Ch. Guys 'N Dolls Honey Grove
Lorien's Lady Arwen	SB-166050	
Lorien's Lady Galadriel	SB-75762	
Guys 'N Dolls Lady Lorien	SA-935096	
Guys 'N Dolls Taste of Honey	SA-936164	
Guys 'N Dolls Spanish Moss	SB-18910	
Guys 'N Dolls Westerly Wind	SB-577008	Ch. Guys 'N Dolls Marie Antoinette
Duke's Tale of Westerly	SB-266655	
Duke's Challenge of Westerly	SB-26652	
Guys 'N Dolls Cutie Singleton	SB-945419	
Guys 'N Dolls Cool Hand Luke	SB-944635	Ch. Guys 'N Dolls Bubbles Browning
Guys 'N Dolls Wild William	SB-986235	
Guys 'N Dolls Rip of Storybook	SA-749255	
Storybook's Pathfinder	SA-776238	Ch. Guys 'N Dolls Lady Eliza
Storybook's MacDuff	SA-780501	
Guys 'N Dolls Rosa Midnight	SA-812865	
Guys 'N Dolls Ziegfield Girl	SA-812864	Ch. Guys 'N Dolls Miss Innocence
Sovereign's Regalia	SB-59103	
Guys 'N Dolls Onassis	SA-707532	
Guys 'N Dolls Oliver Ridgedale	SA-707533	Ch. Lady Dana of Ellendale
Guys 'N Dolls Ophelia	SA-707534	
Raybar's Grand Gusto	SA-813268	
Raybar's Show Stopper of Wesley	SA-721148	Ch. Raybar's Ain't She Sweet
Guys 'N Dolls Gentry of Raybar	SA-844379	
Tahills Juniper Jeeves	SA-609386	
Tahills Ponderosa Polly	SA-609385	Ch. Raybar's Orange Blossom
Ta-Mar's Tangy	SA-602996	
Sage Hill's Silver Plume	SB-295492	
Sage Hill's Vindicator Mine	SC-184184	Belset Wind-Lass
Sage Hill's Sterling Silver	SB-333767	
Seamrog Johnny Appleseed	SB-49310	
Seamrog Apple Annie	SB-36286	Ch. Guyline's Lady Chatterly
Guyline's Seamrog Shaman	SA-931301	
Clariho Checkmate of Critt-Du	SA-816573	
Clariho Kristofer of Critt-Du	SA-731148	Clariho Pell of Stone Gables
Clariho Caper of Critt-Du	SA-738515	
Flecka's Sandpiper of Raybar	SA-775831	
Raybar's Secret Agent	SA-808270	Ch. Anita of Cherry Lane
Lorien's Evenstar	SA-935098	
Lorien's Mistress Rose	SB-75764	Ch. Empire's Roxanne
Keynote's Sunshine	SA-858173	
Keynote's Candidate	SA-858172	Ch. Emma Peel of Makepeace
Excalibur's Extempore	SB-542822	
Excalibur's Exemplar	SB-638531	Excalibur's Lady Luck
Guys 'N Dolls Big Jon of Wileire	SC-250856	
Guys 'N Dolls Lizzy T of Wileire	SC-136062	Ch. Guys 'N Dolls Elizabeth Taylor
Caraglin Shambray Chianti	SB-516980	
Marset's Shambray Chablis	SB-422078	Arnee's Silhouette, C.D.
Guys 'N Dolls Broadway Joe	SB-872410	Ch. Edwardian Gibson Girl, C.D.
Mary Marksman Mary Marksman	SC-24092	Exceptionell Bell 'O The Ball
Solheim's Miss Sundance	SB-152606	Ch. Fivesmith's Heidi
Guys 'N Dolls Lemon Drop Kid	SB-18908	Ch. Guys 'N Dolls Miss Adelaide

Guys 'N Dolls Shalimar Duke (continued)

Fairhaven's Jeb Stuart	SB-683360	Ch. Hiddenlane Beth of Fairhaven
Andrew of Argyll	SB-672108	Ch. Oleander of Lonesome Lane
Fireline's Golden Mist	SB-23482	Shadow Hills Miss Muffin
Shalimar Princess Splendor	SB-235246	Chaucer's Doll of Stone Gables
Chearta Manlove Charade	SB-872461	Manlove's Merry Sherry

CH. GUYS 'N DOLLS ZIEGFIELD GIRL, C.D.

AKC No. SA-812864   Whelped May 29, 1970   Bitch
Height - 25 inches   Orange Belton
Owner: Shirley Hoeflinger, Verdes, Ca.   OFA # ES-542-T
Breeder: Neal & Harron Weinstein

Ch. Skidby's Sturdy Tyke
Ch. Hillsdale Sentinel
Ch. Hillsdale Susan
Ch. Guys 'N Dolls Shalimar Duke
Ch. Sir Guy of Ellendale
Ch. Guys 'N Dolls Bridget O'Shea CD
Lady Jill of Ellendale

Ch. English Accent of Valley Run
Ch. Merry Rover of Valley Run
Wamlay's Merry Minx
Ch. Guys 'N Dolls Miss Innocence
Ch. Hillsdale Sentinel
Ch. Guys 'N Dolls Miss Adelaide
Ch. Guys 'N Dolls Bridget O'Shea CD

Ch. Ben-Dar's Advance Notice
Ch. Hillsdale Susan
Can. Ch. Pollyana
Ch. Ludar of Blue Bar
Ch. Manlove of Ellendale
Ch. Manloves Mona
Ch. Skyline of Stone Gables
Ch. Manloves Mona
Ch. Rock Falls Racket
Ch. Starbright of Valley Run
Ch. Mike of Meadboro
Cinderella of Oak Valley
Ch. Skidby's Sturdy Tyke
Ch. Hillsdale Susan
Ch. Sir Guy of Ellendale
Lady Jill of Ellendale

Dam of 10 Champions: Sired by:

Guys 'N Dolls On The Money	SB-76243	
Guys 'N Dolls Bristol Cream	SB-218056	
Seamrog April of Guys 'N Dolls	SB-753078	Ch. Guys 'N Dolls Onassis
Seamrog Seabring Solitaire	SB-721863	
Seamrog Blue Note	SB-502387	
Seamrog Ballad in Blue	SB-493607	
Seamrog Moody Blues O'Kenwood	SB-619309	Ch. Raybar's Blue Line
Seamrog Stargazer	SC-505824	
Seamrog Tyson of Palomar	SC-41555	
Seamrog Holly Hobbie	SB-982173	Ch. Arnee's Nell'Son of Nor'Coaster

CH. HELJAX TOP HAT

AKC No. SA-657272 — Whelped September 17, 1968 — Dog
Height - 26 inches — Weight - 68 pounds — Orange Belton
Breeder-Owner: Heljax Kennels, Avon, Ct.

Ch. Ben-Dar's Winning Stride
Ch. Buff's Pride
Bunnydale's Daisy Belle
Ch. Bayonet Point Preakness
Heljax Cye
Heljax Black Eyed Susan
Ch. Heljax Sweet Lady

Ch. Rock Falls Racket
Ch. Aspetuck's Shadow
Ch. Aspetuck's Diana
Bilmar's Orphan Annie
Raymond of Blue Bar
Winickset Lady Gwendolyn
Sycamore Lodge Lydibelle

Ch. Ludar of Blue Bar
Yorkley Wisp O'Heather
Ch. Dill of Blue Bar
Martie of Blue Bar
Heljax Invasion of Scyld
Silvermine Blue Mist
Ch. Rock Falls Colonel
Heljax Rebecca
Ch. Rock Falls Cavalier
Ch. Rock Falls Belle
Sturdy Max II
Aspetuck's Red Sumac
Ch. Rube of Blue Bar
Jenifer of Blue Bar
Ch. Rock Falls Cavalier
Ch. Rock Falls Belle

Sire of 15 Champions: **Out of:**

Tra-Bon Lindsay Burlingham	SB-864025	
Tra-Bon Chelsea Burlingham	SB-186206	
Tra-Bon's Sam	SB-235825	
Tra-Bon's Orange Haze	SB-264805	Ch. Meadowset's Smooth Sailing
Tra-Bon's Orange Sunshine	SB-264806	
Heljax Drummer Boy of Tra-Bon	SB-398602	
Meadowset's Patience of Tamara	SB-202081	
Five Oakes Top Lass	SA-847718	
Five Oakes Snow Flake	SA-847719	Tansy of Five Oakes
Johnny Reb of Five Oakes, C.D.	SA-829942	
Manlove's Crumpet of Scotsmar	SB-710482	Manlove's Misty of Lenape Farm
Manlove's Liberty	SB-769930	
White Pillar's Tam of Scotsmar	SB-542348	White Pillar's Popover
Meadowset's Yankee Peddler	SB-350156	Ch. Clariho Souvenir
Guinevere of Meadowset	SA-954170	Domino of Meadowset

CH. HIDDEN LANE'S BENCHMARK

AKC No. SA-964238   Whelped June 4, 1971   Dog
Height - 26 inches   Weight - 66 pounds   Orange Belton
Owner: Robert B. Anderson, Edina, Mn.
Breeder: Marge O'Connell & John Tomlinson

Mister Mar-Jon	Ch. Ben-Dar's Carbon Copy
Ch. Hiddenlane's Busy Imp	Notice-Me of Carylane
Duchess of Westfield	Ch. Hiddenlane's Mark Me
Ch. Hiddenlane's Blue Turquoise	Darbella's Cimmaron Frost
Ch. Ben-Dar's Carbon Copy	Ch. Ludar of Blue Bar
Hiddenlane's Blue Surprise	Ch. Silvermine Chambray
Notice-Me of Carylane	Ch. Ben-Dar's Advance Notice
	Black Imp of Caryland
Ch. Ben-Dar's Winning Stride	Ch. Ludar of Blue Bar
Ch. Hiddenlane's Mark Me	Yorkley Wisp O'Heather
Enid of Cherry Lane	Ch. Ernford Highflier
Harmony Lane Windsor Castle	Bunnydale's Daisy Belle
Ch. Ben-Dar's Carbon Copy	Ch. Ludar of Blue Bar
Ch. Camelot Candace	Ch. Silvermine Chambray
Ch. Cynthia Darbella	Ch. Ben-Dar's Winning Stride
	Linda

Sire of 15 Champions: **Out of:**

Xceptionell's Drummer Boy	SB-344442	
Xceptionell's Old Glory	SB-432401	
Xceptionell's Royal Salute	SB-428541	Ch. Hidden Lane's Xceptionell
Xceptionell's Parader	SB-394782	
Raybar's Webster of Marksman	SC-035089	
Raybar's Marksman Texas Toast	SC-63394	Ch. Raybar's Kismet of Cherry Lane
Marksman Flintlock of Raybar	SC-35088	
Thistledown's Charisma	SB-860030	Excalibur's Lady Luck
Marksman Maid Marion	SC-015287	Moonshine's Aquarius
Roustabout's Mr. Mac Byrd	SB-588070	Ch. Margand Merry of Jaccard Hill
Cameron's Diamond Lil	SB-704859	Ch. Cameron's Cham Cham Girl
Windem's Fallen Angel	SC-590177	The Argentine Firecracker
Woodridge Wonder Woman	SB-239845	
Woodridge Chandelle Waterlu	SB-162415	Ch. Chandelle's Etcetera
Woodridge Wild Oats	SB-178318	

CH. HIDDENLANE'S BLOOMFIELD BABU

AKC No. SA-676325   Whelped May 23, 1966   Bitch
Height - 25½ inches   Orange Belton
Owner: Mrs. Marge O'Connell, Livonia, Mi.
Breeder: Mrs. Bruce Campbell

Ch. Rock Falls Racket
Ch. English Accent of Valley Run
Ch. Starbright of Valley Run
Ch. Merry Rover of Valley Run
Ch. Mike of Meadboro
Wamlay's Merry Minx
Cinderella of Oak Valley

Ch. Ben-Dar's Carbon Copy
Mister Mar Jon
Notice Me of Carylane
Ch. Hiddenlanes Broker's Tip
Ch. Hiddenlanes Barnstormer
Ch. Hiddenlane Scheherazade
Ch. Susie Chubb

Ch. Rock Falls Cavalier
Ch. Rock Falls Belle
Ch. Sturdy Max II
Silvermine Confection
Thelan Sir Rocklyn
Lady McBeth
Ch. Sharoc's Monty of Oak Valley
Gold Dust of Oak Valley
Ch. Ludar of Blue Bar
Ch. Silvermine Chambray
Ch. Ben-Dar's Advance Notice
Black Imp of Carylane
Ch. Ben-Dar's Winning Stride
Enid of Cherry Lane
Ch. Ben-Dar's Winning Stride
Dag Mar Little Lady

Dam of 7 Champions: **Sired by:**

Hiddenlane's King George, U.D.	SB-75015	Ch. Hiddenlane's Busy Imp
Hidden Lane's Xceptionell	SA-971369	
Hidden Lane Lisa	SB-488119	
Hidden Lane's Brandy Snap	SA-951141	Ch. Hiddenlane's Merry Max
Hiddenlane's Jagersbo Banner	SA-83029	
Hiddenlane's Pace Setter	SB-272229	
Hiddenlane Beth of Fairhaven	SB-242	
Hiddenlane Special Delivery	SB-455469	Ch. Hiddenlane Turk-Son of Mayhew
Hiddenlane's Golden Talisman	SB-406108	

CH. HIDDENLANE'S MERRY MAX

AKC No. SA-507784   Whelped April 8, 1967   Dog
Height - 26 inches   Orange Belton
Breeder-Owner: Marge O'Connell

Ch. Ludar of Blue Bar	Ch. Sir Herbert of Kennelworth
Ch. Ben-Dar's Carbon Copy	Manlove's Goldie
Ch. Silvermine Chambray	Ch. The Snark of Scyld
Mister Mar-Jon	Silvermine Wanita
Ch. Ben-Dar's Advance Notice	Ch. Ludar of Blue Bar
Notice Me of Carylane	Ch. Silvermine Chambray
Black Imp of Carylane	Topper of Stan Royal
	Ch. Parpoint Aragon Present
Ch. Ben-Dar's Winning Stride	Ch. Ludar of Blue Bar
Ch. Hiddenlane's Mark Me	Yorkley Wisp O'Heather
Enid of Cherry Lane	Ch. Ernford Highflier
Ch. Hiddenlane's Nelle	Bunnydale's Daisy Belle
Ch. Ben-Dar's Carbon Copy	Ch. Ludar of Blue Bar
Darbella's Cimmaron Frost	Ch. Silvermine Chambray
Ch. Cynthia Darbella	Ch. Ben-Dar's Winning Stride
	Linda

Sire of 18 Champions: **Out of:**

Name	Number	Out of
Hiddenlane Liza	SB-488119	
Hiddenlane Beth of Fairhaven	SB-242	
Hiddenlane's Brandy Snap	SA-951141	
Hiddenlane's Jagersbo Banner	SB-83029	Ch. Hidden Lane Bloomfield Babu
Hiddenlane's Pace Setter	SB-272229	
Hidden Lane's Xceptionell	SA-971369	
Topper of Pleasant Point	SA-689386	
Rogue of Pleasant Point	SA-689385	
Cameo of Pleasant Point	SA-645483	Frenessa of Pleasant Point
Lord Nelson of Pleasant Point	SA-644373	
Belset Wind-Lass	SA-945762	
Belset Grand Slam	SA-844985	Yorkley Honi of Lonesome Lane
Blue Diamond's Drambuie	SA-772831	
Blue Diamond's Digby	SA-772830	Ch. Blue Diamond's Mist
Benchmark Bess	SB-31195	Ch. Margand Martha
Stoneybrook's Mister Crook	SB-566161	Ch. Blue Diamond's Benedictine
Hiddenlane Bloomfield Peg	SA-901835	Ch. Hidden Lane's Broker's Tip
Oakwind's Prize Package	SB-94655	Lorric's Peaches 'N Cream

CH. HIDDENLANE TURK-SON OF MAYHEW

AKC No. SB-084191   Whelped October 10, 1971   Dog
Height - 27½ inches   Weight - 79 pounds   Blue Belton
Owners: Marge O'Connell and George Quigley
Breeder: Elizabeth & Richard J. Burandt

Ch. Hiddenlane's Busy Imp
Ch. Hiddenlane's Blue Turquoise
Ch. Hiddenlane's Blue Surprise

Mister Mar-Jon
Duchess of Westfield
Ch. Ben-Dar's Carbon Copy
Notice-Me of Carylane

Ch. Remittance Man of Lazy F
Ch. Lady Tracey of Mayhew
Mayhew's Game Girl

Ch. Windsor of Cherry Lane
Ch. Lady Lark of Panthorn
Ch. End O'Maine White Rock
Ch. Wallis of Cherrylane

Sire of 13 Champions:

Out of:

Harmony Lane Sportin Life	SC-170523 ⎤	
Harmony Lane's Daffodil	SC-174227 ⎦	Ch. Harmony Lane Sure Nuf Jubilee
Harmony Lane Pot of Honey	SC-356384 ⎤	
Heritage Bush Pilot	SC-315385 ⎦	Ch. Thistledown Doll O'Willow Run
Hiddenlane's King Henry, C.D.	SB-259622 ⎤	
Hiddenlane's Smoky Blue	SB-284492 ⎦	Hiddenlane's Jacqueline
Hiddenlane's Golden Talisman	SB-406108 ⎤	
Hiddenlane Special Delivery	SB-455469 ⎦	Ch. Hiddenlane Bloomfield Babu
Fantail's Mandarin Orange	SB-915800 ⎤	
Fantail's Orange Crusher	SB-941415 ⎦	Ch. Fantail's Snowboots
Parpoint Peppacorn	SB-679278 ⎤	
Manlove's Mr. Chips	SB-455386 ⎦	Ch. Parpoint Placater
Hiddenlanes Bold Strike	SB-297713	Harmony Lane's Windsor Castle

305

CH. HIGHLANDS WHIP OF PENMAEN

AKC No. SA-607617   Whelped June, 1968   Dog
Height - 26 inches   Blue Belton
Owner: Mason H. Stone Jr.   OFA # ES-45
Breeder: Betty W. Sly & Susan S. Maire

Ch. Ulysses of Blue Bar	Rube of Blue Bar
Ch. Mt. Mansfield's Tilt	Ripple of Blue Bar
Mt. Mansfield's Mata Hari	Yorkley Statesman
Ch. Mt. Mansfield's William	Mt. Mansfield's Tear Drop
Ch. Tioga King Arthur	Tioga Robin Hood
Ch. Mt. Mansfield's Forget Me Not	Tioga Wild Honey
Ch. Shiplake Skyblue	Shiplake Swift
	Shiplake Simone
Ch. Ben-Dar's Advance Notice	Ch. Ludar of Blue Bar
Ch. Top O'Tamerlaine	Silvermine Chambray
Flecka's Hush Puppy	Lep of Blue Bar
Ch. Penmaen Wood Sprite	Feather of Blue Bar
Wamlay's Mike Chism	Ch. Mike of Meadboro
Ch. Skidby's Cambridge Miss	Chism's Queenie
Royal Blue of Stone Gables	Ch. Raskalus Raff of Stone Gables
	Tower Hill To and Again

Sire of 15 Champions: Out of:

Ace of Pheasant Ridge	SB-417920	
Penmaen Nutmeg and Clove	SB-415932	
Penmaen Here Comes the Sun	SB-469727	Ch. Penmaen Petunia of Northwood
Penmaen P.T. Lillibet	SB-707336	
Fern Rocks First Edition	SB-379901	
Fern Rocks Jandal's Claribel	SB-639200	
Fern Rocks Betsy Ross Charlin	SB-630958	Ch. Clariho Conversation Piece
Fern Rocks Whipper Snapper	SB-557978	
Heritage Daniel Boone	SB-809152	
Heritage Betsy Ross	SB-809153	Ch. Thistledown Doll O'Willow Run
Harmony Lane London Fog	SB-875754	
Sunswept Milord of Hemlock Lane	SB-802905	Ch. Hemlock Lane Social Event
Sportin' Man of Button Ball	SB-528820	Hi-Hat of Button Ball
Velvet's Blue Moon	SB-142063	Ch. Meadowset's Blue Velvet
Penmaen Blueberry Muffin	SA-775373	Ch. Penmaen Blue Cambric

AM./CAN. CH. JAMES OF CHERRY LANE

AKC No. SA-312329   Whelped April 24, 1964   Dog
Height - 25 inches   Orange Belton
Owner: Wayne C. Gould and Arthur L. Shapera   OFA # ES-118
Breeder: Dorothy S. Reiter

Ch. Sir Herbert of Kennilworth
Am/Can. Ch. Ludar of Blue Bar
Ch. Manlove's Goldie
Am/Can. Ch. Ben-Dar's Winning Stride
Ch. Sunny Jim
Yorkley's Wisp O'Heather
Ch. Southern Lady of Aragon

Ch. Rip of Blue Bar
Vivacious Doll of Vilmar
Ch. Dean of Blue Bar
Ch. Manlove's Goldie of Stagboro
Ch. Commander Richey
Prune's Own Patricia
Tom of Merrie Sherwood
Orange Empress of Aragon

Ch. Sir Herbert of Kennelworth
Ch. Bunnydale's Orange Vulcan
Ch. Norma of Blue Bar
Ch. Pretty Maid of Cherry Lane
Ch. Ernford Highflier
Enid of Cherry Lane
Bunnydale's Daisy Belle

Ch. Rip of Blue Bar
Vivacious Doll of Vilmar
Ch. Lem of Blue Bar
Zo of Blue Bar
Ernford Apollo
Teal of Yaresyde
Dill of Blue Bar
Martie of Blue Bar

Sire of 10 Champions:

		Out of:
Manlove's Chearta First Step	SB-269477	
Chearta Manlove Worried Man	SB-325858	Manlove's Merry Sherry
Chearta Manlove Circe	SB-324306	
Chearta Wil-Bet Golden Blaze	SB-240713	
Lansdowne's Lady Aristocrat	SA-799563	Oxford's Flair of Stone Gables
Sir Lars of Lansdowne	SA-807728	
Fitzpatrick of Lansdowne	SA-934574	Sunswift Misty of Kaynor
Lady Greta of Deerfield Manor	SA-934574	
Gregory of Cherry Lane	SA-928412	Ch. Teresa of Cherry Lane
Elizabeth of Lansdowne	SA-945623	

307

CH. LORIEN'S LADY GALADRIEL

AKC No. SB-75762   Whelped January, 1972   Bitch
Height - 25 inches   Orange Belton
Breeder-Owner: Jeffrey and Irene M. Bottrell

Ch. Skidby's Sturdy Tyke	Ch. Ben-Dar's Advance Notice
Ch. Hillsdale Sentinel	Ch. Hillsdale Susan
Ch. Hillsdale Sparkle	Ch. Ludar of Blue Bar
Ch. Guys 'N Dolls Shalimar Duke	Can. Ch. Pollyanna
Ch. Sir Guy of Ellendale	Ch. Manlove of Ellendale
Ch. Guys 'N Dolls Bridget O'Shea C.D.	Ch. Manlove's Mona
Lady Jill of Ellendale	Ch. Skyline of Stone Gables
	Ch. Manlove's Mona
Ch. English Accent of Valley Run	Ch. Rock Falls Racket
Ch. Merry Rover of Valley Run	Ch. Starbright of Valley Run
Wamlay's Merry Minx	Ch. Mike of Meadboro
Ch. Guys 'N Dolls Honey Grove	Cinderella of Oak Valley
Ch. Hillsdale Sentinel	Ch. Skidby's Sturdy Tyke
Ch. Guys 'N Dolls Miss Adelaide	Ch. Hillsdale Sparkle
Ch. Guys 'N Dolls Bridget O'Shea C.D.	Ch. Sir Guy of Ellendale
	Lady Jill of Ellendale

Dam of 6 Champions: **Sired by:**

Lorien's Ringbearer	SB-559910 ⎤	
Lorien's Lord of Rohan	SB-623864 ⎬	Ch. Raybar's Blue Line
Lorien's Lightfoot	SB-457964 ⎦	
Lorien's American Flyer	SC-263522 ⎤	
Lorien's American Gal	SC-263523 ⎦	Ch. Manlove's All American
Lorien's Blue Sapphire	SB-861855	Ch. Clariho Warpaint

CH. LYNDA'S MELYNDA OF TEL-MO CD

AKC No. SA-155316   Whelped May 19, 1962   Bitch
Height - 24½ inches   Weight - 50 pounds   Orange Belton
Owner: Lynda (Maudsley) Lucast, Shakopee, Mn.
Breeder: Harry B. & Leona N. Kurzrok

Ernford Apollo
Ch. Ernford Highflier
Teal of Yarside
Ch. Pirate of Polperro
Ch. Rock Falls Racket
Ch. Betsworth Gold Flake
Aspetuck's Red Sumac

Silvermine Friar Tuck
Silvermine Sky Chief
Silvermine Wanita
Ch. Panthorn Valley Run Samantha
Ch. Silvermine Whipcord
Ch. Panthorn Gold of Pleasure
Silvermine Decal

Ernford Easter Parade
Ernford Cilldara Silver
Ensign Remor
Tarnock Fiona of Remor
Ch. Rock Falls Cavalier
Ch. Rock Falls Belle
Ch. Silvermine Showman
Ch. Suzette of Setterfield
Ch. Sturdy Max II
Silvermine Nylon
Ch. Silvermine Wagabond
Racket's Gene of Silvermine
Ch. The Snark of Scyld
Silvermine Wanita
Ch. Sturdy Max II
Silvermine Swift

Dam of 6 Champions: **Sired by:**

Tel-Mo's Groovy Gidget	SA-590233 ⎤	
Black Oak's Brett of Tel-Mo	SA-313786 ⎟	
Tel-Mo's Lady Debora	SA-348217 ⎟	Ch. Chandelle's Anchor Man
Gal's Gay Debut of Tel-Mo	SA-542015 ⎟	
Excalibur's Anchors Aweigh	SA-395370 ⎦	
Tel-Mo's Tuffer-N-Hell	SB-32070	Trodgers Cyclamen

AM., CAN. & MEX. CH. LA MAY'S PLAYMATE'S GUNNER, SA-58910
(Ch. La May's Jim Dan Dee x Manlove's Judy)

Sire of 10 Champions:

		Out of:
Quiet Hills Brotherly Love	SA-101371	Ch. La May's Playmate
Farthest North Heather	SA-152351	Farthest North Patches, C.D.
Can. Ch. Quiet Hills Gun Butt	743078	Ch. Farthest North Heather
Bret Harte of Rocky Nevada	SA-133369	
Mark Twain of Rocky Nevada	SA-133371	
Rocky Nevada's Reno Girl	SA-133366	
Rocky Nevada's Shoshone Belle	SA-133368	Can. & Am. Ch. Madame Hi-Tone
Kit Carson of Rocky Nevada	SA-133372	of Rocky Nevada
Pogonip of Rocky Nevada	SA-133373	
Toiyabe of Rocky Nevada	SA-133367	

310

AM. & CAN. CH. LUDAR OF BLUE BAR, S-454627

Ch. Dean of Blue Bar
Ch. Rip of Blue Bar
Ina of Blue Bar
Ch. Sir Herbert of Kennelworth
Banker of Fallondale
Vivacious Doll of Vilmar
Delta of Larana

Ch. Mallhawk's Jeff
Ch. Dean of Blue Bar
Ch. Lakeland's Peaches
Ch. Manlove's Goldie
Ch. Rummey Boy of Stagboro
Ch. Manlove's Goldie of Stagboro
Viola of Stagboro

Ch. Mallhawk's Jeff
Ch. Lakeland's Peaches
Roy of Blue Bar
Ch. Fly of Stagboro
Can. & Am. Ch. Maxie of Stagboro
Ch. Grayland Orange Blossom
Ch. Sturdy Max
Ch. Lakeland's Dawn
Ch. Mallhawk's Rackets Boy
Flora Mallhawk
Rummey Stagboro
Lakeland's Nymph
Rummey Stagboro
Ch. Rose of Stagboro
Rummey Stagboro
Winsome of Stagboro

Sire of 26 Champions:

			Out of:
Can. & Am. Ch. Ben-Dar's Replica	S-689328	⎤	
Can. Ch. Ben-Dar's Special Edition	S-689329		
Yorkley's Statesman	S-689326	⎬ Yorkley Wisp O'Heather	
Can. & Am. Ch. Ben-Dar's Winning Stride	S-689327	⎦	

311

Can. & Am. Ch. Hillsdale Susan	S-747434	
Can. & Am. Ch. Hillsdale Betty	S-663940	
Hillsdale Surprise	S-689350	Can. Ch. Pollyanna
Can. Ch. Hillsdale Sparkle	347752	
Can. & Am. Ch. Ben-Dar's Advance Notice	S-568625	Ch. Silvermine Chambray
Sir Gallant of Panthorn	S-761457	Ch. Silvermine Decal
Tioga Wild Honey	S-688128	Ch. Tioga Dotted Swiss
Dover's Wall Street	S-946627	Ch. Confetti of Calamity Lane
Can. & Am. Ch. Krisquier's Flambeau O'Ludar	S-801138	Can. & Am. Ch. Hillsdale Susan
Can. & Am. Ch. Darby of Carylane	S-660482	Ch. Silvermine Chambray
Lady of Carylane	S-776704	Ch. Silvermine Matchless
Can. & Am. Ch. Ben-Dar's Carbon Copy	S-655200	Ch. Silvermine Chambray
Ben-Dar's Sweet Sue	S-689331	Yorkley Wisp O'Heather
Dover's Replica of Ludar	S-949336	Ch. Confetti of Calamity Lane
Can. & Am. Ch. Ludar's Ludette	451838	Ch. Lady Marco
Dover's Ticker Tape	S-924006	Ch. Confetti of Calamity Lane
Can. Ch. Ben-Dar's Little Slam	340693	Ch. Silvermine Chambray
Can. Ch. Wendy of Algoma	365333	Jill of Algoma
Lady Lark of Panthorn	S-761460	Ch. Silvermine Decal
Dover's Par Value	S-939358	Ch. Confetti of Calamity Lane
Dover's Sir-Plus, C.D.	S-925080	
Sir Lance of Panthorn	S-761458	Ch. Silvermine Decal

Can. and Am. Ch. Ludar's Ludette

AM. & CAN. CH. MADAM HI-TONE OF ROCKY NEVADA, S-980585
(Ch. Rocky Nevada x Ch. Blue Cinders of Blue Bar)

Dam of 7 Champions: **Sired by:**

Rocky Nevada's Shoshone Belle	SA-133368	
Kit Carson of Rocky Nevada	SA-133372	
Bret Harte of Rocky Nevada	SA-133369	Am. & Can. Ch. La May's
Mark Twain of Rocky Nevada	SA-133371	Playmate's Gunner
Rocky Nevada's Reno Girl	SA-133366	
Pogonip of Rocky Nevada	SA-133373	
Toiyabe of Rocky Nevada	SA-133367	

MALLHAWK MALLIE OF ELM KNOLL, S-538880
(Mallhawk Heather Grouse x Mallhawk Quail)

Dam of 6 Champions: **Sired by:**

Eadie of Elm Knoll	S-637788	
Fusilier of Elm Knoll	S-637793	
Emilie of Elm Knoll	S-637787	Ch. Earl of Elm Knoll
Lancer of Elm Knoll	S-637797	
Elaine of Elm Knoll	S-637790	
Ellen of Elm Knoll	S-637791	

CH. MANLOVE'S COLONEL, S-740461
(Am., Can. & Cuban Ch. Rock Falls Colonel x Ch. Manlove's Patsy Lee)

Sire of 10 Champions: **Out of:**

Cabin Hill Blue Belle	S-977764	Ch. Waseeka's Memphis Belle
Flecka's Dutchess of Dunwick	S-991236	
Flecka's Flash of Cabin Hill	SA-3977	Ch. Princessa de Rancho Tranquilo
Flecka's Charlie	S-989553	
Kerry of Berriwood	SA-219087	
Sir Kippford of Berriwood	SA-216002	
Krackerjack of Berriwood	SA-217268	Ch. Popcorn of Berriwood
Koko of Berriwood	SA-219088	
Kernel of Berriwood	SA-220647	
Dover's Dawn of Scotchmoor	SA-242297	Ch. Dover's Ticker Tape

313

Ch. Manlove's Colonel

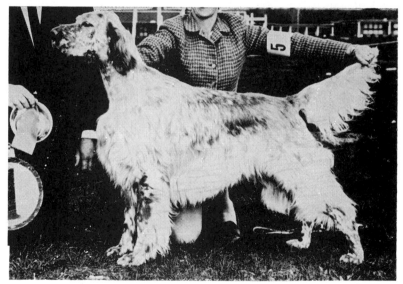

Ch. Flecka's Flash of Cabin Hill (Ch. Manlove's
Colonel — Ch. Princess de Rancho Tranquila

CH. MANLOVE'S ALL AMERICAN

AKC No. SA-435974   Whelped July 1, 1966   Dog
Height - 25½ inches   Weight - 72 pounds   Orange Belton
Breeder-Owner: Judy L. Graef, Verona, N. J.   OFA # ES-125

Ch. Ludar of Blue Bar
Ch. Ben-Dar's Winning Stride
Yorkley Wisp O'Heather
Ch. Buff's Pride
Ch. Dill of Blue Bar
Bunnydale's Daisy Belle
Martie of Blue Bar

Ch. Ben-Dar's Replica
Ch. Krisquier's Lone Eagle
Ch. Hillsdale Susan
Ch. Manlove's Cover Girl
Ch. Rock Falls Colonel
Ch. Manlove's Lovely Lady
Manlove's Lady Juliet

Ch. Sir Herbert of Kennelworth
Ch. Manlove's Goldie
Ch. Sunny Jim
Ch. Southern Lady of Aragon
Ch. Rip of Blue Bar
Schoolgirl Sue of Havertown
Ch. Rummey Sam of Stagboro
Kanandarque Goldie
Ch. Ludar of Blue Bàr
Yorkley's Wisp O'Heather
Ch. Ludar of Blue Bar
Can. Ch. Pollyanna
Ch. Rock Falls Cavalier
Ch. Rock Falls Belle
Ch. Sir Herbert of Kennelworth
Ch. Manlove's Goldie

CH. MANLOVE'S ALL AMERICAN

Sire of 21 Champions: **Out of:**

Manlove's Cap and Gown	SC-436920	⎤
Manlove's Ike	SC-381552	Ch. Manlove's Chearta First Step
Manlove's Sarah	SC-278210	⎦
Drummont's Tasty's Billy	SC-408484	⎤
Drummont's American Eagle	SC-408487	Ch. Guys 'N Dolls Taste of Honey
Drummont's Tasty's Applause	SC-408485	⎦
Erinshire Swinging Liza of B	SC-170913	⎤
Erinshire Chearta Admiration	SC-204577	Ch. Chearta Manlove Circe
Lorien's American Flyer	SC-263522	⎤
Lorien's American Gal	SC-263522	Ch. Lorien's Lady Galadriel
Malmwood Seth	SA-572519	⎤
Manlove's Sir Jeffrey	SA-512942	Ch. Manlove's Priscilla
Pacar's Johnny Appleseed	SA-914299	Miss Ginger of Hershey
Manlove's Molly Magee	SB-608135	Manlove's Lady Winifred
Birdhaven American Legacy	SB-305973	Maeve of Birdhaven
Manlove's American Heidi	SB-176627	Manlove's Heidi of Oaklyn
Manlove's Lancer	SB-459829	Ch. GoGo Girl of Glenarm
Saybrooks Blue Jennie	SB-488572	Manlove's Lady In Blue
Hemlock Lane Holly of Mayhew	SB-841579	Ch. Mayhew's Dabs of Sienna
Riverrun Herbert of Manlove, C.D.	SC-484226	Ch. Katie of Cherry Lane
Chearta's Lancer of Briarclif	SC-568600	Ch. Chearta Manlove Cantique

Ch. Manlove's Cover Girl

316

CH. MANLOVE'S COVER GIRL

AKC No. SA-241419   Whelped July 1, 1963   Bitch
Height - 23½ inches   Weight - 55 pounds   Orange Belton
Breeder-Owner: Judy L. Graef, Verona, N.J.

Ch. Ludar of Blue Bar
Ch. Ben-Dar's Replica
Yorkley Wisp O'Heather
Ch. Krisquier's Lone Eagle
Ch. Ludar of Blue Bar
Ch. Hillsdale Susan
Can. Ch. Pollyanna

Ch. Rock Falls Cavalier
Ch. Rock Falls Colonel
Ch. Rock Falls Belle
Ch. Manlove's Lovely Lady
Ch. Sir Herbert of Kennelworth
Manlove's Lady Juliet
Ch. Manlove's Goldie

Ch. Sir Herbert of Kennelworth
Ch. Manlove's Goldie
Ch. Sunny Jim
Ch. Southern Lady of Aragon
Ch. Sir Herbert of Kennelworth
Ch. Manlove's Goldie
Rummey Sunbeam of Stagboro
Pamela
Ch. Grayland's Racket Boy
Ch. Linda Lou of Blue Bar
Ch. Grayland's Racket Boy
Nocturne of Crowlcroft
Ch. Rip of Blue Bar
Vivacious Doll of Vilmar
Ch. Dean of Blue Bar
Ch. Manlove's Goldie of Stagboro

Dam of 6 Champions:		Sired by:
Manlove's Chimney Sweep	SA-629842	Ch. Sir Timothy of Valley Run
Manlove's Blue Moon	SA-580972	
Manlove's Cover Charge	SA-854826	Manlove's Steve
Manlove's Cover Story	SA-876257	
Manlove's Daisy Mae	SA-748197	Sundridge Halcyon
Manlove's All American	SA-435974	Ch. Buff's Pride

Manlove's Merry Sherry

317

MANLOVE'S MERRY SHERRY

AKC No. SA-854827   Whelped May, 1968   Bitch
Height - 24 inches   Weight - 60 pounds   Orange Belton
Owner: Richard Butterer & Judy L. Graef   OFA # ES-469
Breeder: Elizabeth Wilson

Ch. English Accent of Valley Run	Ch. Rock Falls Racket
Ch. Merry Rover of Valley Run	Ch. Starbright of Valley Run
Wamlay's Merry Minx	Ch. Mike of Meadboro
Ch. Stan The Man of Valley Run	Ch. Cinderella of Oak Valley
Ch. Pirate of Polperro	Ch. Ernford Highflier
Ch. Valley Run Dinah-Mite	Ch. Betsworth Gold Flake
Ch. Panthorn Valley Run Samantha	Silvermine Skychief
	Ch. Panthorn Gold of Pleasure
Ch. Ben-Dar's Winning Stride	Ch. Ludar of Blue Bar
Ch. Buff's Pride	Yorkley Wisp O'Heather
Bunnydale's Daisy Belle	Ch. Dill of Blue Bar
Manlove's Cinnamon Stick	Martie of Blue Bar
Ch. Krisquier's Lone Eagle	Ch. Ben-Dar's Replica
Ch. Manlove's Cover Girl	Ch. Hillsdale Susan
Ch. Manlove's Lovely Lady	Ch. Rock Falls Colonel
	Manlove's Lady Juliet

Dam of 9 Champions: **Sired by:**

Chearta Manlove Cantique	SB-102584	⎤
Chearta Crescent of Manlove	SB-105661	⎥ Ch. Penmaen Canto
Manlove Countess of Polperro	SB-45240	⎥
Manlove's Penny Candy	SB-34302	⎦
Chearta Manlove Circe	SB-324306	⎤
Chearta Manlove Worried Man	SB-325858	⎥ Ch. James of Cherry Lane
Chearta Wil-Bet Golden Blaze	SB-240713	⎥
Manlove's Chearta First Step	SB-269477	⎦
Chearta Manlove Charade	SB-872461	Ch. Guys 'N Dolls Shalimar Duke

318   Ch. Margand Lord Baltimore

Ch. Buzz of Haon
Margand El Capitan
Dutchess's Blue Artemis
Ch. Margand Lord Calvert
Ch. Els-Har Jake
Margand Princess Anne
Ch. Talphant Lady Elizabeth

Ch. Rock Falls Cavalier
Ch. Rock Falls Colonel
Rock Falls Belle
Ch. Phantom Brook's Petticoat
Ch. Ken of Blue Bar
Ch. Phantom Brook's Deductible
Ch. Babe of Blue Bar II

Rummey Stagboro
Ch. Knollcroft Nancy Lou
Prediction's Test Pilot
Rummey Ann's Blue Duchess
Ch. Marbar's Little John
Ch. Merry Sunshine of Maple Lawn
Ch. Mallhawk Orange Lad
Mid-Oak Pride
Ch. Grayland Rackets Boy
Ch. Linda Lou of Blue Bar
Ch. Grayland Rackets Boy
Nocturne of Crowlcroft
Ch. Jesse of Blue Bar
Ora of Blue Bar
Ch. Rip of Blue Bar
Bette of Blue Bar

Sire of 24 Champions:

Out of:

Margand Mary Jane	S-964786	Ch. Stagmore's Lady Jane
Chandelle's Anchor Man	SA-95127	
Chandelle's Air Mail, C.D.	SA-95126	Ch. Chandelle Lady
Chandelle's Allspice	SA-95130	
Chandelle's Littlest Angel	SA-95128	
Robinwood's Angel	SA-143364	Ch. Robinwood's Dot
Robinwood's Big Hunter	SA-157723	
Margand Meteor of Dogstar	SA-234567	Ch. Margand Mary Jane
Stellaire Debute of Ramar	SA-215559	Mary of Haleridge
Chandelle's Bambi	SA-250902	
Chandelle's Bittersweet	SA-250905	Ch. Chandelle Lady
Chandelle's Butterscotch	SA-250903	
Chandelle's Billet-Doux	SA-250904	
Margand Alexandra	SA-208001	Margand Brown Girl
Margand Duke of Baltimore	SA-188370	
Jaccard Hill Alastaire	SA-317411	Ch. Top O' Yankee Doodle Candace
Jaccard Hill Amelia	SA-317412	
Margand Masquerader	SA-363373	Margand Jacquelyne
Margand Jennifer	SA-348398	
Lo-Eris Golden Girl of Golden Q	SA-405891	Ch. Quinn's Golden Dawn Lady
Margand King of Golden Q	SA-363365	
Lady Meg of Shallegan	SA-432211	Ch. Parpoint Prett-Tri
Fedric's Lord Pepper Jacquard	SA-325189	Ch. Top O'Yankee Doodle Candace
Margand Artemis	SA-363370	Margand Jacquelyne

319

CH. MARGAND METEOR OF DOGSTAR

AKC No. SA-234567   Whelped June 13, 1963   Dog
Owner: James H. & Gladys J. Wallace   Orange Belton
Breeder: Margand Kennels

Margand El Capitan	Ch. Buzz of Haon
Ch. Margand Lord Calvert	Dutchess's Blue Artemis
Margand Princess Anne	Ch. Els-Har Jake
Ch. Margand Lord Baltimore	Ch. Talphant Lady Elizabeth
Ch. Rock Falls Colonel	Ch. Rock Falls Cavalier
Ch. Phantom Brook's Petticoat	Ch. Rock Falls Belle
Ch. Phantom Brook's Deductible	Ch. Ken of Blue Bar
	Ch. Babe of Blue Bar II
Ch. Margand Lord Calvert	Margand El Capitan
Ch. Margand Lord Baltimore	Margand Princess Anne
Ch. Phantom Brook's Petticoat	Ch. Rock Falls Colonel
Ch. Margand Mary Jane	Ch. Phantom Brook's Deductible
Ch. Rock Falls King Charles	Ch. Rock Falls Cavalier
Ch. Stagmoor's Lady Jane	Ch. Rip's Miss Dusky Havertown
Lil of Blue Bar	Ricky of Blue Bar
	Ch. Mary of Blue Bar

Sire of 17 Champions: **Out of:**

Gemody's Danny Boy	SA-457261	
Gemody's Star Dust	SA-457263	
Gemody's Gidget Goes Hawaiian	SA-457266	
Gemody's Ina Darling	SA-457267	
Gemody's Barbara Gal	SA-457270	
Gemody's Rambling Laddie	SA-457260	Ch. Dione Duchess of Dogstar
Gemody's Gemini of Dogstar	SA-460394	
Gemody's Sophisticated Lady	SA-457268	
Gemody's Aquarius	SB-94465	
Gemody's Taste of Honey	SA-234567	
Gemody's Mischievous Cecilia	SA-885872	
Gal's Tough-Enough	SA-894030	
Gal's Gabbi Girl	SA-832487	Ch. Gal's Gay Debut of Tel-Mo, C.D.
Gal's Fantasia	SA-915897	
Parpoint Pacifica	SB-376230	Ch. Parpoint Placater
Benchmark Amy	SA-744051	Ch. Margand Martha
Merry Meteor of Dogstar	SA-404752	Quiet Hills White Cloud

320

CH. MEADOWSET'S SMOOTH SAILING

AKC No. SA-961250
Height - 24 inches
Owner: Barbara Panos
Breeder: Janet E. Miner

Whelped April 12, 1971

Bitch
Orange Belton

Ch. Sidby's Bosun of Stone Gables
Ch. Sir Kip of Manitou
High-Tor's Spicy Lady
Ch. Clariho Rough Rider
Ch. Prince of Deerfield
Clariho Piper of Stone Gables
Candy of Clariho

Ch. Ben-Dar's Winning Stride
Ch. Buff's Pride
Bunnydales Daisy Belle
Ch. Calumet of Makepeace
Ch. Merry Rover of Valley Run
Ch. Valley Run Dinah's Damoselle
Ch. Valley Run Dinah-Mite

Can. Ch. Wamlay's Mike Chism
Royal Blue of Stone Gables
Ch. Cinnabar of High-Tor
Blue Mountain Plain Jane
Ch. The Rock of Stone Gables
Ch. Frosty of Stone Gables
Ch. The Rock of Stone Gables
High-Tor's Spicy Lady
Ch. Ludar of Blue Bar
Yorkley Wisp O'Heather
Ch. Dill of Blue Bar
Martie of Blue Bar
Ch. English Accent of Valley Run
Wamlay's Merry Minx
Ch. Pirate of Polperro
Ch. Panthorn Valley Run Samantha

Dam of 7 Champions:

Sired by:

Tra-Bon Lindsay Burlingham	SB-864025	
Tra-Bon Chelsea Burlingham	SB-186206	
Tra-Bon's Sam	SB-235825	
Tra-Bon's Orange Haze	SB-264805	Ch. Heljax Top Hat
Tra-Bon's Orange Sunshine	SB-264806	
Heljax Drummer Boy of Tra-Bon	SB-398602	
Meadowset's Patience of Tamara	SB-202081	

CH. MERRY ROVER OF VALLEY RUN, SA-116098

Ch. Rock Falls Cavalier
Ch. Rock Falls Racket
Ch. Rock Falls Belle
Ch. English Accent of Valley Run
Sturdy Max II
Ch. Starbright of Valley Run
Silvermine Confection

Thelan Sir Rockland
Ch. Mike of Meadboro
Lady MacBeth
Wamlay's Merry Minx
Ch. Sharoc's Monty of Oak Valley
Cinderella of Oak Valley
Gold Dust of Oak Valley

Ch. Grayland Rackets Boy
Ch. Linda Lou of Blue Bar
Ch. Grayland Rackets Boy
Nocturne of Crowlcroft
Ch. Lakeland's Yuba
Ch. Dora of Maridor
Ch. Dean of Blue Bar
Silvermine Wanita
Ch. Jack O'Racket
Rock Falls Lady Marilyn
Ch. Honor's Even Marksman
Royal Whirl
Sturdy Max II
Ch. Sharoc Dolly Madison
Ch. Golden Boy of Fairlawn
Judy of Stoughton

Sire of 30 Champions: **Out of:**

Thenderin Starstream of Delta	SA-499657	
Thenderin Merry Belle O'Delta	SA-436794	
Thenderin Jessabelle O'Delta	SA-505716	
Thenderin Revor of Delta	SA-413620	Ch. Thenderin Golden Dream
Thenderin Headliner of Delta	SA-461548	
Thenderin Class-E-Lady O'Delta	SA-461547	
Bem's Sir Anthony of O'Delta	SA-400906	

322

Guys 'N Dolls Lady Eliza	SA-493240	
Guys 'N Dolls Society Max	SA-493235	
Guys 'N Dolls Honey Grove	SA-493239	Ch. Guys 'N Dolls Miss Adelaide
Guys 'N Dolls Hickory Slim	SA-493238	
Bold Bidder of Bloomfield	SA-405530	
Breeze of Bloomfield	SA-407864	Ch. Hidden Lane's Broker's Tip
Hidden Lane Bloomfield Babu	SA-676325	
Scheherazade of Forest	SA-513288	
Merry Mist of Forest	SA-513292	Ch. Penmaen Suzanne of Forest
Forest Richard The Crusader	SA-513291	
Merry Rose of Valley Run	SA-433293	
Pinney Paige of Valley Run	SA-454463	Ch. Valley Run's Sabrina Fair
Rusty of Valley Run	SA-415290	
Stan The Man of Valley Run	SA-24088	Ch. Valley Run Dinah-Mite
Sir Timothy of Valley Run	SA-259096	
Meadowset Gay Go of Valley Run	SA-578472	Domino of Meadowset
Meadowset Cindy of Valley Run	SA-535144	
Meadowset's Polly Flinders	SA-292913	Blue Serenade of Stone Gables
Valley Run's Windfall	SA-307697	
Judy's Gingersnap	SA-345161	Ch. Rebecca of Cherry Lane
Valley Run's English Muffin	SA-346590	
Top Man of Meadboro	SA-395038	Ch. Flirtation of Meadboro
Bambi-Two of Bloomfield	SA-405529	Ch. Bambi of Bloomfield

Ch. Stan The Man of Valley Run

CH. MIKE OF MEADBORO, S-415928

Ch. Grayland Rackets Boy
Ch. Jack O'Rackets
Ch. Linda of Blue Bar
Thelan Sir Rocklyn
Ch. Grayland Rackets Boy
Ch. Rock Falls Lady Marilyn
Nocturne of Crowlcroft

Ch. Maro of Maridor
Ch. Honor's Even Marksman
Ch. Rodger Dale Dean
Lady McBeth
Ch. Rummey Sam of Stagboro
Royal Whirl
End O'Maine Tangerine

Rummey Stagboro
Blenheim Violet
Ch. Blue Bar Limited
Gretta of Blue Bar
Rummey Stagboro
Blenheim Violet
Ch. Blaze of Fallondale
Romance of Crowlcroft
Ch. Sturdy Max
Ch. Lakelands Dawn
Ch. Sturdy Max
Ch. Nellie of Stagboro
Rummey 2nd of Stagboro
Kate of Stagboro
Ch. Cedric of Delwed
Margarine Penelope

Sire of 19 Champions:

		Out of:
Sir Rellim of Stone Gables	S-717651	Ch. Prize Par-Sal of Stone Gables
Mt. Mansfield's Smuggler	S-670594	Reveille's Pandora
The Rock of Stone Gables, C.D.	S-770432	Ch. Vivacious Sally of Vilmar
Weloset Yankee Boy	S-729866	Cinderella of Oak Valley
Weloset Silver Ripple	S-706319	Wamlay Snow White
Phantom Brook's Thunderbolt	S-819203	Ch. Phantom Brook's Popcorn
Chism's Cherokee Mike	S-812186	Chism's Queenie
Pretty Romper of Panthorn	S-847494	Ch. Silvermine Decal
Kings Ransom Timberdoodle	S-804912	Ch. Hillsdale Surprise

Mike of Meadboro (continued)

Can. Ch. Wamlay's Mike Chism	S-812817	Chism's Queenie
Agene's Mi-Bo	S-591977	Ch. Agene's Holli-Jo
Thelan Memory of Nocturne	S-507406	Ch. Rock Falls Lady Marilyn
Wamlay's Lollypop	S-749782	Ch. Vivacious Sally of Vilmar
Phantom's Brook's Blizzard	S-819202	Ch. Phantom Brook's Popcorn
Thelan Mark of Distinction	S-507401	Ch. Rock Falls Lady Marilyn
Pheasant Point Hottentot	S-782526	Ch. Rock Falls Virginia Date
Jean's Pearl Buttons	S-832852	Breezy Acres Spitfire
Robin Roy of Stone Gables	S-877442	Ch. Prize Par-Sal of Stone Gables
Jean's Eldorado	S-884871	Breezy Acres Spitfire

CH. MT. MANSFIELD TEAR DROP, S-582157
(Ch. Prune's Own Parade x Reveille's Pandora)

Dam of 6 Champions:

Sired by:

Mt. Mansfield Spring Song	S-928030	Ch. Ulysses of Blue Bar
Mt. Mansfield Rum Runner	S-866758	Ch. Mt. Mansfield Smuggler
Mt. Mansfield Sugar Bush	S-928028	Ch. Ulysses of Blue Bar
Mt. Mansfield Flanders Field	S-981024	Ch. Yorkley Statesman
Mt. Mansfield Moonbeam	SA-60161	Ch. Ulysses of Blue Bar
Can. Ch. Mt. Mansfield Hill Billy	513636	

325

CH. MT. MANSFIELD'S WILLIAM

AKC No. SA-412075   Whelped September 24, 1965   Dog
Breeder-Owner: Rosamond A. Chambers   Blue Belton

Ch. Rube of Blue Bar	Ch. Sir Herbert of Kennelworth
Ch. Ulysses of Blue Bar	Ch. Norma of Blue bar
Ch. Ripple of Blue Bar	Ch. Lep of Blue Bar
Ch. Mt. Mansfield's Tilt	Ch. Penny of Happy Valley
Ch. Yorkley Statesman	Ch. Ludar of Blue Bar
Mt. Mansfield's Mata Hari	Yorkley Wisp O'Heather
Ch. Mt. Mansfield's Tear Drop	Ch. Prune's Own Parade
	Reveille's Pandora
Tioga Robin Hood	Ch. Ulysses of Blue Bar
Ch. Tioga King Arthur	Countess of Blue Bar
Ch. Tioga Wild Honey	Ch. Ludar of Blue Bar
Ch. Mt. Mansfield's Forget-Me-Not	Ch. Tioga Dotted Swiss
Shiplake Swift	Rombalds Templar
Eng./Am. Ch. Shiplake Sky Blue	Truslers Freckles of Frejender
Shiplake Simone	Shiplake Sweet William
	Shiplake Medeshamstead Delphine

Sire of 20 Champions: **Out of:**

Delta's Cover Girl	SA-949904	
Delta's Charatan	SA-949903	
Thenderin Jenny Luv of Delta	SA-888202	
Thenderin Big Dream of Delta	SA-764875	
Thenderin Maggie Now of Delta	SA-755044	Ch. Thenderin Golden Dream
Thenderin Mr. Rad of Delta	SA-848600	
Thenderin Miss O'Dell of Delta	SA-788493	
Bem's Sir Philip of Delta	SA-753315	
Mt. Mansfield's Golden Rod	SA-876981	
Knighttown Back Again	SB-364376	
Knighttown Billy The Kid	SB-364377	Nocturne's Jenny of Knighttown
Knighttown Lawdy Lawdy	SB-159851	
Highland's Whip of Penmaen	SA-607617	Ch. Penmaen Wood-Sprite
Mt. Mansfield's Wistful	SA-597255	
Mt. Mansfield's Sun Rise	SA-886929	Dapplewhite Dawn
Mt. Mansfield's Dusk	SA-886930	
Delta's Blue Charisma	SB-173289	Yorkley Hope of Lonesome Lane
Delta's Pepper	SB-153560	
Rumpelstiltskin of Bryn Mawr	SA-857740	Idlenot's Dancers Daughter
Idlenot's Nu Blu	SA-942026	Ch. Hiddenlane's Penny Candy

CH. PANTHORN VALLEY RUN SAMANTHA, S-956900
(Silvermine Sky Chief x Ch. Panthorn's Gold-of-Pleasure)

Dam of 6 Champions: **Sired by:**

Lady Jane of Polperro	SA-154899	
Valley Run Dinah-Mite	SA-163052	
Lynda's Melynda of Tel-Mo	SA-155316	Ch. Pirate of Polperro
Puck of Polperro	SA-154898	
Valley Run Samantha's Birdie	SA-350122	Ch. Flecka's Charlie
Misty Sample of Valley Run	SA-370858	

326

CH. PARPOINT PLACATER

AKC No. SA-484561   Whelped September, 1966   Bitch
Height - 24¾ inches   Weight - 60 pounds   Orange Belton
Owner: Gordon M. Parham, Salem, Mi.
Breeder: Dr. Harry E. Schneiter

Ernford Kingfisher	Kirket Kerryboy
Ch. Ernford Oriole	Eng. Ch. Ernford Evening Flight
Eng. Ch. Ernford Cildara Felicity	Grouse of Capard
Ch. Margand Wildcatter	Minx of Medeshamstead
Ch. Margand Lord Baltimore	Ch. Margand Lord Calvert
Ch. Margand Lady Jane	Ch. Phantom Brooks Petticoat
Ch. Stagmoor's Lady Jane	Ch. Rock Falls King Charles
	Lil of Blue Bar
Ernford Kingfisher	Kirket of Kerryboy
Ch. Ernford Oriole	Eng. Ch. Ernford Evening Flight
Eng. Ch. Ernford Cildara Felicity	Grouse of Capard
Ch. Parpoint Pretti Tri	Minx of Medeshamstead
Ch. Darby of Carylane	Ch. Ludar of Blue Bar
Ch. Parpoint Precarious	Ch. Silvermine Chambray
Ch. Silvermine Matchless	Ch. Silvermine Wagabond
	Ch. Silvermine Swift

Dam of 9 Champions: Sired by:

Margand Huck Finn	SA-941288	
Margand London Boy	SA-952698	
Margand Merry of Jaccard Hill	SA-962756	
Margand Rusty Ann	SA-941286	Ch. Jaccard Hill Alastaire
Margand Marjorie	SA-941287	
Kelpare Model of Parpoint	SB-13315	
Parpoint Peppacorn	SB-679278	
Manlove's Mister Chips	SB-455386	Ch. Hiddenlane Turk-Son of Mayhew
Parpoint Pacifica	SB-376230	Ch. Margand Meteor of Dogstar

CH. PENMAEN WANDERING HOME

AKC No. SA-274296   Whelped June 29, 1964   Bitch
Height - 24¼ inches   Orange Belton
Owner: James & Susan L. Hanson, Haddam, Ct.
Breeder: Susan S. Maire

Ch. Ludar of Blue Bar   Ch. Sir Herbert of Kennelworth
Ch. Ben-Dar's Advance Notice   Ch. Manlove's Goldie
Ch. Silvermine Chambray   Ch. The Snark of Scyld
Ch. Top O' Tamerlaine   Silvermine Wanita
Ch. Lep of Blue Bar   Ch. Matt of Blue Bar
Flecka's Hush Puppy   Dora of Blue Bar
Ch. Flecka Feathers of Blue Bar   Ch. Silvermine Wagabond
                                         Winkie of Blue Bar

Ch. Mike of Meadboro   Thelan Sir Rocklyn
Can. Ch. Wamlay's Mike Chism   Lady McBeth
Chism's Queenie   Ch. Rock Falls Skyway
Ch. Skidby's Cambridge Miss   Colonel's Manlove Lady
Ch. Raskalus Raff of Stone Gables   Silvermine Hot Shot
Royal Blue of Stone Gables   Cinderella of Oak Valley
Tower Hill To and Again   Rock Falls White Cloud
                                         April of Blue Bar

Dam of 7 Champions: Sired by:

Northwood's Miss Poise 'N Ivy   SB-66526
Northwood's Prodigal Son   SA-797399
Northwood's Lancelot   SA-729650
Northwood Rebel Rouser   SA-955928   Ch. Galahad of Polperro
Valiant of Northwood   SA-738203
Lady Shea of Northwood   SB-129981
Penmaen Petunia of Northwood   SA-775327

CH. PHANTOM BROOK'S DEDUCTIBLE, S-482279

Roy of Blue Bar
Ch. Jesse of Blue Bar
Ch. Lovely Lady of Stucile
Ch. Ken of Blue Bar
Ch. Dean of Blue Bar
Ora of Blue Bar
Ch. Gem of Blue Bar

Ch. Dean of Blue Bar
Ch. Rip of Blue Bar
Ina of Blue Bar
Babe of Blue Bar II
Ch. Rummey Sam of Stagboro
Bette of Blue Bar
Kanandarque Goldie

Ch. Mallhawk's Jeff
Kanandarque Lovelyness
Rummey Stagboro
Ch. Modern Maid of Stucile
Ch. Mallhawk's Jeff
Ch. Lakeland's Peaches
Kanandarque Rackets Boy
Inglehurst Matchless
Ch. Mallhawk's Jeff
Ch. Lakeland's Peaches
Roy of Blue Bar
Ch. Fly of Stagboro
Rummey II of Stagboro
Kate of Stagboro
Ch. Dean of Blue Bar
Ch. Gem of Blue Bar

Dam of 8 Champions:

		Sired by:
Phantom Brook's Petticoat	S-607395	Can., Am. & Cuban
Phantom Brook's Capital Gains	S-865996	Ch. Rock Falls Colonel
Phantom Brook's Popcorn	S-607396	
Phantom Brook's Frolic	S-658352	Ch. Phantom Brook's Crown
Phantom Brook's Excess Profit	S-865997	Can., Am. & Cuban
Phantom Brook's Gold Digger	S-866000	Ch. Rock Falls Colonel
Phantom Brook's Chip	S-989999	Phantom Brook's Cholmondley
Phantom Brook's Dale	S-990000	

PHANTOM BROOK'S FOREVER YOURS, SA-87976
(Mt. Mansfield's Spruce Peak x Ch. Phantom Brook's Popcorn)

Dam of 6 Champions:

		Sired by:
Raybar's Orange Blossom	SA-346878	
Raybar's Brandy	SA-344333	
Raybar's Champagne Velvet	SA-345008	
Raybar's Boilermaker	SA-345782	Ch. Spark 2nd of Cherry Lane
Raybar's Mai Tai of Taporcan	SA-410686	
Raybar's Early Times	SA-357836	

POSIE OF BLUE BAR, S-738432
(Ch. Lep of Blue Bar x Ginny of Blue Bar)

Dam of 7 Champions:

		Sired by:
Gentleman Jim of Valley Run	SA-86980	
Prince Charlie of Valley Run	SA-104105	
Valley Run Dixie Barbu	SA-58256	Ch. English Accent of Valley Run
Valley Run Cinnamon Cindy	SA-88582	
Valley Run's Miss Cassandra	SA-119254	
Valley Run's Sabrina Fair	SA-119253	
Quiambaugh Scotch Lassie	S-884701	Ch. Rock Falls Cavalier

329

CH. PRINCE OF DEERFIELD

AKC No. SA-55588   Whelped July, 1960   Dog
Height - 26 inches   Weight - 65 pounds   Orange Belton
Owner: Bethny Hall Mason, Yardley, Pa.
Breeder: Frank Hurdis

Thelan Sir Rocklyn	Ch. Jack O'Rackets
Ch. Mike of Meadboro	Rock Falls Lady Marilyn
Lady McBeth	Ch. Honor's Even Marksman
Ch. The Rock of Stone Gables, CD	Royal Whirl
Ch. Rip of Blue Bar	Ch. Dean of Blue Bar
Ch. Vivacious Sally of Vilmar	Ina of Blue Bar
Vivacious Lass of Vilmar	Banker of Fallondale
	Delta of Larana
Silvermine Hotshot	Ch. Silvermine Wagabond
Ch. Raskalus Raff of Stone Gables	Ch. Ship Cape Speckles
Cinderella of Oak Valley	Ch. Sharoc Monte of Oak Valley
Ch. Frosty of Stone Gables	Gold Dust of Oak Valley
Rock Falls White Cloud	Ch. Rock Falls Colonel
Tower Hill To and Again	Ch. Linda Lou of Blue Bar
April of Blue Bar	Ch. Dean of Blue Bar
	Ch. Tibby of Blue Bar

Sire of 15 Champions: **Out of:**

Clariho Fieldstone Carousel	SA-430994 ⌉	
Clariho Blossom Slosson	SA-429885	
Clariho Joint Account	SA-429884	Ch. Tiffany of Clariho
Clariho Pym of Stone Gables	S-292346 ⌋	
Peppermint of Clariho	SA-279557 ⌉	
Clariho Pell of Stone Gables	SA-429885	Candy of Clariho
Clariho Piper of Stone Gables	SA-296427 ⌋	
Blue Talisman of Stone Gables	SA-295904 ⌉	
Duke of Whittenton	SA-287087	Blue Ecstasy of Stone Gables
Raff's Replica of Stone Gables	SA-495782 ⌋	
Prince William of B	SA-523978 ⌉	
Prince Charles of B	SA-523979 ⌋	Margand Evening Flight of B
Ranger of Stone Gables	SA-341925	Roxanne of Stone Gables
Jolly Rector of Stone Gables	SA-634553	Thenderin Meg of Dunemere
Westward Ho of Stone Gables	SA-813874	Clariho Blue Horizon

CH. RAYBAR'S AIN'T SHE SWEET

AKC No. SA-408241   Whelped April 24, 1966   Bitch
Height - 23½ inches   Orange Belton
Owner: Ray & Barbara Parsons, Las Cruces, NM.
Breeder: Ray S. & Barbara J. Parsons & Joan R. Stainer

Ch. Ben-Dar's Winning Stride
Ch. Windsor of Cherry Lane
Bunnydale's Daisy Belle
Ch. Spark II of Cherry Lane
Ch. Bunnydale's Orange Vulcan
Lady of Cherry Lane
Ch. Lady of Carylane

Ch. Ludar of Blue Bar
Yorkley Wisp O' Heather
Dill of Blue Bar
Martie of Blue Bar
Ch. Sir Herbert of Kennelworth
Ch. Norma of Blue Bar
Ch. Ludar of Blue Bar
Ch. Silvermine Matchless
Ch. Sir Herbert of Kennelworth
Ch. Manlove's Goldie
Ch. Bullet of Calamity Lane
Ch. Rock Candy of Calamity Lane
Ch. Yorkley Ensign Roberts
Ch. Candy of Blue Bar
Ch. Rock Falls Lieutenant
Ch. Candy of Blue Bar

Ch. Ludar of Blue Bar
Dover's Doc Holliday
Ch. Confetti of Calamity Lane
Ch. Frenessa of Calamity Lane
Ch. Bullet of Calamity Lane
Ch. Calamity of Calamity Lane
Ch. Rock Candy of Calamity Lane

Dam of 6 Champions:

		Sired by:
Raybar's Grand Gusto	SA-813268	
Raybar's Show Stopper of Wesley	SA-721148	Ch. Guys 'N Dolls Shalimar Duke
Guys 'N Dolls Gentry of Raybar	SA-844379	
Raybar's Hat Trick	SA-546317	
Raybar's Sweepstakes	SA-540440	Raybar's Boilermaker
Raybar's Rachel	SB-92348	Ch. Raybar's Secret Agent

CH. RAYBAR'S BLUE LINE

AKC No. SA-702351   Whelped December 25, 1968   Dog
Owner: Robert & Nancy Praiswater   Blue Belton
Breeder: C.A. Welborn   OFA # ES-379

Ch. Ben-Dar's Winning Stride	Ch. Ludar of Blue Bar
Ch. Windsor of Cherry Lane	Yorkley Wisp O'Heather
Bunnydale's Daisy Belle	Ch. Dill of Blue Bar
Ch. Spark II of Cherry Lane	Martie of Blue Bar
Ch. Bunnydale's Orange Vulcan	Ch. Sir Herbert of Kennelworth
Lady of Cherry Lane	Ch. Norma of Blue Bar
Ch. Lady of Carylane	Ch. Ludar of Blue Bar
	Ch. Silvermine Matchless
Flecka's Scout	Flecka's Mr. Trax
Ch. Flecka's Fancy Chips	Ch. Princessa de Rancho Tranquillo
Ch. Fancy Feathers	Jeff of Blue Bar
Flecka's Starr Fire	Flecka's Fancy
Bowbrae He's Mine	Rasputin Jones
Belle Starr	Ch. Kiko Kiko of Lua Lua Lei
Flecka's Powder Puff	Ch. Mallhawk Bob White
	Ch. Flecka's Powder

Sire of 16 Champions: **Out of:**

Seamrog Blue Note	SB-502387	⎫	
Seamrog Ballad In Blue	SB-493607		
Seamrog Moody Blues O'Kenwood	SB-619309		Ch. Guys 'N Dolls Ziegfield Girl, C.D.
Seamrog Stargazer	SC-505824	⎭	
Lorien's Ringbearer	SB-559910	⎫	
Lorien's Lord of Rohan	SB-623864		Ch. Lorien's Lady Galadriel
Lorien's Lightfoot	SB-457964	⎭	
Timbertrails Tickertape	SB-942104	⎤	
Timbertrail Peaches 'N Cream	SB-912746	⎦	Ch. Heatherhope Cindy Meg
Raybar's Flecka Patterns	SB-191356	⎤	
Flecka's Sandpiper Parader	SB-180883	⎦	Ch. Flecka's Sandpiper of Raybar
Tedmar Fallin In Love Again	SB-637826		Lady Allison of Tedmar
Wyncastle Showoff of Starvue	SB-860481	⎤	
Wyncastle Affair To Remember, C. D.	SC-253935	⎦	Ch. Storybooks Merry Wyncastle
Arnee's Nell'Son of Nor'Coaster	SA-843058		Ch. Hidden Lane's Nelle
Raybar's Macarthur	SA-957385		Ch. Raybar's Champagne Velvet

CH. ROCK FALLS CAVALIER, S-131384

Spiron Jagersbo
Rummey Stagboro
Selkirk Snooksie
Ch. Grayland Rackets Boy
   Int. Ch. Rackets Rummey
Bleheim Violet
   Principe Bonnie

   Kanandarque Rackets Boy
Ch. Blue Bar Limited
   Inglehurst Matchless
Ch. Linda Lou of Blue Bar
   Ch. Mallhawk Jeff
Gretta of Blue Bar
   Ch. Lakeland's Peaches

Int. Ch. Spiron
Arbu Lala B
Int. Ch. McConnell's Nori
Int. Ch. Selkirk Juliet
Ch. Mallwyd Ralph
Stylish Pretty Polly
Snowdon Ralph
Graylands Belle
Ch. Mallhawk Rackets Boy
Selkirk's Mallhawk Juliet
Ch. Sir Orkney Willgress
Inglehurst Mary
Ch. Mallhawk Rackets Boy
Flora Mallhawk
Rummey Stagboro
Lakeland's Nymph

Sire of 21 Champions:

		Out of:
Can., Am. & Cuban Ch. Rock Falls Colonel	S-329961	Ch. Rock Falls Belle
Rock Falls Racket	S-254264	
Wilbert's Snooksie	S-709092	Hyde's Kip
Rock Falls Troubadour	S-370334	Ch. Manlove's Goldie of Stagboro

Rock Falls King Charles	S-446142	Ch. Rip's Miss Dusky of Havertown
Rock Falls Rhett Butler	S-804176	Rock Falls Libby
Carolina's Adorable Lady	S-360849	Prune's Own Sweetheart
King's Ransom Bufflehead	S-477791	Ch. Suave of Scyld
Rock Falls Virginia Dare	S-504564	Ch. Rock Falls Belle
Hadceda Jewel 2nd	S-461501	Ch. Rip's Miss Dusky of Havertown
Flush of Blue Bar	S-524585	Ch. Mary of Blue Bar
Rock Falls Blue Baron	S-402086	Ch. Manlove's Goldie of Stagboro
Rocky Nevada	S-504146	Ch. Miss Tilly of Blue Bar
Al-Kay's Gold Fever	S-625813	Ch. Thelan Memory of Nocturne
King's Ransom Lord Jeff	S-477790	Ch. Suave of Scyld
Manlove's Patsy Girl	S-468759	Manlove's Rose Dee
Hadceda Cavalier	S-461499	Ch. Rip's Miss Dusky of Havertown
Rock Falls Crystal	S-850903	Ch. Rock Falls Mamie
Rock Falls Lancelot	S-370333	Ch. Manlove's Goldie of Stagboro
Rock Falls Galahad	S-256844	Ch. Rock Falls Belle
Quiambaugh Scotch Lassie	S-884701	Posie of Blue Bar

The great Ch. Rock Falls Colonel, son of Cavalier
and winner of 101 Bests in Show, with his owners.

334

AM., CAN. & CUBAN CH. ROCK FALLS COLONEL, S-329961

Rummey Stagboro
Ch. Grayland Rackets Boy
Bleheim Violet
Ch. Rock Falls Cavalier
    Ch. Blue Bar Limited
Ch. Linda of Blue Bar
Gretta of Blue Bar

Rummey Stagboro
Ch. Grayland Rackets Boy
Bleheim Violet
Ch. Rock Falls Belle
    Ch. Blaze of Fallondale
Nocturne of Crowlcroft
Romance of Crowlcroft

Spiron Jagersbo
Selkirk Snooksie
Int. Ch. Rackets Rummey
Principe Bonnie
Kanandarque Rackets Boy
Inglehurst Matchless
Ch. Mallhawk Jeff
Ch. Lakeland's Peaches
Spiron Jagersbo
Selkirk Snooksie
Int. Ch. Racket's Rummey
Principe Bonnie
Ch. Mark of Stagboro
Ch. Grayland Orange Blossom
Ch. Ladysman of Jagersbo
Patrician Lady of Jagersbo

Sire of 30 Champions:

		Out of:
Manlove's Colonel (10)	S-740461	Ch. Manlove's Patsy Girl
Phantom Brook's Capital Gains	S-865996	Ch. Phantom Brook's Deductible
Manlove's Lady Wolfscroft	S-855790	Manlove's Jenny Lee
Cabin Hill Sensation	S-880887	Rock Falls Amber

335

Sig of Snowfeather	S-545355	Ch. Dame Bonny of Snowfeather
Phantom Brook's Petticoat	S-607395	Ch. Phantom Brook's Deductible
Heljax Sweet Lady	S-642275	Heljax Rebecca
Phantom Brook's Popcorn	S-607396	Ch. Phantom Brook's Deductible
Can. & Am. Ch. Rock Falls Manlove Peter Pan	S-581673	Alliene of Blue Bar
Rock Falls Mamie	S-623498	Rock Falls Eve
Rock Falls Dixie Darling	S-614218	Rock Falls Amber
Destiny's Small Talk	S-541769	Jubalee's Destiny
Manlove's Dawn	S-581239	Ch. Manlove's Goldie
Phantom Brook's Lyric	S-665384	Ch. Phantom Brook's Fortune
Craiglare's Major's Command	S-681766	Bolton Rebound
Can. & Am. Ch. Manlove's Ike	S-621883	Rock Falls Eve
Rolling Greens Marysam	S-714231	Ch. Caroline's Adorable Lady
Rock Falls Sky Way	S-585551	Rock Falls Peggy
Bishop of Highbridge Acres	S-654228	Blue Lady of Highbridge Acres
Manlove's Anna Lee	S-740464	Ch. Manlove's Patsy Girl
Rock Falls Lieutenant	S-519226	Jacklinn-O-Rackets
Rock Falls Daisy Mae	S-614213	Rock Falls Eve
Phantom Brook's Gold Digger	S-866000	Ch. Phantom Brook's Deductible
Manlove of Ellendale	S-907448	Ch. Manlove's Dawn
Phantom Brook's Excess Profit	S-865997	Ch. Phantom Brook's Deductible
Cabin Hill Hostess	S-880889	Rock Falls Amber
Manlove's Mona	S-810218	Ch. Rip's Miss Dusky of Havertown
Manlove's Belle	S-810216 ⎤	
Colonel Robert E. Lee	S-838435 ⎦	Ch. Manlove's Patsy Girl
Manlove's Lovely Lady	S-987652	Manlove's Lady Juliet

336

CH. ROCK FALLS RACKET, S-254264

Rummey Stagboro
Ch. Grayland Rackets Boy
Blenheim Violet
Ch. Rock Falls Cavalier
    Ch. Blue Bar Limited
Ch. Linda of Blue Bar
    Gretta of Blue Bar

Rummey Stagboro
Ch. Grayland Rackets Boy
Blenheim Violet
Ch. Rock Falls Belle
    Ch. Blaze of Fallondale
Nocturne of Crowlcroft
    Romance of Crowlcroft

Spiron Jagersbo
Selkirk Snooksie
Int. Ch. Rackets Rummey
Principe Bonnie
Kanandarque Rackets Boy
Inglehurst Matchless
Ch. Mallhawk Jeff
Ch. Lakeland's Peaches
Spiron Jagersbo
Selkirk Snooksie
Int. Ch. Racket's Rummey
Principe Bonnie
Ch. Mark of Stagboro
Ch. Grayland Orange Blossom
Ch. Ladysman of Jagersbo
Patrician Lady of Jagersbo

Sire of 29 Champions:

		Out of:
Can. & Am. Ch. Silvermine Jackpot	S-491402	Silvermine Corrine
Aspetuck's Red Letter	S-648297	Aspetuck's Red Sumac
Can. & Am. Ch. Chatterwood's Hot Toddy	S-696509	Ch. Aspetuck's Diana
Betsworth Gold Flake	S-601825	Aspetuck's Red Sumac
Silvermine Roderick 2nd	S-651705	Wamlay Snow White
Chatterwood on the Rocks	S-696508	Ch. Aspetuck's Diana

337

Silvermine Roulette	S-491401	Silvermine Corinne
Ike of Blue Bar	S-586365	Ch. Rip Tide of Blue Bar
Can. & Am. Ch. Silvermine Custom Maid	S-491405	Silvermine Corinne
Zamitz Exciting Expose	S-660334	Ch. Zamitz Bread and Butter
Chatterwood Lyric	S-824737	Aspetuck's Diana
Aspetuck's Chief Waramaug	S-883218	Ch. Aspetuck's Feather
English Accent of Valley Run	S-893847	Ch. Starbright of Valley Run
Waseeka's Jiminy Cricket	S-778397	Ch. Scyld's The Black Widow
Zamitz Export Edition	S-660332	Ch. Zamitz Bread and Butter
Deepwood Danny	S-669036	Ch. Aspetuck's Feather
Betsworth Blue Print	S-663667	Ch. Scyld's The Black Widow
Aspetuck's Golden Touch	S-696515 ⎤	
Chatterwood Marmalade	S-824735 ⎦	Ch. Aspetuck's Diana
Betsworth It's A Racket	S-635115 ⎤	
Candlewood Destiny	S-668475 ⎦	Duchess of Iversley
Valley Run Starbright's Gina	S-918827	Ch. Starbright of Valley Run
Zamitz Early Edition	S-660329	Ch. Zamitz Bread and Butter
Aspetuck's Shadow	S-957593	Ch. Aspetuck's Diana
Star Rocket of Valley Run	S-976906 ⎤	
Sweet Suzanna	S-858168 ⎦	Ch. Starbright of Valley Run
Aspetuck's Red Satin, C.D.	S-915777	Ch. Aspetuck's Diana
Archibald of Valley Run	S-983561	Ch. Starbright of Valley Run
Cedar Retreat's Rocket	S-853876	Folly of Cedar Retreat

Ch. Chatterwood on the Rocks

CH. THE ROCK OF STONE GABLES, C.D.—S-770432

Ch. Jack O'Rackets
Thelan Sir Rocklyn
Ch. Rock Falls Lady Marilyn
Ch. Mike of Meadboro
Ch. Honor's Even Marksman
Lady McBeth
Royal Whirl

Ch. Dean of Blue Bar
Ch. Rip of Blue Bar
Ina of Blue Bar
Ch. Vivacious Sally of Vilmar
Banker of Fallondale
Vivacious Lass of Vilmar
Delta of Larana

Ch. Grayland Rackets Boy
Ch. Linda Lou of Blue Bar
Ch. Grayland Rackets Boy
Nocturne of Crowlcroft
Can. & Am. Ch. Maro of Maridor
Ch. Rodger Dale Dean
Ch. Rummey Sam of Stagboro
End O'Maine Tangerine
Ch. Mallhawk's Jeff
Ch. Lakeland's Peaches
Roy of Blue Bar
Ch. Fly of Stagboro
Can. & Am. Ch. Maxie of Stagboro
Ch. Grayland Orange Blossom
Ch. Sturdy Max
Ch. Lakeland's Dawn

Sire of 12 Champions:

		Out of:
Autumaura Carefree Bev	S-985345	
Autumaura Corpsman Joe, C.D.	S-985348	Ch. Elaine of Elm Knoll
Autumaura Corporal Chet	S-985347	
Skyline of Stone Gables	S-898822	Pleiades Electra of Deer Run
Autumaura Cheery Miss	S-985343	Ch. Elaine of Elm Knoll
Blue Rex of Stone Gables	SA-20547	Blue Bess
Can. Ch. Truebarn's Baroness	476346	Can. Ch. Skidby's Deborah
Prince of Deerfield	SA-55588	Ch. Frosty of Stone Gables
Autumaura Captain Jim	S-985350	Ch. Elaine of Elm Knoll
Thenderin Friar of Chiltern	SA-106711	Ch. Autumaura Carefree Bev
Swagger Boy of Stone Gables	SA-49061	Blue Bess
Thenderin Maid Merian of Kent	SA-144089	Ch. Manlove's Mona

339

Rummey Stagboro
Ch. Sturdy Max
Rummey Girl of Stagboro
Ch. The Snark of Scyld
Rummey Stagboro
Ch. Samantha of Scyld
Jane of Maridor

Ch. Rhett Butler of Silvermine
Can. & Am. Ch. Silvermine Wagabond
Keyfield Judy
Silvermine Wanita
Vera's Adonis of Jagersbo
Rackets Gene of Silvermine
Ch. Sandy's Racket Gene

Spiron Jagersbo
Selkirk Snooksie
Ch. Pat II
Selkirk Snooksie
Spiron Jagersbo
Selkirk Snooksie
Ch. Sturdy Max
Hi Nellie P.S.
Rummey Stagboro
Lady Dian of Silvermine
Fox Flame
Lavender Lady
Can. & Am. Ch. Rackets Rummey
Molly Jagersbo
Ch. Sandy D
Heather Gale

Dam of 6 Champions:

		Sired by:
Can. & Am. Ch. Ben-Dar's Advance Notice	S-568625 ⎤	
Can. & Am. Ch. Darby of Carylane	S-660482 ⎥	Can. & Am. Ch. Ludar of Blue Bar
Can. & Am. Ch. Ben-Dar's Carbon Copy	S-655200 ⎦	
Can. & Am. Ch. Hidden Lane's Michael	S-854561	Can. & Am. Ch. Manlove's Ike
Can. Ch. Ben-Dar's Little Slam	340693	Can. & Am. Ch. Ludar of Blue Bar
Silvermine Citadel	S-474604	Sturdy Max 2nd

AM./CAN./BDA. CH. SIR KIP OF MANITOU

AKC No. SA-240824   Whelped November 3, 1963   Dog
Owner: Mr. & Mrs. Stanley Silverman   Orange Belton
Breeder: Richard S. Howe

Ch. Mike of Meadboro		Thelan Sir Rocklyn
Wamlay's Mike Chism		Lady McBeth
Chisms Queenie		Ch. Rock Falls Sky Way
Ch. Skidby's Bosun of Stone Gables		Colonels Manlove Lady
Ch. Raskalus Raff of Stone Gables		Silvermine Hotshot
Royal Blue of Stone Gables		Cinderella of Oak Valley
Tower Hill To and Again		Rock Falls White Cloud
		April of Blue Bar
		Ch. Toby of Setterfield
Sycamore Lodge Lord Geoffrey		Ch. Rock Falls Belle
Ch. Cinnebar of High-Tor		Ch. Toby of Setterfield
Sycamore Lodge Champagne		Sycamore Gustine
High-Tor's Spicy Lady		Ch. Silvermine Wagabond
Ch. Silvermine Messenger		Ch. Silvermine Swift
Blue Mountain Plain Jane		Ch. Prunes Own Mariner
Mariner's Blue Imp		Ginger Mountain Girl

Sire of 42 Champions: **Out of:**

Clariho Bit O'Candy	SA-410611	
Clariho Rough Rider	SA-402848	
Tom Terrific of Stone Gables	SA-411562	
The Hallmark of Stone Gables	SA-411561	Clariho Piper of Stone Gables
Clariho Luck Be A Lady	SA-781259	
Clariho Encore of Critt-Du	SA-806253	
Clariho Zuercher Aristocrat	SA-781675	
Clariho Candy Bar	SA-393185	

Name	Reg. No.	Dam/Grouping
Clariho Moonraker	SA-655891	⌉
Clariho Sir Duke of Bon Air	SA-611573	
Clariho Army Blue	SA-655708	Clariho's Once In a Blue Moon
Clariho Moonlight Cocktail	SA-660455	
Clariho I'm Blue of Manitou	SA-727723	⌋
Clariho Cascade	SA-626843	⌉
Clariho Blue Horizon	SA-513092	Druids Brew of Stone Gables
Sir Eric of Valley Heights	SA-540294	⌋
Clariho'Ey Luv of Manitou	SA-711740	⌉
Clariho Conversation Piece	SA-872175	Ch. Lemon Delight of Carowa
Clariho Brandy Belle	SA-625301	⌋
Stone Gable's Seafield Romany	SA-537798	⌉
Ye Country Boy of Stone Gables	SA-605377	Clariho Pell of Stone Gables
Surrey's Charm of Stone Gables	SA-563193	⌋
Clariho Double O Seven	SA-478741	⌉
Clariho Mayflower	SA-478744	Canberra's Copper of Clariho
Clariho Copper Coin	SA-478745	⌋
Prince Rex of Kimba	SA-685138	⌉
Duke Stephen of Kimba	SA-685141	⌋ Ch. Clariho Mayflower
Fieldstone Arpege of B	SA-852539	⌉
Fieldstone Wind Song of B	SA-882702	⌋ Ch. Clariho Fieldstone Carousel
Guyline's Jet Setter	SA-731940	⌉
Guyline's Flying Tiger	SA-731942	⌋ Ch. Guyline's Lady Chatterly
Clariho Tres Gay of Somerset	SA-441687	⌉
Leelynn's Top Brass of Clariho	SA-400988	⌋ Navy Blue of Stone Gables
Social Climber of Lazy F	SA-516435	⌉
Laeurce's Courtney Cricket	SA-572081	⌋ Ch. Mayhew's Deb of Lazy F
Brandyrun's Santana Canta	SA-723677	Brandyrun's Bonnie Buffy
Wragge Run's Hey Charlie	SA-930779	Clariho Out Of The Blue
Clariho Sweet Sue	SB-267006	James' Lady of Lansdowne
Thunder Bolt of Ora-Blue	SB-180500	Dorabelle of Ora-Blu
Clariho Major of Meadowset	SA-866405	Ch. Clariho Bit O'Candy
Frosty of Honeyset	SA-903699	Gorsebrook Blue Honey
Ben-Wen's Jamie Boy	SA-738120	Manlove's Suzy of Valleywood

AM. & CAN. CH. SKIDBY'S CAMBRIDGE MISS, SA-94250
(Can. Ch. Wamlay's Mike Chism x Royal Blue of Stone Gables)

Dam of 10 Champions:

		Sired by:
Top O'Penmaen Lord Willin'	SA-266552	
Penmaen Wandering Home	SA-274296	
Top O'Penmaen Widsith	SA-266553	Ch. Top O' Tamerlaine
Penmaen Wood Sprite	SA-274298	
Penmaen With Love	SA-274297	
Shawsheen's Penmaen Camber	SA-148073	
Penmaen Suzanne of Forest	SA-143385	Ch. Shawsheen High Tide
Penmaen Canto	SA-694592	
Penmaen's Meg of Gypsy Lane	SA-512960	Ch. Gilroy's Chancellor
Penmaen Blue Cambric	SA-510511	

343

CH. SOLHEIM'S GINGER SNAP

AKC No. SA-814742   Whelped April, 1969   Bitch
Height - 24½ inches   Orange Belton
Owners: Joan E. Solheim & Yvonne Ward, Peoria, Az.
Breeders: Allan D. & Joan E. Solheim

Ch. English Accent of Valley Run	Ch. Rock Falls Racket
Ch. Merry Rover of Valley Run	Ch. Starbright of Valley Run
Wamlay's Merry Minx	Ch. Mike of Meadboro
Ch. Guys 'N Dolls Society Max	Cinderella of Oak Valley
Ch. Hillsdale Sentinel	Ch. Skidby's Sturdy Tyke
Ch. Guys 'N Dolls Miss Adelaide	Ch. Hillsdale Sparkle
Ch. Guys 'N Dolls Bridget O'Shea CD	Ch. Sir Guy of Ellendale
	Lady Jill of Ellendale
	Ch. Ben-Dar's Winning Stride
Ch. Windsor of Cherry Lane	Bunnydale's Daisy Belle
Ch. Remittance Man of Lazy F	Ch. Ludar of Blue Bar
Ch. Lady Lark of Panthorn	Ch. Silvermine Decal
Ch. Fivesmith's Heidi	Ch. Mike of Meadboro
Ch. Phantom Brook's Thunderbolt	Ch. Phantom Brook's Popcorn
Phantom Brook's Zypher	Ch. Bunnydale's Orange Vulcan
Ch. Pretty Maid of Cherry Lane	Enid of Cherry Lane

Dam of 17 Champions: Sired by:

Sunburst Gingerbread Girl	SB-825904	
Sunburst Shalimar of R-Lew	SB-907008	
Sunburst Peaches 'N Cream	SB-825905	
Sunburst Rhinestone Cowboy	SB-825906	
Sunburst Special Edition	SB-337619	
Sunburst Shelly	SB-183943	
Sunburst Button 'N Bows	SB-183943	
Solheim's Star Attraction	SB-498069	Ch. Guy 'N Dolls Shalimar Duke
Solheim's Royal Duke	SB-60119	
Solheim Checkerberry	SB-221635	
Solheim Ravishing Ruby	SB-348053	
Solheim Razzleberry, C.D.	SB-153134	
Sixpence Kelly of Sunburst	SB-499001	
Captain Jack of Ennistar		
Sunburst Hasten Down The Wind	SC-169663	
Sunburst All Spice	SC-146008	Ch. Guys 'N Dolls Onassis
Sunburst Gold Dust	SB-683860	Ch. Tom Terrific of Stone Gables

CH. SPARK II OF CHERRY LANE
(Ch. Windsor of Cherry Lane × Lady of Cherry Lane)

AKC No. SA-159967   Whelped   April 21, 1962   Dog
Owners: Ray S. and Barbara Parsons   Orange Belton
Breeder: Dorothy S. Reiter

Sire of 12 Champions:		**Out of:**
Sparkson of Ramar	SA-298010	Mary of Haleridge
Raybar's Orange Blossom	SA-346878 ⎤	
Raybar's Brandy	SA-344333	Phantom Brooks Forever Yours
Raybar's Champagne Velvet	SA-345008	
Raybar's Boilermaker	SA-345782 ⎦	
Raybar's Wisp of Lonesome Lane	SA-418085 ⎤	Ch. Frenessa of Calamity Lane
Raybar's Ain't She Sweet	SA-408421 ⎦	
Anita of Cherry Lane	SA-506730	Belinda of Cherry Lane
Raybar's Mai Tai of Taporcan	SA-410686 ⎤	Phantom Brooks Forever Yours
Raybar's Early Times	SA-357836 ⎦	
Raybar's Dennis of Rockport	SA-627710	Ch. Eliza Doolittle of Kaynor
Raybar's Blue Line	SA-702351	Flecka's Starr Fire

345

CH. STONE GABLES SEAFIELD ROMANY

AKC No. SA-537798   Whelped November 17, 1967   Bitch
Height - 23½ inches   Weight - 50 pounds   Orange Belton
Owner: Kathleen M. & Stephen B. Osterling, Lexington, N.C. OFA # ES-260
Breeder: Thomas W. Hall

Can. Ch. Wamlay Mike Chism	Ch. Mike of Meadboro
Ch. Skidby's Bosun of Stone Gables	Chism's Queenie
Royal Blue of Stone Gables	Ch. Raskalus Raff of Stone Gables
Ch. Sir Kip of Manitou	Tower Hill To And Again
Ch. Cinnabar of High-Tor	Sycamore Lodge Lord Geoffrey
High-Tor's Spicy Lady	Sycamore Lodge Champagne
Blue Mountain Plain Jane	Ch. Silvermine Messenger
	Mariner's Blue Imp
Ch. The Rock of Stone Gables CD	Ch. Mike of Meadboro
Ch. Prince of Deerfield	Ch. Vivacious Sally of Vilmar
Ch. Frosty of Stone Gables	Ch. Raskalus Raff of Stone Gables
Ch. Clariho Pell of Stone Gables	Tower Hill To And Again
Ch. The Rock of Stone Gables	Ch. Mike of Meadboro
Candy of Clariho	Ch. Vivacious Sally of Vilmar
High-Tor's Spicy Lady	Ch. Cinnebar of High-Tor
	Blue Mountain Plain Jane

Dam of 7 Champions: **Sired by:**

Seafield's Virginia Storm	SB-597986 ⎤	
Seafield's Tickle My Fancy	SB-695746	Ch. Clariho Kristofer of Critt-Du
Seafield's Holiday Mystique	SB-701975 ⎦	
Seafield's Catamaran of Teplr	SB-327310 ⎤	
Seafield's Sandcastle	SB-711789 ⎦	Ch. Clariho Checkmate of Critt-Du
Seafield's Tidal Wave	SB-190258	Ch. Clariho Moonraker
Seafield's Pride of Brooklawn	SB-981197	Ch. Guyline's Flying Tiger

STURDY MAX 2nd, S-750816

Spiron Jagersbo
Rummey Stagboro
Selkirk Snooksie
Ch. Lakeland's Yuba
Can. & Am. Ch. Rackets Rummey
Lakeland's Nymph
Lakeland's Fascination

Int. Ch. Spiron
Arbu Lala B
Can. & Am. Ch. McConnell's Nori
Can. & Am. Ch. Selkirk Juliet
Ch. Mallwyd Ralph
Stylish Pretty Polly
Meadowdale Mallwyd Count
Myer's Blue Bird
Spiron Jagersbo
Selkirk Snooksie
Ch. Pat II
Selkirk Snooksie
Spiron Jagersbo
Selkirk Snooksie
Can. & Am. Ch. Rackets Rummey
Lakeland's Fascination

Rummey Stagboro
Ch. Sturdy Max
Rummey Girl of Stagboro
Ch. Dora of Maridor
Rummey Stagboro
Ch. Lakeland's Dawn
Lakeland's Nymph

Sire of 14 Champions:

		Out of:
Aspetuck's Red Robin	S-569092	Aspetuck's Red Sumac
Silvermine Citadel	S-474604	Ch. Silvermine Chambray
Silvermine Delicious	S-509709	Ch. Silvermine Swift
Starbright of Valley Run	S-545136	Silvermine Confection
Silvermine Decal	S-509712 ⎤	
Silvermine Delightful 2nd	S-509711 ⎦	Ch. Silvermine Swift
Aspetuck's Diana	S-622274	Aspetuck's Red Sumac
Silvermine Domino	S-570672	Silvermine Wanita
Sharoc's Monte of Oak Valley	S-279044	Ch. Sharoc Dolly Madison
Aspetuck's Feather	S-584358	Aspetuck's Red Sumac
Prune's Own Amber	S-105416	Peggy Jane
Orange Man Machold	S-297568	Rummey Sam's Sally
Mr. Watt	S-235418 ⎤	
Chief of Armsworth	S-213489 ⎦	Maxson's Delight

CH. SUKARLA'S SANDPIPER

AKC No. SA-802859 Whelped May 5, 1970 Dog
Owner: Mary Ciszek, Barrington, Il. Orange Belton
Breeder: John P. & Mary N. Nielsen

Ch. Margand Lord Calvert
Margand Lord Baltimore
Ch. Phantom Brook's Petticoat
Ch. Chandelle's Anchor Man
Ch. Rock Falls Lieutenant
Ch. Chandelle Lady
Duchess Rugged Honey

Margand El Captain
Margand Princess Anne
Ch. Rock Falls Colonel
Ch. Phantom Brooks Deductible
Ch. Rock Falls Colonel
Jacklin O'Rackets
Rugged Boy
Rubins Honey Maid

Ch. Rock Falls Racket
Ch. Aspetuck's Shadow
Ch. Aspetuck's Diana
Ch. Sukarla's Serendipity
Ch. Margand Lord Baltimore
Ch. Chandelle's Bambi
Ch. Chandelle Lady

Ch. Rock Falls Cavalier
Ch. Rock Falls Belle
Sturdy Max II
Aspetuck's Red Sumac
Ch. Margand Lord Calvert
Ch. Phantom Brooks Petticoat
Ch. Rock Falls Lieutenant
Duchess Rugged Honey

Sire of 10 Champions:		**Out of:**
Maraspelle Lady of Belton Bay	SC-168444	
Georgia Luv of Belton Bay	SC-206936	
Barnstormer of Belton Bay	SB-861402	
Beau Brummel of Belton Bay	SB-709785	Ch. Chandelle's First Love
Chandelle's Great Day	SB-520517	
Mr. Chips of Belton Bay	SB-543020	
Luv's Niklgrab 'R of Belton Bay	SC-438364	
Cannongate Shades of Grey	SC-253072	Heatherhope Junie Moon
Tattershall Amy of Marimaque	SB-523499	Ch. Brynnestone So-Rite
Kaynor's Once in a Lifetime	SB-275751	Ch. Sukarla's Sweet Bippy of Kaynor

CH. SUKARLA'S SERENDIPITY

AKC No. SA-403013   Whelped May, 1966   **Bitch**
Height - 25 inches   Weight - 58 pounds   Orange Belton
Breeders-Owners: John P. & Mary N. Nielsen,

Ch. Rock Falls Cavalier	Ch. Grayland's Racket's Boy
Ch. Rock Falls Racket	CH. Linda Lou of Blue Bar
Ch. Rock Falls Belle	Ch. Grayland's Racket Boy
Ch. Aspetuck's Shadow	Nocturne of Crowlcroft
Study Max II	Ch. Lakeland's Yuba
Ch. Aspetuck's Diana	Ch. Dora of Maridor
Aspetuck's Red Sumac	Ch. Silvermine Showman
	Ch. Suzette of Setterfield
Ch. Margand Lord Calvert	Margand El Capitan
Ch. Margand Lord Baltimore	Margand Princess Anne
Ch. Phantom Brooks Petticoat	Ch. Rock Falls Colonel
Ch. Chandelle's Bambi	Ch. Phantom Brooks Deductible
Ch. Rock Falls Lieutenant	Ch. Rock Falls Colonel
Ch. Chandelle Lady	Jacklin O'Rackets
Duchess Rugged Honey	Rugged Boy
	Rubin's Honey Maid

Dam of 6 Champions: **Sired by:**

Sukarla's Samantha Sue	SA-838051 ⎤	
Sukarla's Sandpiper	SA-802859 ⎬	Ch. Chandelle's Anchor Man
Sukarla's Sorceress	SA-815481 ⎦	
Sukarla's Dan-Di Chelsea	SB-148805 ⎤	
Sukarla's Happy Day Chancell'r	SB-160022 ⎬	Ch. Sukarla's Sock It To Me
Sukarla's Rocket Man	SB-130048 ⎦	

CH. SUKARLA'S SOCK IT TO ME

AKC No. SA-717826   Whelped May 11, 1972   Dog
Owner: John P. & Mary N. Nielsen   Blue Belton
Breeder: John P. & Mary N. Nielsen

		Ch. Mike of Meadboro	Thelan Sir Rocklyn
	Mt. Mansfield's Spruce Peak		Lady MacBeth
	Reveille's Pandora		Ch. Silvermine Wagabond
Ch. Dover's Blue Sky			Gwen du Hameau
	Ch. Bullet of Calamity Lane		Ch. Yorkley's Ensign Robert
	Ch. Confetti of Calamity Lane		Ch. Candy of Blue Bar
	Ch. Rock Candy of Calamity Lane		Ch. Rock Falls Lieutenant
			Ch. Candy of Blue Bar
		Ch. Margand Lord Calvert	Margand El Capitan
	Ch. Margand Lord Baltimore		Margand Princess Anne
	Ch. Phantom Brook's Petticoat		Ch. Rock Falls Colonel
Ch. Chandelle's Bambi			Ch. Phantom Brook's Deductible
	Ch. Rock Falls Lieutenant		Ch. Rock Falls Colonel
	Ch. Chandelle's Lady		Jacklin O'Racket
	Duchess Rugged Honey		Rugged Boy
			Rubin's Honey Maid

Sire of 14 Champions: **Out of:**

Sunnybrae's Sunstruck Ida	SB-838027	
Sunnybrae's Sunrock	SB-851304	Excalibur's Echo O'Sunnybrae
Sunnybrae's Zachariah	SB-861346	
Sukarla's Dan-Di Chelsea	SB-148805	
Sukarla's Happy Day Chancell'r	SB-160022	Ch. Sukarla's Serendipity
Sukarla's Rocket Man	SB-130048	
Heatherhope Rossmoor Brandy	SA-889979	
Heatherhope Arabian Nights	SA-828561	Clariho April Dancer
Heatherhope Heidi	SA-858091	
Popkin's Sophisticated Miss	SA-854256	
Popkin's Dazzling Star	SA-944599	Ch. Popkins Sweet Polly Pure Bred
Morgental's Brass Mist	SB-218659	Ch. Gemody's Gidget Goes Hawaiian
Cameron's Cham Cham Girl	SA-950441	Ch. Chandelle's Chambray
Argent's Blue Belle	SB-852010	Excalibur's Exuberant Ms

CH. THENDERIN GOLDEN DREAM

AKC No. SA-328321   Whelped March 8, 1964   Bitch
Height - 26 inches   Weight - 67 pounds   Orange Belton
Owner: B.J. Miller, Clarksburg, Calif.
Breeder: Dr. David J. Sayles

Ch. Mike of Meadboro	Ch. Thelan Sir Rocklyn
Ch. The Rock of Stone Gables CD	Lady Macbeth
Ch. Vivacious Sally of Vilmar	Ch. Rip of Blue Bar
Ch. Thenderin Friar of Chilltern	Vivacious Lass of Vilmar
Ch. The Rock of Stone Gables CD	Ch. Mike of Meadboro
Ch. Autumaura Carefree Bev	Ch. Vivacious Sally of Vilmar
Ch. Elaine of Elm Knoll	Ch. Earl of Elm Knoll
	Mallhawk Mallie of Elm Knoll
	Ch. Rock Falls Racket
Ch. Zamitz Export Edition	Ch. Zamitz Bread & Butter
Ch. Zamitz Jumpin Jack	Shawsheen Bo-Sun
Shawsheen Fini	Rossland's Princess
Autumaura Christmas Debut	Ch. Case's General Jackson
Ch. Earl of Elm Knoll	Reba of Blue Bar
Ch. Elaine of Elm Knoll	Mallhawk Heather Grouse
Mallhawk Mallie of Elm Knoll	Mallhawk Quail

Dam of 15 Champions: Sired by:

Delta's Cover Girl	SA-949904	
Thenderin Jenny Luv of Delta	SA-888202	
Thenderin Big Dream of Delta	SA-764875	
Thenderin Maggie Now of Delta	SA-755044	Ch. Mt. Mansfield's William
Thenderin Mr. Rad of Delta	SA-848600	
Thenderin Miss O'Dell of Delta	SA-788493	
Bem's Sir Philip of Delta	SA-753315	
Mt. Mansfield's Golden Rod	SA-876981	
Thenderin Starstream of Delta	SA-499657	
Thenderin Merry Belle O'Delta	SA-436794	
Thenderin Jessabelle O'Delta	SA-505716	
Thenderin Revor of Delta	SA-413620	Ch. Merry Rover of Valley Run
Thenderin Headliner of Delta	SA-461548	
Thenderin Class-E-Lady O'Delta	SA-461547	
Bem's Sir Anthony of Delta	SA-400906	

CH. THENDERIN SARAH BROWN, SA-750422
(Ch. Thenderin Revor of Delta x Autumaura Endearment)

Dam of 6 Champions: Out of:

Charlin Rudolph	SB-41243	
Charlin Eric	SB-41246	
Charlin Valentina	SB-41245	Ch. Guys 'N Dolls Onassis
Charlin Tiny Tim	SB-41247	
Charlin Christina	SB-41244	
Charlin Billy Jack	SB-382216	

351

CH. ULYSSES OF BLUE BAR, S-654297

Ch. Rip of Blue Bar
Ch. Sir Herbert of Kennelworth
Vivacious Doll of Vilmar
Ch. Rube of Blue Bar
Ch. Lem of Blue Bar
Ch. Norma of Blue Bar
Zo of Blue Bar

Ch. Matt of Blue Bar
Ch. Lep of Blue Bar
Dora of Blue Bar
Ch. Ripple of Blue Bar
Happy Valley Creole Chief
Ch. Penny of Happy Valley
Happy Valley Cobalt Queen

Ch. Dean of Blue Bar
Ina of Blue Bar
Banker of Fallondale
Delta of Larana
Lone Ace of Kanandarque
Lovely Dawn of Kanandarque
Ch. Dean of Blue Bar
Ch. Rita of Blue Bar
Ch. Pilot of Crombie of Happy Valley
Inglehurst Matchless
Ch. Jesse of Blue Bar
Ch. Lola of Blue Bar
Happy Valley Punch
Lipstick of Stucile
Happy Valley Ragged
Happy Valley Lady Mallhawk

Sire of 10 Champions:		Out of:
Zamitz Invader	S-793017 ⎤	
Zamitz Intended	S-793023 ⎦	Silvermine Athalee
Mt. Mansfield Independence	S-949182	Mt. Mansfield Sugar Slalom
Mt. Mansfield's Sugar Bush	S-928028 ⎤	
Mt. Mansfield Spring Song	S-928030 ⎦	Ch. Mt. Mansfield's Tear Drop
Mt. Mansfield Gregarious	SA-70045	Mt. Mansfield Mata Hari
Mt. Mansfield Moonbeam	SA-60161	Ch. Mt. Mansfield's Tear Drop
Mt. Mansfield's Pumpkin	SA-70240	Ch. Phantom Brook's Pepper Corn
Mt. Mansfield's Tilt (1)	SA-172553	Mt. Mansfield Mata Hari
Can. Ch. Mt. Mansfield's Hillbilly	513636	Ch. Mt. Mansfield's Tear Drop

352

Other Sires and Dams: In a compilation of this type it is impossible, due to expense, to list every stud and dam worthy of attention. The pictures and pedigrees you have just seen give you the dogs found in the majority of recent pedigrees in the United States and Canada.

However, a few dogs that had not produced ten or more champions of record when this compilation was made are deserving of mention. Some of the following may well become the top producers of tomorrow.

Sires with Nine Champions

Excalibur's Extempore
Ch. Hiddenlane's Blue Turquoise
Ch. Jaccard Hill Alastaire
Ch. Margand Masquerader

Sires with Eight Champions

Ch. Arnee's Nell'Son of Nor'Coaster
Ch. Excalibur's Explosion
Ch. Harmony Lane Marquis
Ch. Manlove's Andy of Saybrook
Ch. Velvet's Blue Moon

Dams with Five Champions

Ch. Blue Diamond Benedictine
Clariho's Once In A Blue Moon
Ch. Tiffany of Clariho
Ch. Daw Anka's Sugar and Spice
Ch. Hiddenlane's Buzz Me Miss Blu
Ch. Cameo of Pleasant Point
Ch. Sukarla's Dan-Di Chelsea
Ch. Sunburst Button 'N Bows
Ch. Thistledown Doll O'Willow Run
Ch. Teresa of Cherry Lane

Dams with Four Champions

Ch. Blue Lupine of Berriwood
Castleroc Duchess of Popkins
Belinda of Cherry Lane
Ch. Clariho Caper of Critt-Du
Clariho April Dancer
Ch. Dolce
Ch. Gal's Gabbi Gal
Ch. Guys 'N Dolls Taste of Honey
Ch. Guys 'N Dolls Westerly Wind
Harmony Lane Windsor Castle
Ch. Hidden Lane's Nelle
Ch. Hidden Lane's Broker's Tip
Ch. Hidden Lane's Xceptionell
Ch. Margand Merry of Jaccard Hill
Ch. Marshfield's Lady Ann
Marchfield's Edwardian Era
Ch. Penmaen Petunia of Northwood
Frenessa of Pleasant Point
Ch. Palomar's Abagail of Scotglen
Ch. Redrah's Gay Feather
Ch. Rossmoor's Captivatin Carrie
Ch. Shady Lane's Sister Sara
Ch. Pinney Paige of Valley Run

Ch. Guys 'N Dolls Miss Adelaide

14

Leading Winners of the 1950's, 1960's and 1970's

A NUMBER of the great producers listed in the previous chapter also distinguished themselves in the show ring. Other English Setters of these three eras also deserve mention for their awards achieved in heavy breed, sporting group and Best in Show competition.

Ch. Rock Falls Colonel and Ch. Rock Falls Racket, litter brothers, did their best winning in the early 1950's. Colonel was well into his fabulous BIS record by the turn of the decade, but the period of 1951 and 1952 saw him virtually invincible. While his brother amassed the top awards, Racket managed to win several Specialties, groups and a few BIS.

In the midwest and Canada, Ch. Ludar of Blue Bar came through strong in the early 1950's with an enviable BIS record of his own. Later in that decade, Ludar's son, Ch. Ben-Dar's Advance Notice, took over for his sire in the same territory.

Ch. Zamitz Jumping Jack

In the east during the middle 'fifties, Racket's sons, Ch. Ike of Blue Bar and Ch. Silvermine Jackpot, and Ch. Mike of Meadboro made a good record for themselves with Ike and Jackpot acquiring several BIS and Mike winning the breed and groups at major events. This period also brought forth a truly great bitch, Ch. Zamitz Bread and Butter, that won a number of sporting groups, a rare accomplishment for one of her sex in those days.

The year 1957 witnessed the rise of a truly superior star in the English Setter sky, Ch. Chatterwood on the Rocks. Never a BIS winner (though in the writer's opinion he deserved it), this great dog dominated the eastern Specialties in his all-too-short span of four years. Most regrettably, he was rarely used at stud. His line — Rock Falls and Sturdy Max II — had proved to be a strong one through other representatives of it.

In the midwest, another Ludar son, Ch. Ben-Dar's Winning Stride, began his move to fame in the later 1950's with Specialty, group and BIS wins. Eastward, the dominant winner became Ch. Zamitz Jumpin' Jack, a tri-color and the first of his pigmentation in a long time to win the breed, group first and Best in Show.

357

The opening year of the 'sixties produced a number of promising winners. While Jumpin' Jack topped the breed's BIS record for the year, Ch. Skidby's Sturdy Tyke—the Canadian dog bred by the Polleys' Skidby Kennels—and Ch. English Accent of Valley Run, Ch. Manlove of Ellendale (in California) and Ch. Margand Lord Baltimore (from the midwest) started their runs of Specialty and group wins, and in the case of Tyke and Lord Baltimore, Bests in Show.

In 1961, English Accent, Jumpin' Jack, Lord Baltimore and a new flyer, Ch. Candlewood Distinction, were the leading breed winners. Two other notable bitches, Ch. Dover's Ticker Tape and Ch. Rebel Roc's Queen of Avalon (another California representative), also scored.

For 1962 and 1963, Ch. Candlewood Distinction and a lovely, smooth-going bitch, Ch. Winifred of Cherry Lane, topped the wins for their respective sexes. In the East, Ch. Flecka's Flash of Cabin Hill won Specialties and groups, and two sons of English Accent, Ch. Gentleman Jim of Valley Run and Ch. Prince Charlie of Valley Run, took Specialties. Ch. Oak Lynn Top Brass and Ch. Chandelle's Anchor Man, from Minnesota, made several strikes in the breed and groups around the center of the

Ch. Candlewood Distinction

country and far west. The midwest claimed another breed topping bitch in Ch. Anne of Sherwood who in 1964 won the first BIS for her sex in many a year.

In 1964, too, Candlewood Distinction increased the celerity with which he was winning groups and BIS; Chandelle's Anchor Man continued his meteoric rise; and a newcomer, Ch. Merry Rover of Valley Run, launched his illustrious career.

Anchor Man and Merry Rover dominated the English setter scene in 1965 and 1966 with substantial group, specialty and BIS wins. I judged both these magnificent specimens a number of times, once together when the decision was the closest and most difficult I have ever adjudicated. In their prime they, and Chatterwood on the Rocks, represented — in my opinion — the finest English Setters during the years they were shown. (In fact, I tried mightily at different times to acquire each!)

For "English Setter of the Year" another flyer, Ch. Sir Kip of Manitou, became a close runner-up to Anchor Man in 1967. And it was in this period that another beautiful bitch made her mark: this was Ch. Valley Run's Dinah-Mite who had taken the measure of male champions at a New England Club specialty in 1965. Dinah-Mite's overall excellence, flawless gait and superb condition won her a BIS from me and several groups from other judges later on. In 1967 Dinah-Mite's son, Ch. Stan the Man of Valley Run, sired by Merry Rover, won two BIS awards and was named the top English Setter of the year under the Phillips' point system.

1967 was also the year that brought a triple tie for the ESAA's Rock Falls Colonel annual award for the breed's leading BIS winners. The three worthy dogs were Chs. Merry Rover of VR, Jaccard Hill Alastaire and Bucket O'Bolts by Law.

The banner year for the breed was 1968 with no less than six BIS winners: Ch. Sir Kip of Manitou, Ch. Stan the Man of VR, Ch. Guys 'N Dolls Miss Adelaide (over a 2,000 all-breed entry), Ch. Bucket O'Bolts by Law, Ch. Jaccard Hill Alastaire, and Ch. Kerry of Berriwood. Sir Kip led these winners by gathering to himself the annual award as English Setter of the Year and the number one rating for the breed in the Phillips System. He also won the ESAA's National Specialty, with over 100 entries, and two regional club specialities.

As the soaring Sixties came to a close, Sir Kip continued his winning ways with BOB at both the ESAA Specialty in New York and its National Specialty in California. A new star in the distaff firmament, Ch. Canberra's Legend, began her career in 1968 with two regional club specialty wins and in 1969 — to the best of memory and research — became but the second bitch to win the breed at the Westminster Kennel Club show in Madison Square Garden.

In 1970 Legend became the first English Setter bitch to win **three** Bests in Show in the breed's American history, all accomplished by her amateur-owner, Joyce Rosen. Legend retired with a record of eight group wins and six specialties which, considering her sex, was remarkable. Also in 1970, Ch. Guys 'N Dolls Shalimar Duke made a splendid Best in Show and group record under the breeder-ownership of Neal and Harron Weinstein. Duke doubled up breed wins at the Combined Setter Specialty in New York and Westminster for that year and in 1971 as well when he was the leading Best in Show winner for the breed.

In 1972 a beautifully marked blue belton, Ch. Highland's Whip of Penmaen, was named English Setter of the Year for having defeated the greatest number in the breed during the year; he was also the breed's leading Best-in-Show winner that year. A tricolor, Ch. Briarpatch of Bryn Mawr, launched his career in 1973 with several sporting group wins.

Briarpatch tied Ch. Charlin Rudolph for Bests in Show though Rudolph took the awards for English Setter of the Year and Sporting Group.

1974 was a banner year for the breed with no less than six English Setters garnering 11 Bests in Show in the United States. Two — the forementioned Briarpatch and the fine orange bitch, Ch. Guys 'N Dolls Annie O'Brien — accounted for six of them with three each. Annie also won the ESAA National and New York Specialties. The other Best in Show winners in that year were Chs. Guyline's Seamrog Shaman, Guys 'N Dolls Oliver Ridgedale, Highland's Whip of Penmaen and Thistledown Duff o' Willow Run.

Annie O'Brien continued her winning ways in 1975 with 10 Bests in Show, 17 Group firsts and Best of Breed again at the National Specialty. Chs. Five Oaks Top Lass and Hidden Lane's Benchmark each won a Best in Show; Benchmark won the New York Specialty with Annie O'Brien going Best of Opposite Sex to him.

In 1976 there was a three-way tie for the Best in Show award with another Guys 'N Dolls bitch, Ch. G 'N D Taste of Honey, Ch. Mister Chips of Belton Bay and Benchmark each having one such award. Annie O'Brien won her third National Specialty in a row and thereby retired the Rock Falls Racket trophy. Taste of Honey received the designation of English Setter of the Year for having defeated the greatest number in the breed.

Top awards were few and far between for English Setters in 1977. In America only one of the breed, Ch. Lourdsdale's Blue Woodsman took a Best in Show. And only one—Ch. Charlin Rudolph—received more than two firsts in the sporting group; he won five. The National Specialty fell to Ch. Sunburst Special Edition and the forementioned Taste of Honey won the winter specialty held with the Combined Setter Club event in New York. The English Setter of the Year award fell to Ch. Story Book's Best Seller.

In 1978 Best Seller repeated his ESY award and won the National Specialty. His kennel mate, Ch. Seasac Knight of Canterbury, won the most points by his placements in the sporting group. Ch. Guys 'N Dolls Wild William captured the Best in Show award and ranked first for the year in number of English Setters defeated and total number of dogs defeated in his group placements; Seasac Knight ranked second to Wild William in this last category. Though not shown in the United States, Am./Can./Bda. Ch. Marengohill's Hello Sunshine amassed five Bests in Show and 33 group firsts in Canada in 1978 which is certainly worthy of mention.

1979 saw Wild William defeating the most in the breed and the English Setter winning the most sporting group points with eleven firsts for the year. Ch. Guys 'N Dolls Damon Runyon won the breed's Best in Show award. In July the ESAA held its largest specialty in its history with 352 dogs entered; the winner was the seven-year-old Ch. Velvet's Blue Moon. Best at the Combined Setter Specialty was Ch. Tattershall Tapestry.

Five American English Setters won Bests in Show in 1980. The leader with three such awards was Ch. Sunburst Shalimar of R-Lew. The other four with one each were Ch. Drummont's Tasty's Billy, Ch. Guys 'N Dolls Barrister Beau, Ch. Mysti's Triumph of Valley Run and Ch. Tamara Runs Modesty. The English Setter of the year was Ch. Lorien's American Flyer. Ch. Garson's Special Prosecutor took the most sporting dog points. The National Specialty winner of the year was Am./Can. Ch. Guys 'N Dolls Molly Bloom, a bitch that four years earlier was best in ESAA's first Futurity.

No other English Setter has yet to come within striking distance of Rock Falls Colonel's record of 101 Bests in Show, and his even greater number of group and breed wins. Only three dogs have surpassed Colonel's BIS achievement — a Boxer, a Pekingese and, in 1980, a Poodle.

And no other English bitch has achieved the amazing number of 13 Bests in Show won by Ch. Guys 'N Dolls Annie O'Brien. In her career she garnered 103 Bests of Breeds with 81 sporting group placings including 43 firsts.

Certain professional handlers seem to enjoy a high affinity and rapport with English Setters. The late Harold Correll campaigned the Blue Bar dogs most successfully, his last being Ch. Ike of Blue Bar. Jane (Kamp) Forsyth piloted a number of this breed to top awards including Chs. Rock Falls Racket, Candlewood Distinction and Ch. Story Book's Best Seller. Ch. Ludar of Blue Bar and his son, Ch. Ben-Dar's Advance Notice, were in the capable hands of Horace Hollands. Robert Forsyth handled Chs. Zamitz Jumpin' Jack, Valley Runs Dinah-Mite and Stan the Man of VR — all Best-in-Show winners — in their careers. The great sire, Ch. Margand Lord Baltimore, did his winning with Richard Cooper as did the more recent Ch. Seasac Knight of Canterbury.

In 1965–69, a handler new to the breed steered two top dogs to their pinnacles. This was William Trainor with Chs. Merry Rover of Valley Run and Sir Kip of Manitou. Dick Webb, now a judge, was another superb professional handler who piloted the successful campaigner, Ch. Guys 'N Dolls Shalimar Duke. Ray McGinnis has shown many English Setters through the years, the most famous being Annie O'Brien and, most recently, Ch. Guys 'N Dolls Wild William. Lately, Bill Trainor has been the "jockey" for another BIS winner, Ch. Drummont's Tasty's Billy, whose dam Ch. Guys 'N Dolls Taste of Honey — also a BIS winner with Trainor holding the lead — has been the only bitch to win the breed at Westminster three times in that illustrious club's 105-year history.

Several amateur owner-handlers gave the professionals a hard race. Though William T. Holt's record of 101 BIS with his Rock Falls Colonel is unlikely to be equalled, other owners merit high praise for campaigning their dogs — Howard Smith with Ch. Mike of Meadboro; Dr. Raymond Chase with Ch. Chatterwood on the Rocks; Rachael Van Buren, for a time, with Chs. English Accent and Merry Rover of VR; Joseph Kaziny with Ch. Chandelle's Anchor Man; Gladys Nichol, also for a time, with Chs. Valley Run's Dinah-Mite and Stan the Man of VR; Neal Weinstein with Ch. Guys 'N Dolls Miss Adelaide; Joyce Rosen with Ch. Canberra's Legend; Ralph Wendels with Ch. Briarpatch of Bryn Mawr; David Baker with Chs. Baker's Northern Lancer and Burr Ridge Constellation, the latter a frequent breed winner and Best of Opposite Sex at specialties; Sarah Sly with Ch. Velvet's Blue Moon—to highlight just a few.

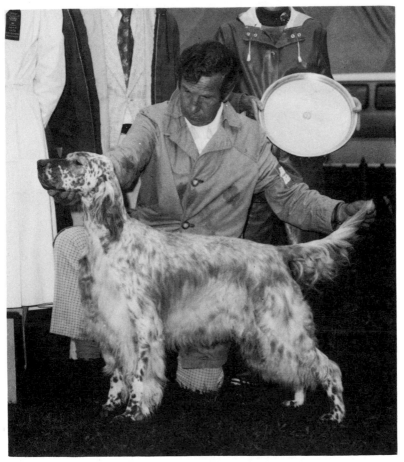

Ch. Five Oakes Top Lass

Ch. Guys 'N Dolls Shalimar Duke

Ch. Canberra's Legend

Ch. Highland's Whip of Penmaen

Ch. Charlin Rudolph

Ch. Guyline's Seamrog Shaman

Ch. Guys 'N Dolls Annie O'Brien

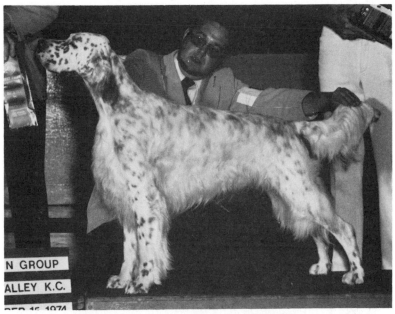

Ch. Thistledown Duff O'Willow Run

Ch. Guys 'N Dolls Oliver Ridgedale

Ch. Hiddenlane's Benchmark

Ch. Guys 'N Dolls Taste of Honey

Ch. Loursdale's Blue Woodsman

Ch. Storybook's Best Seller

Ch. Seasac Knight of Canterbury

Ch. Guys 'N Dolls Wild William

Am/Can/Bda Ch. Marengohill's Hello Sunshine

Ch. Guys 'N Dolls Damon Runyon

Ch. Mister Chips of Belton Bay

Ch. Rogue's Dapper Dan

372

Ch. Velvet's Blue Moon, winner of the 1979 ESAA National
Specialty

Ch. Drummont's Tasty's Billy, winner of the 1981 ESAA
National Specialty

15

The English Setter
Association of America

F̲ORMED IN 1934, the breed's parent club has flourished nicely over the past thirty years. In 1950 its membership numbered approximately 75 fanciers, only 15 of whom attended the annual meeting in New York City. In early 1981 its membership totalled 987. Since less than 1,400 English Setters were registered by the American Kennel Club in 1980, the ESAA membership is truly remarkable; many clubs for breeds with much greater registrations have much fewer members.

ESAA's growth over the past 30 years is attributable to two major developments. In 1951 the association's constitution was changed to include the election of *regional* vice presidents to represent those areas in the United States most active in the breed's interest. This worthy step was the brain child of Davis Tuck, the club's newly elected president at that time. It has stimulated the formation of local clubs which hold their own match shows, specialties and other activities beneficial to the breed and its fanciers.

In 1968, the parent club voted to hold two specialties each year, one in the New York area and the other, to be known as the National Specialty, rotated around the country with a local club serving as host. ESAA's annual meetings are held with the National Specialties.

The other salutary development in the ESAA is the superb dedication of its officers and committee chairmen to the interests of the breed. The parent club has been most fortunate in having presidents, secretaries, treasurers and *workers* who labor selflessly to achieve its objectives.

ESAA publishes two splendid, informative periodicals for its members. The monthly Newsletter, free to members, covers important show wins including specialty awards, columns on the breed in the field, and all sorts of items of interest and value to ES fanciers. The Newsletter also serves as the carrier for members' ballots on the election of officers, judges for parent club specialties and proposed changes in the ESAA constitution.

The other publication is the magnificent ESAA *Annual*, a durably hardbound volume lavishly and beautifully illustrated with photos of the year's top winners, new champions, and sires and dams. The *Annual* lists the winners of the yearly ESAA awards and includes the reports of the year's developments in the local clubs. If published commercially the ESAA *Annual* would have to be priced at $25.00. To active members of the ESAA it is available for a fraction of that amount.

Membership in the English Setter Association of America is hugely satisfying and rewarding to active fanciers of the breed. The name and address of ESAA's current secretary can be obtained from the American Kennel Club, 51 Madison Avenue, New York, N. Y. 10010.